YOU CANNOT BE SERIOUS

MATTHEW NORMAN is a journalist and broadcaster in many forms. He writes about sport in the *Daily Telegraph*, for which he is also the restaurant reviewer. He has been the British Press Awards Food and Drink Writer of the Year (2004) and Columnist of the Year (2008). He is married with a son and lives in London.

MATTHEW NORMAN

You Cannot Be Serious

The 101 Most Infuriating Things in Sport

FOURTH ESTATE • *London*

Fourth Estate
An imprint of HarperCollins*Publishers*
77–85 Fulham Palace Road
Hammersmith
London W6 8JB

This Fourth Estate paperback edition published 2011

1

First published in Great Britain by Fourth Estate in 2010

Copyright © Matthew Norman 2010

Matthew Norman asserts the moral right
to be identified as the author of this work

A catalogue record for this book
is available from the British Library

ISBN 978-0-00-743873-0

Typeset in Minion by G&M Designs Limited,
Raunds, Northamptonshire

Printed and bound in Great Britain by Clays Ltd, St Ives plc

MIX
Paper from
responsible sources

FSC
www.fsc.org **FSC® C007454**

FSC™ is a non-profit international organisation established to promote
the responsible management of the world's forests. Products carrying the
FSC label are independently certified to assure consumers that they come
from forests that are managed to meet the social, economic and
ecological needs of present and future generations,
and other controlled sources.

Find out more about HarperCollins and the environment at
www.harpercollins.co.uk/green

To Rebecca and Louis, implacable enemies of sport
in all its myriad guises

INTRODUCTION

I love sport. I love it with a passion so obsessive that it strikes me as indistinguishable from mental illness, as my wife would be gracious enough to confirm. In May 1991, three days into the commencement of our courtship, she awoke at 6.30 a.m. to hear me announce that I was leaving the flat to tie a shoelace on the northbound Northern Line platform at Embankment underground station. Spurs were playing Nottingham Forest in that afternoon's FA Cup final, I explained as her absolute indifference gave way to mild alarm, and because such a shoelace-tying had prefaced our victory over Manchester City in the replayed Cup final of 1981, it had to be done again. She didn't say anything.

Nor was she capable of speech four months later when, a week into our honeymoon, I checked us out of a quaint Shaker inn in rural Massachusetts and into a filthy, cockroach-infested motel room, on the grounds that the former had no cable TV and the latter did, allowing us (me) to watch the peerlessly melodramatic dénouement to that year's Ryder Cup.

Almost two decades later, the deranged love for sport remains unabated by the ravages of middle age. I can, and do, spend untold unbroken hours not only watching sport – any sport, other perhaps than dressage, rowing and ten-pin bowling – on television, but also taking comfort from studying cricket averages, the sequence of winners in golfing majors, and the results from the early rounds of 1970s tennis Grand Slam events. When I confess that one of my more thrilling experiences in recent years was chancing upon a website that included the scores from the qualifying competitions for World Snooker Championships, which I duly attempted to memorise, you may understand why I have come to know the condition as spautism. I regard myself as a little less far along the spectrum than those who have not missed an away fixture played by their football team in forty years, or have visited all ninety-two league grounds; but not by much, and more thanks to indolence than anything else.

Hand in hand with any all-consuming, sanity-threatening love, there inevitably travels a portion of its opposite. I resent sport as a whole for its imperious hold over me, as the stalker perhaps does the stalkee, or a heroin addict the weakness of which the drug use is manifestation rather than cause. And I resent those involved in playing, describing and administering it, both as agents of that time-sucking dominion, and in many cases for themselves.

The frustrations, distastes, rages and loathings acquired over forty years have made the writing of this book a painful task. How does one whittle down so many thousands of irritants, dullards, hypocrites, narcissists and plain horrors to a mere 101? On what possible grounds can no space be found for Cristiano Ronaldo or Vinnie Jones, Iron Mike Tyson or Sam Allardyce? What brand of imbecile would put his name to a list devoid of such titans of administrative cluelessness as cricket's Giles Clark, or Sir Dave Richards, who somehow vaults the towering conflict-of-interest hurdle to remain a power at both the Football Association and the Premier League? Whence the sheer gall to include Colin Montgomerie, yet not Nick Faldo? How in the name of all the saints did Chas and Dave avoid an appearance for 'Snooker Loopy'?

You will each have your own fierce criticisms, as much for the inclusion of those you admire (Peter Alliss's popularity with many sound judges must, however bemusing, be acknowledged) as for the omissions of those you detest. The ranking of the 101 will also inevitably displease.

If you believe you could do it better, you are almost certainly right. Events since the publication of the hardback edition a year ago already confirm that I could and should have done it better myself. Some of those featured now appear flattered by their comparatively lowly positions (see Sepp Blatter, no. 27), while Colin Montgomerie's unexpectedly calm and dignified captaincy of the European Ryder Cup team has at least partially redeemed him. In my defence, others, notably Andy Gray (see no. 36) and Sir Ian Botham, who had the decency to confirm a reference in his entry (see no. 42) by starting a ruck with Ian Chappell in an Adelaide car park during the 2010–11 Ashes tour, have gratifyingly franked the form.

I have left the rankings unaltered, however, and updated entries only where strictly demanded by events. The judgements made in 2010 must take their chances, if I might go that extra mile in the flight from pomposity, against the sweep of future sporting history. If they choose to make the author look a fool, they will be joining a long and distinguished line.

All I can say in my own defence is that every word of what follows comes from the heart – not from one of that organ's more gentle or engaging ventrical chambers, perhaps, but from the heart nonetheless.

Matthew Norman
September 2010

101

Roger Federer

Setting aside the bleeding obvious (genius beyond compare, blah blah), it must be admitted, with reluctance and sadness, that the Fed has become something of a wanker.

It isn't easy to say, and people continue to shy away from saying it, for such is the reverence for the indecent beauty of his tennis and so capacious is the storehouse of glorious memories the Swiss has deposited in those, like me, who have followed his career obsessively for almost a decade. I can't think of a sportsman who has given me half as much televisual joy as Federer. I've barely missed a match he's played since he announced himself as a generational talent at Wimbledon in 2001 with a thrilling five-set win over the seemingly unbeatable apeman Pete Sampras (see no. 17). Even now, with his decline apparently established and picking up pace, there is no one you'd rather watch.

So it is with far more regret than relish that the masturbatorial quality he increasingly exhibits must, in the interests of the rigorous honesty that defines this book, be noted.

First of all, there are the gleaming white blazers – vaguely nautical, with hints of both seventies disco and something worn on the bridge of the USS *Enterprise*, invariably with some boastful statistic (fifteen major titles, for instance) stitched into them – he has taken to wearing. With the notable exception of the Green Jacket presented to winners of the US Masters, there are no naffer garments known to world sport.

More disturbing, meanwhile, is the self-pity. The infantile crying fit that followed his defeat to Rafael Nadal in the Australian Open final of 2009, when he had to abandon his loser's speech, although not the first of its kind, was an embarrassment to behold. For a while after that, it seemed that the birth of his twin girls and his maiden French Open win in the summer of that year had matured him. Admittedly his victory speech at Wimbledon, after edging out a heroic Andy Roddick 16–14 in the fifth, was not impressive. A man with fifteen major titles informing another with just the one, and that years ago, that he knew the agony of narrow defeat, lacked sensitivity. The relief was that Roddick was too traumatised by his loss to take in the clumpingly misplaced condescension.

Worse by far would come after the following year's shock quarter-final defeat to Tomáš Berdych, when Federer blamed everything – a back injury, a sore leg, bad bounces, Denis Compton and the alignment of Uranus in Mars's seventh house – other than himself, and offered the faintest and most grudging of praise for the Czech. 'I definitely gave away this match,' he said. But he hadn't. He'd simply been on the wrong end of the sort of hiding he has dished out a thousand times, and lacked not only the humility to accept it, but the will to simulate that humility. No one sane expects epochal titans like Roger Federer to be genuinely humble. You don't dominate a sport for years without a rapacious ego. All we ask is that they have the wit to give the appearance of modesty on the rare occasions it's demanded, and this now seems beyond Federer's grasp.

The emperors of Rome had slaves positioned behind them at all times with the sole purpose of reminding them of their humanity by whispering the mantra, 'You too shall die, Lord.' Federer could do with one of those as his career comes to what one hopes will, for all the irritation he can generate, be a very slow and gentle close. That, and a style counsellor on the lines of Reginald Jeeves, who always found a way to prevent Bertie Wooster from wearing one of those white smoking jackets he'd bought in Monte Carlo that were capable of cauterising the retina at twenty paces.

100

Neville Neville

Excuse the self-indulgent lurch into personal philosophising, but I have two iron rules of human existence, and two alone.

The first is that anyone who imagines that something as infinitely complex and perplexing as human existence is susceptible to an iron rule is, axiomatically, an imbecile.

The second is this. Never trust anyone who has the same name twice. Humbert Humbert was Lolita's paedo-stepfather, and Sirhan Sirhan shot Bobby Kennedy. Like so many iron rules, this has its one exception (Lord Chief Justice Igor Judge, or Judge Judge, seems a good judicial egg). Neville Neville, on the other hand, serves only to confirm it.

Can you honestly blame a man, you might ask, for his parents' startling lack of imagination? Of course not. What you can and must blame him for is not availing himself of the cheap and simple remedy that is deed poll. What the advantages of hanging on to both names could be, apart perhaps from halving the time required in adolescence to practise the signature, I can't imagine.

But it's not the wilful refusal to jettison at least one of those Nevilles that earns this double namer – a football agent with just the two clients (can you guess? Go on, have a crack) – his berth in this book. That refusal did, after all, inspire what may be the second-best football chant of the last twenty years. The first is the Chelsea ditty about Gianfranco Zola, sung to the tune of the Kinks' 'Lola', that went thus:

> If you think we're taking the piss
> Just ask that cunt Julian Dicks
> About Zola
> Who-oo-oo-o Zola ...

The brilliance, I've always felt, lies in how the Sondheims of Stamford Bridge eschewed substituting that 'piss' with the 'mick' that would have made it very nearly rhyme. This deliberate avoidance of the obvious strips away any lingering threat of Hallmark-greeting-card tweeness, and imbues the song with an emotional force, even poignancy, it would otherwise have lacked.

The Old Trafford chant regarding our subject, sung in the earliest days of his issue's Manchester United careers to the tune of Bowie's 'Rebel Rebel', was barely less uplifting, if bereft of the assonant genius celebrated above. This is it:

> Neville Neville, they're in defence
> Neville Neville, their future's immense
> Neville Neville, they ain't half bad
> Neville Neville, the name of their dad.

With one of the brothers, this was also uncannily prescient. The future of Gary 'Our Kid' Neville, with club and country, was indeed immense. More than that, Gary, one of the more articulate native players in the Premier League (he speaks English almost as well as the less fluent Dutchmen), would prove to be football's most influential trade unionist in the years between Jimmy Hill masterminding the scrapping of the maximum wage in the 1960s and John Terry's heroically flawed attempt to spearhead a mutiny against Fabio Capello during the World Cup of 2010.

You may recall how Gary, the Lech Wałęsa of his generation, nobly led the England dressing room in threatening to withdraw

4

their labour in protest over the ban imposed on his clubmate and fellow England defender Rio Ferdinand for the amnesiac skipping of a drugs test; and how he spearheaded the snubbing of the media after one international in umbrage at their criticism. Anyone on several million quid per annum who can bring the flavour of the Gdansk shipyard to the England dressing room is more than all right with me.

Philip, alas, is quite another matter. More gormless and less gifted by far than his elder brother, his career has contained just the one moment of immensity: the immense act of foolishness that concluded England's involvement, under the riotously clueless stewardship of Kevin Keegan, in Euro 2000. England, astonishingly incompetent even by their own standards in the final group game against Romania, had inexplicably recovered from conceding an early goal to lead 2–1 at half time.

The plucky little Ceauşescu-executors duly equalised in the second half, but with a couple of minutes remaining England had the draw they needed to make laughably ill-deserved progress to the knockout stage. And then, for no apparent reason, with Viorel Moldovan heading harmlessly towards the byline, Our Philip chose to scythe him to the turf. Short of picking the ball up and dribbling it around the box in homage to the Harlem Globetrotters' Meadowlark Lemon, he could not have gifted Romania a more blatant penalty.

An admirably distraught Phil would eventually receive full punishment (a transfer to Everton), but from Neville Neville there has been not a word of regret for his own central role – part genetic, no doubt, but surely part nurture as well – in the creation of this national humiliation.

Shameless Shameless.

99

Adolf Hitler

On 28 May 1940, Winston Churchill held the most important Cabinet meeting in British history. With the Foreign Secretary Lord Halifax championing the majority view that the military situation was so hopeless that the only option was to sue for peace, the new Prime Minister had a desperate fight on his hands to keep buggering on against the Hun. The need to win round his ministers elicited from him what is regarded as even his greatest speech – the fight must continue even if it meant every one of them bleeding to death in the dust, he said, because a nation that is conquered can rise again, but one that surrenders is finished for ever. The memory always amuses when a peevish politician does what Hillary Clinton did in the spring of 2008, and insists that fancy oratory ain't worth diddly.

For all that, I can't help wondering if Winston could have spared himself the rhetorical bother had he known then what we know now about Hitler and cricket. In the event, all he would have needed to do was inform the Cabinet, take a vote and go back to his bath.

In fact this outrage didn't emerge for another seven decades, when a contemporary account by a Hitler-loving Tory MP, one Oliver Locker-Lampson, was unearthed. This related how in 1923 Hitler came across some British expats enjoying a genteel game of cricket and asked if he could watch them play. Happy to oblige, these thoroughly decent coves went that extra mile for post-Versailles Treaty hatchet-burial by writing out the rules of the game for his perusal. Hitler, having duly perused, returned a few days later with his own team and took them on. The score-card of this Anglo–German clash has never been published, but from what followed we may presume that the result pre-empted the one to follow in 1945.

In an unwonted flash of intolerance, Hitler took umbrage at the rules, declaring the game 'insufficiently violent for German fascists' (Bodyline, which might have changed his thinking there, had yet to come). To this end, and with a novel way of training troops in mind, he suggested tweaking the rules by introducing a larger, harder ball, and abandoning pads. The absence of any masterplan to jettison the protective box may well be further evidence of that rumoured gonadic deficit. With only one to protect, imaginary Nazi cricket scholars posit, why bother?

If the Führer had entirely misunderstood the point of the game, failing to appreciate the languor, subtlety, nuance and infinite complexities that make Test cricket the most captivating of sports, perhaps he can be forgiven. He was never a chap easily imagined daydreaming at deep fine leg, or taking four hours to score 23 on a flat wicket.

Even so, and however unsuccessfully, he had blazed the trail of cheap-thrills pseudo-cricket that would find its apotheosis in Twenty20, and for that, among other things, he cannot lightly be forgiven.

98
Simon Barnes

'I suppose the problem,' observed the chief sportswriter of *The Times* once, when contemplating the crazy misconception that he merits the teasing of the inferior and the envious, 'is that some people can't come to terms with the idea that intelligent people like sport, and might want to read someone who tries to write about sport in an intelligent way.' How true this is, how very, very true. I mean, it's hardly as if there are incredibly bright and thoughtful writers like Hugh McIlvanney in the *Sunday Times* and the *Mail on Sunday*'s Patrick Collins out there covering this turf, is it? It's not as if Mike Atherton, Matthew Syed, Marina Hyde, Paul Hayward, Oliver Holt and others sate the appetite for smart and insightful sportswriting. 'My attempts to do so have met,' Mr Barnes went on, 'with a bewildering hostility in some quarters.'

Bewildering indeed. To be a lone oasis of intellectualism in an arid wasteland of moronic cliché must be a grievous weight on the shoulders of this most engagingly unpompous of hacks. Yet, like Atlas, he bears his burden stoically and without complaint. 'Occasionally I've come up with some high-faluting notion,' said this Pseuds Corner fixture, 'and somebody will say, "What if *Private Eye* got hold of it?" I say, "Well, fuck them. Let them get hold of it. I'm setting the bloody agenda here, not these guys." '

It's that 'occasionally' I love. At his best, when writing about his Down's Syndrome son and even every now and then about sport, Mr Barnes – an eerie doppelganger, with his lupine face and ponytail, for the Satanic character Bob in *Twin Peaks* – is very good indeed. At one iota less than his best, when presenting himself as what someone identified as a 'posturing narcissist' –

well, suffice it to say that another hack once expressed bewilderment of his own on finding him using the words 'unpretentious' and 'unselfconscious' (of Amir Khan) with apparent admiration.

From the canon of Simon Barnes, you could pluck many hundreds, perhaps thousands, of examples to illustrate the massive range and power of his mind, or indeed his commitment to wearing his learning lightly. Sometimes, for example, he will restrict the Nietzsche references to no more than one a paragraph (I'm a Heidegger man myself, with the odd Hegelian twist). But space is short, so let us leave it to this all-time personal favourite to give the flavour. Roger Federer, Mr Barnes once declared, is 'as myriad-minded as Shakespeare ever was'.

Sometimes, as the agenda-setter himself might be the very last to agree, there simply are no words.

97

The Argentine Polo Player

The abundant ridiculousness of the sport itself need not detain us here. That it appeals to male members of the House of Windsor within a death or two of the throne is ample comment on its mingling of needless physical danger and grotesque unaffordability. Its appeal to the female sex is predicated on something else, of course, as close students of Jilly Cooper's *oeuvre* will need little reminding. Why frustrated women *d'une certaine age* prefer the ogling of equestrians, and inter-chukka traipsing around fields stamping down displaced pieces of turf to work off some of that ardour, to availing themselves of the splendid pornography so freely available on cable television, I cannot say. All we know is that the Argentine polo player, that prancing ponce of the aristo sporting world, makes the polo field cougar paradise.

Invariably sickeningly handsome and repulsively dashing, this archetype of gentrified machismo has correctly identified the tight-buttocked, muscle-bulging activity of riding around swinging a mallet as the speediest route to a life of idle riches. For decades, long before the trail was blazed by Sarah Ferguson's mother, wealthy English and American women have been alighting on the pseudo-gaucho talent pool as a source of mid-life gratification.

Exactly how many of the players are descended from gentlemen who hurriedly fled central Europe in the mid-1940s is unknown, though any genetic inheritance from Prussian cavalrymen would obviously be handy for horsemanship. One of the age's finest players, meanwhile, glories in the first name of Adolfo.

Yet it is not for us to visit the sins of the great-grandfathers on the great-grandsons. What it is for us to do is point out that these show ponies are essentially glamourised gigolos with nothing on their minds but the servicing of Anglo-American sugar mummies and the cushy lives their capacious purses will thenceforth provide. What polo represents to the Argentine, in other words, is a hole with a mint.

96
Blake Aldridge

So much nauseating drivel is intoned by sports people about the primacy of the collective effort – the striker insisting he couldn't care about scoring so long as the team wins, for example, when he'd massacre an orphanage for a hat-trick in a 3–9 defeat – that any expression of individuality in a group context generally acts as an anti-emetic. When, however, a member of that group, even a group as small as two, pinpoints the midst of competition as the time to slag off his partner, the antidote loses its efficacy. When that same group member chooses to do so at the side of an Olympic pool, by speaking to his mother in the crowd on his mobile phone, you know you're dealing with a fool of the very first water.

The diving prodigy Tom Daley, who represented Britain in the 2008 Olympics at an age when others are gingerly ditching the armbands, was admittedly an irritant himself, with all the robotic references to his sponsor. He paid tribute to 'Team Visa' with all the frequency and sincerity Barry McGuigan lavished on 'my manager Mr Barney Eastwood' before the two went to attritional courtroom war.

But then, precocious fourteen-year-olds are irritating, as parents and *Britain's Got Talent* viewers need no reminding. They also tend, inexplicably, to lack Olympic experience, which perhaps explained the sub-par performance in the Beijing synchronised diving event of a pubescent boy who would confirm his talent a year later by winning an individual world title in Rome.

Aldridge, although more than a decade older, allowed him no such latitude, publicly criticising Daley during the competition despite the experts identifying Aldridge himself as the weaker performer. As for the phone call, filial piety is a wonderful thing, but there are times and places to demonstrate it. Seldom since Oedipus has a public figure found a less appropriate method of showing the world how much he loves his mummy.

Aldridge's punishment was not the putting out of his own eyes, but a lurch into a new sport also covered by live cameras. Sadly, he seems to have as much talent for shoplifting as for diving, winning his first conviction in May 2009, a few months before Daley won his gold in Rome. He was fined £80 by police for nicking stuff from B&Q.

Encouragingly, he appears to be showing more sticking power in this career. He was arrested again in February 2010 on suspicion of stealing wine from Tesco and assaulting the security guard who caught him at it. His trial awaits at the time of writing, and we wish him well. If and when it takes place – if it hasn't already – a word of advice. Whatever the temptation, try not to call your mother in the spectator seats at the back from the dock. Judges hate that. And however badly you think your barrister is performing, Blake, on no account criticise him publicly until the verdict is in. In court, as on the diving board, it is essential to work as a team.

95
Peter Fleming

John McEnroe's old doubles partner may be the most unnervingly weird character ever to analyse any sport on television. His air of intellectual superiority may be well-founded, as it would be for anyone with an IQ over ninety sharing airtime with Barry Cowan, but it does tend to grate.

Although he behaves himself during Wimbledon, when he works for the BBC, Fleming seldom hears a question on Sky that isn't beneath his dignity. His preferred mode of expressing disdain, particularly towards presenter Marcus Buckland, a modest and charming soul, is the exaggerated pause. How, Mr Buckland once asked him, would he explain the amazing abundance of talent in the men's game today? Eunuchs grew rabbinical beards in the time Fleming took to ponder this, before offering a desolate 'I dunno,' and lapsing into quietude once more.

On a good day, the silence in response to a seemingly unchallenging enquiry – Does Novak Djokovic's second serve look a bit off? Are Rafa Nadal's knees playing up? What is the time? – puts you in mind of Pinter performed by the Theatre of the Mute. On a bad one, you could write a wistful rite-of-passage memoir in the style of Alan Bennett in the time he requires to address a wayward Andy Murray two-hander down the line.

Occasionally, when Fleming feels that the foolishness of the question requires more peremptory treatment, he might wince, snort or raise his eyebrows to the crown of his head. Now and again, he will stare in disbelief, the gaze apparently in homage to Jack Nicholson in *The Shining* or Javier Bardem in *No Country for Old Men*.

When Mr Fleming, facially a hybrid between the Addams Family's butler Lurch and Jay Gatsby, does deign to share an opinion, it's invariably worth hearing. He is an extremely bright guy, and he certainly has a presence (that of a Harvard philosophy professor stunned into an existential crisis at mysteriously finding himself redeployed as a third-grade teaching assistant). Tennis, like darts and nothing else, is a sport Sky covers well, and the languid gloss Fleming lends to its broadcasts does much to explain that bucking of the form book. I wouldn't be without him for the world.

Nor, however, would I wish to get into a big-money staring contest with him, much less be the Chairman of the Joint Chiefs in the Situation Room at the White House demanding an instant decision from a President Fleming about how to respond to worryingly raised activity levels in an Iranian nuclear silo.

Tony Green

The most perplexing event in the sporting calendar is the BDO World Darts Championship, broadcast each New Year by the BBC. The tortured history of the great darting split, as featured in a hilarious edition of BBC2's documentary strand *Trouble at the Top*, needn't detain us long. Suffice it to say that in the 1990s a trickle of BDO stars flowed away to form the rival PDC, now run with typical commercial *élan* by Barry Hearn, and that the trickle later became a torrent.

Where the PDC is dart's equivalent of football's Premier League – a point it subtly underscores by naming a competition 'the Premier League of Darts' – the BDO is, at best, its Conference. So robbed of talent has it become that the trades descriptions people risk a class action for negligence by failing to have it restyled The World Championship for People Who Try Hard, Bless 'Em But Just Aren't Terribly Good at Darts. An averagely well coordinated male who threw the first arrow of his life on Christmas Day could expect to reach the quarter-finals, at least, a fortnight later.

The timing of the BDO event, which starts immediately after Phil 'The Power' has retained the real world title on Sky Sports, is the equivalent of rescheduling Wimbledon as a warm-up for a satellite event in Cleethorpes, and adds an additional layer of poignancy that isn't strictly required. That the work of lead commentator Tony Green perfectly reflects the quality of the darts completes a startlingly surreal picture.

Best known to students of game show theory as Jim Bowen's *Bullseye* stooge ('And Bully's special priiiiize … a reverse lobotomy!'), this John Prescott lookalike, and alas soundalike, must be the most clueless commentator in the history of televised sport. Like the former deputy PM he so closely resembles in girth and jowls, Mr Green boldly pioneers aphasia as a mainstream lifestyle choice.

His trademarks may be boiled down to two. Whenever the director shows a cutaway shot of a palpably bored crowd sullenly watching the apology for top-flight darts on a giant screen (and isn't that the special appeal of a live event? It's so qualitatively different from watching at home) he will respond with an elongated 'Yeeeeeessssss, there they are!' Technically, it's hard to pick a fight with that. There is invariably where they were. On other levels … well, it's not Richie Benaud, is it?

The other signature dish is to respond to a cosmically witless pre-prepared pun from co-commentator David Croft with the wheezy breath of an obese hyena dying from emphysema. This death rattle is then followed by 'Dear, dear … oh dear,' to suggest a psycho-geriatric-ward fugitive reacting with a mixture of delight and shame to a bladder accident induced by unquenchable mirth at Arthur Askey affecting, on the London Palladium stage in 1957, to be a busy, busy bee.

How Mr Green has been retained by the BBC for so long, in defiance of the verbal facility of the inter-stroke victim, is less mysterious than it seems. The BDO is effectively the property of a cabal – a couple of veteran players, chairman Olly Croft, master of ceremonies Martin Fitzmaurice (the sea monster who screams 'Are you ready? Let's. Play. Darts'), cackling sub-Kray blingmaster Bobby George, and Mr Green himself.

Between them, this bunch have transformed the BDO into a hybrid of kitschily ironic entertainment, aversion therapy for those terrified of becoming hooked on televised darts, and crèche for those who might one day grow up to join the PDC.

Mr Green himself refuses to acknowledge the existence of the rival organisation, which unusually for him makes some sense. The immortal Sid Waddell, his one-time BBC colleague, is of course the PDC's main commentator, and even Mr Green can see the danger of drawing attention to the contrast. Even when the BDO version was won by a disabled man unable to extend his arm fully when throwing, the Australian haemophiliac Tony David in 2001, Mr Green's confidence in its supremacy remained unshaken.

'Yeeeessssss,' is how he greeted the winning double that day, 'it's Tony Davis!' After two weeks of the tournament and two hours of final action, how cruel to come within a single space on the middle line of the Qwerty keyboard of calling the new champion's name right. For once, Mr Green had stumbled on a certain eloquence. Albeit unwittingly, and with unwonted succinctness, he had told his audience all it needed to know, if only about himself, in a syllable.

93

Frank Warren

How a man of such exquisite sensitivity has survived and made money in the rough and Runyonesque world of boxing is one of the miracles of the age. Mr Warren's vulnerability to criticism does him nothing but credit. Where others become hardened by long careers in the big-fight game, he has been softened remarkably.

Other than offering sincere admiration, what can you say about the adorably florid-faced boxing promoter and gunshot survivor? Not a dickie bird. While Frank lives up to his own belief that when people have an opinion, 'they are entitled to express it' – for example, he repeatedly expressed his opinion of me ('moron', for example) in his *News of the World* column – experience teaches that this passion for freedom of speech is a one-way street. Even the most affectionate of teasing will provoke from Frank the threat of an action for libel. In fact, he'll more than likely sue over this.

'If it pleases your lordship, my client Mr Frank Warren, a man of the most blameless character, a pillar of his local community, a tireless worker for many deserving charities, is profoundly distressed by the implication that he may tend toward the mildly litigious, and seeks substantial damages for the injury to his feelings and reputation …' Somewhere in such an action we might sniff out the stirrings of a defence, should it come to that. And it's even money that it will.

92

Graeme Souness

Even in the legalised GBH halcyon era of the 1970s and early eighties, English football knew no more vicious a would-be maimer than Graeme Souness. With the thick moustache and bubble perm regarded as mandatory at Liverpool at the time, he may have joined team-mate Mark Lawrenson (see no. 14) as a prototype for the Village People's construction worker. But had you found yourself sharing a YMCA dormitory or navy bunk with Souness, you'd soon enough have swapped the warmth for a street doorway or Davy Jones's locker, for fear of being on the wrong end of a studs-up leg-breaker in the middle of the night.

No one ever took such unsmiling satisfaction from endangering careers. His most infamous assault, late in his career for Glasgow Rangers against Steaua Bucharest, crystallised the purity of his malevolence. About the raising and spiteful stamping of his right boot onto the thigh of one Dmitri Rotario there was nothing unusual. What was so refreshingly novel was that Souness, whose reaction to this arrestable offence was to clutch his own leg in mock agony, was in possession of the ball at the time.

The best to be said of Souness's commitment to violence is that it never lacked integrity. Just as with Roy Keane, who is excused an entry thanks to the accurate character reading he offered Mick McCarthy (see no. 31), he was too magnificent a player to need the brutality. There was no design or purpose to it whatever. This was the Edmund Hillary of football hatchet men: he sought to rupture cruciate ligaments because they were there.

Souness went on to earn his berth on Sky Sports, where despite the hot competition he shines out as a beacon of charisma-free witlessness, in the traditional manner. Only having repeatedly proved his uselessness as a manager, with Liverpool, Blackburn Rovers and Newcastle among others, was he deemed fit to point out their inadequacies to coaches in current employment.

Despite the rich catalogue of failures, his self-confidence remains as strident as it is misplaced. A few years ago I came across him in a bar during one of Tottenham's then perpetual managerial crises, and asked if he fancied himself the guy to turn Spurs around. 'Son,' he said, leaning magisterially back on his stool, 'the club I couldnae turn round has yet to be built.'

Inexplicably, this remains a judgement shared by no one else. Indeed, in a nice instance of life imitating art imitating life, Souness has come to emulate Yosser Hughes, with whom he famously appeared in a *Boys From the Black Stuff* cameo (excellent he was, too). Time and time again he has invited chairmen to 'Gizza job,' and been answered with a sarcastic chuckle. Although not, one suspects, to his face.

91

Kriss Akabusi

It pays testament to his enduring genius to irritate that even today, years after last setting eyes and (worse) ears on the man, it remains impossible to do the late-night channel-flick of the insomniac philistine without a frisson of terror that Kriss Akabusi might crop up in an ancient repeat of *A Question of Sport.*

As a useful 400-metre runner over hurdles and on the flat, specialising in stirring last legs of the relay, Akabusi seemed a harmless enough soul. Yet even then the exaggerated can-do enthusiasm of his post-race interviews – for all that they often came moments after he had proved that he couldn't do, and indeed hadn't done – hinted at the horrors to come.

Television executives evidently noticed them, and concluded that what the viewing public needed in the deep recession of the early 1990s was the human equivalent of one of those executive toys which, at the faintest touch, produce an extended burst of deranged giggling. If laughter is indeed the best medicine, Akabusi will live to be 140. The problem for the rest of us is that while he was getting all the health benefits, we were stuck in the placebo group. Worse than that, the insane chortling that was doing him such a power of good had the disturbing side effect of raising the blood pressure in the rest of us.

If there is an unflatteringly jealous tone in the above, the reason for that is simply put. Of all the human traits, the one I envy most is the Akabusian gift of being easily amused. In a dark and gruesome world, what ineffable bliss it must be to laugh uncontrollably at nothing until the ribcage creaks and the bladder screams for mercy.

In what passed for his televisual heyday, when he was a presenter on *Record Breakers* and a guest on just about everything else, nothing – not one thing – Akabusi could hear would fail to strike him as outlandishly amusing. If the Shipping Forecast on Radio 4 revealed a high ridge of pressure moving towards South Utsira, he'd squeal with mirth. If the Hang Seng index in Hong Kong had been marked sharply up in brisk early trading, he would yelp and shake with merriment. If his GP had told him that he'd developed gangrene in both legs, and required an immediate double amputation, he'd have collapsed with mirth and crawled around on the floor until the limbs detached themselves of their own accord. In his commitment to laughing uncontrollably at the studiedly unfunny, he was a one-man Michael McIntyre audience long before that alleged comedian emerged to raise fresh doubts about the taste and even the sanity of his compatriots.

Whether the unceasing screeching was genuine, possibly due to an undiagnosed neurological condition, or the stand-out feature of a construction designed to get him media work, it is impossible to be sure. I don't remember his eyes laughing in tune with his mouth, but it was all a blessedly long time ago.

Today, Mr Akabusi does what retired sportsmen with a TV future buried in the past tend to do. He is a motivational speaker, using silly voices, demented changes of decibel level (whispering one moment, yelling the next, neither volume remotely explained by the text), anecdotes and archive footage of relay triumphs to give new meaning and direction to the lives of those unable to find a televangelist at the right price.

No doubt he makes a decent living from reliving the highlights of a decent career, and explaining to those unable to better the late King of Tonga's personal best for the 60-metre dash how to adapt his athletic experiences to become better, happier and richer people. I hope so. There is no obvious malice in the man, and I wish him well.

For all that, I can't help thinking that that the only people for whom a talk from Kriss Akabusi would constitute an effective motivational force are members of the voluntary euthanasia society Exit.

90

Ronnie O'Sullivan

For this possessor of the purest natural talent ever known to British sport – or games, for those who believe that a *sine qua non* of any authentic sport is that it leaves the player needing a shower – lavish allowances must be made. He is the scion of a family next to which the kith and kin of John Terry, engagingly Runyonesque though they are, look like the Waltons.

Rocket Ronnie's father remains a house guest of Her Majesty for murdering an alleged Kray associate in a restaurant in 1982, although he is up for parole, while the mother did a bit of bird herself for tax evasion. You needn't have a doctorate in clinical psychology, or be a close student of the parental poetry of Philip Larkin, to appreciate the effects on a formative mind.

The extent of Ronnie's confusion and vulnerability was spotlighted a few years ago when, flailing about to make sense of his life, a little (a very little, perhaps) like Woody Allen in *Hannah and Her Sisters*, he turned for a spiritual guide to the boxer Naseem Hamed. Mr Hamed narrowly failed to shepherd Ronnie into the Muslim faith. He never did become Rahquet Rhani al Sull'ivan, but it was apparently a close call.

However unlikely the image of this tortured, saturnine figure being called to prayer by the muezzin, the external discipline might have helped a man who conceded a best-of-seventeen-frame match to Stephen Hendry when 0–4 behind with a terse 'I've had enough mate', and whose notion of good grace in defeat, at the China Open of 2008, extended to bragging about the girth of his penis at the press conference, and inviting a female reporter to fellate him, before giving her a helpful demonstration by mistaking the head of his microphone for a lollipop.

In the absence of that religious discipline, it becomes ever harder to overlook the contempt with which he treats his genius. At times, in fact, genius has seemed an inadequate word. Roger Federer is a genius, but always had to work devilishly hard to cope with the raging Mallorcan bull Rafael Nadal (and usually failed), and even the likes of Novak Djokovic and Andy Murray.

At his best, O'Sullivan appears not to be working at all, potting balls at ridiculous speed and with absurd ease with either hand. Perhaps this explains why he seems not to value his gift at all. Often, in fact, he seems to resent it, and to wish it dead. As a fabled wit once observed – Oscar Wilde, perhaps, or possibly John Virgo – each man kills the thing he loves. Ronnie hasn't killed it yet, but it seldom blossoms as gorgeously as it did, or as it should.

Still harder to excuse is the contempt he shows his public. Whether or not his lip-curling disdain for snooker is sourced in insecurity he tries to cloak in contrived diffidence, his concession of frames when he needs a single snooker to win them has been getting on the top ones for too long.

The disrespect he shows almost every rival other than John Higgins is more a comment on him, needless to say, than on them. Whenever the likable Mark Selby, who has the nickname 'Jester' for the compelling comedic rationale that he hails from Leicester, wins the last four frames to beat him, Ronnie makes it crystal clear that he doesn't rate him, and hints at having thrown the match away because scrapping against so palpable an inferior is beneath his dignity.

As for the continual threats to quit, no public figure in history has announced their retirement so often – yes, Streisand, that includes you – and reneged. He knows he can behave as boorishly, lewdly and disrespectfully as he wishes without that retirement being forced on him because he remains the biggest draw, if not the only one, in snooker, and that without him the dangerous decline of the game (a world championship sponsored by Pukka Pies, forsooth) might well become terminal. But the little-boy-lost act ran out of whatever minimal charm it had long ago. There comes a time in every wounded lamb's life when, however much they fucked him up, his mum and dad, the leonine thing to do is not to roar but stoically to hide the misery and behave. At thirty-five, that time is now. If not, the next time he announces his retirement, he might find that the majority reaction isn't a plea to reconsider, or even a weary shrug, but a sigh of relief.

89

Pelé

If Pelé had shown the same talent with his feet as he has exhibited since retiring with his mouth, he would have been, at best, Emile Heskey. Never has the old saw that former sportsmen should be neither seen nor heard been more perfectly illustrated – and that includes such fellow entrants in this work as Mark Lawrenson, Sue Barker, Sebastian Coe and even Kriss Akabusi.

Genius that he was on the pitch, off it he struggles to make the cut as a half-wit. You can barely wade through five pages of his autobiography without encountering a variant of 'Once again, my business judgement sadly betrayed me.' So it was that money troubles obliged him to advertise Viagra, thereby betraying our memories of the wonderfully lithe, natural seventeen-year-old striking talent who devastated Sweden in the 1958 World Cup final, and later electrified the 1970 tournament. The last thing you want from a sporting god is the image of him struggling with flaccidity.

The same talent for misjudgement that caused his frequent flirtations with bankruptcy (you could sell him a batch of $103 bills for twice their face value) extends to his reading of the one thing he might be expected to know a little about. As a football pundit, Pelé is barely less mythical a figure than he once was in the yellow and blue of Brazil. Romario, a successor as leader of the Brazilian attack, once said, 'Pelé is a poet when he keeps his mouth shut,' while the World Cup-winning coach and briefly manager of Chelsea Luiz Felipe Scolari chipped in with this little gem: 'I believe Pelé knows nothing about football. His analysis always turns out to be wrong. If you want to win a title, you have to listen to Pelé and then do the opposite.'

The Sadim of football punditry (like Midas in reverse, everything he touches turns to lead) has made too many sensationlly daft predictions for them all to be catalogued here, so we must confine ourselves to a few favourites.

Pelé's pick for the 1994 World Cup was Colombia. Suffice it to say that the Colombian defender Andrés Escobar had been shot dead in a Medellin car park before the final was played. In 1998 he went for Norway. Norway. Four years later, the scorer of more than 1,000 career goals studied the World Cup field, and plumped – I'm not making this up – for England. To repeat, that's England. E.N.G.L.A.N.D.

Over his insistence, long ago, that Nicky Barmby would become a player of unarguably world class, and his categorical statement that an African nation would win the World Cup before the year 2000, let us lightly pass. Perhaps the highlight of highlights from the mouth of this soothsayer of soothsayers was his contemptuous dismissal of his own country's chances in 2002 (the year, you may recall, he predicted an England victory). Brazil, insisted Pelé, would not survive the group stage. How tantalisingly close the team came to fulfilling his expectation, as they became the first country ever to win all seven games in normal time en route to lifting the Jules Rimet Trophy.

Whoever would have believed back in 1986 that of the two players universally acknowledged, then as now, as the greatest of all time, it would be Diego Maradona – much too adorably deranged nowadays to warrant an entry of his own in this volume – who went on to become the more beloved, and Pelé who would establish himself, even in football, as the imbecile's imbecile? If only there were a Viagran equivalent for a limp and lifeless brain.

88

Brian Barwick

When Caligula set the template for hilarious over-promotion, who would have thought that the day would dawn when the Football Association of England would make the creation of a horse as Consul of Rome seem a tediously conventional employment decision? In fact, giving his horse Incitatus that much-prized post was the sanest thing (not the highest of bars to clear, in truth) Caligula ever did. Its purpose was purely ironic. He intended to satirise the cravenness of his Senators by obliging them to celebrate the appointment as a masterstroke. As, to a Senator, what with being in terror of their lives, they did.

What Brian Barwick's ironic intent in hiring Steve McClaren as England football coach might have been, on the other hand, I've no idea, because the only thing satirised there was the luminescent idiocy of Barwick himself and the FA of which he was chief executive. However, since the only other possible explanation is that he regarded Mr McClaren (see no. 25) as a gifted international coach, there is no option but to hail him as the world's first, and doubtless last, kamikaze satirist.

Truth be told, this erstwhile TV sports executive looks nothing like an anarcho-comic genius. With the wide, bald dome and bristly little moustache, he more closely resembles Mr Grimsdale, the 1950s middle-management archetype in all those side-splitting Norman Wisdom flicks that still have them queuing round the block in downtown Tirana.

Mr Grimsdale can be excused for repeatedly hiring Norman, having noted the calamitous results of doing so in thirty-three previous films, on the grounds that he was a fictional character conforming to somebody else's script. Mr Barwick wrote his own, yet no one but he was vaguely surprised that McClaren's England stint concluded beneath a deluge of farce (brolly and all) of which a coalition of the Keystone Kops, Laurel and Hardy, Jim Carrey and our own Chuckle Brothers could barely have dreamed. McClaren's inadequacies were so evident to all but Mr Barwick that the first obituary to his England career was published the day after his appointment was announced. This was at least a day late.

Still more humiliating than the act of panic itself (in such a state was Barwick after his fiascoid failure to hire the Brazilian Luiz Felipe Scolari that he'd have given the job to a hat stand with the requisite coaching badge) was the way in which he chose to present it. Fans of Gordon Brown's blanket denial in the summer of 2009 that he had intended to fire Alistair Darling as Chancellor should note that Brian Barwick had blazed that trail. He donned his straightest face to inform us that Mr McClaren had been his 'first-choice candidate' all along, within days of allowing himself to be filmed at Heathrow en route to talk to Scolari in Lisbon – the very act of amateur-hour incompetence which provoked the media frenzy that in turn frightened Scolari into telling Mr Barwick to stuff the job up his jacksie. And in the sense that Mr McClaren dwelt in a holiday cottage a few inches to the south of Mr Barwick's upper colon at the time, this is precisely what he did.

Two years later, soon after McClaren had masterminded the epochal disaster at Wembley that saw England lose to Croatia and fail to qualify for Euro 2008, old Grimsdale followed him out of the FA. His involvement in football now rests with his place on the board of Hampton & Richmond Borough FC. So let us end this appreciation on an uplifting and life-enhancing note by congratulating Brian Barwick on finding his level at last. Long may he enjoy it.

87
Sledging

All that strictly needs to be said of the relationship between this cricketing branch of low-level bullying and genuine wit is this: of all the cricket-playing nations, sledging is beloved solely by the Australians.

There was a time, long ago, when it may have had some appeal. When W.G. Grace reacted to having his stumps clattered by informing the bowler, "Twas the wind which took the bail orf, good sir,' and the umpire chipped in, 'Indeed, doctor, and let us hope the wind helps thee on thy journey back to the pavilion,' the coalescence of mannerliness and the lingo of the Amish barn-builder lent the exchange some charm. Nothing there to induce the enquiry, 'Where is thy ribcage repair kit, good doctor, when thou most sorely requireth it?' perhaps, but rather sweet for all that.

By the time, some half a century later, that F.S. Trueman was advising an incoming Aussie batsman who shut the gate to the pavilion behind him, 'Don't bother, son, you won't be out there long enough,' the art of sledging may already have been in decline. Another half a century on, and it is virtually impossible to find any sledge that is not predicated on either the batsman's girth or the conceit that his wife has a sexual appetite so rapacious that her reflex observation, having serviced the entire Household Cavalry, is to ask after the whereabouts of the Scots Dragoons.

Perhaps this is too harsh. It could be that Shane Warne was indeed a larrikin Mark Twain, and Adam Gilchrist an ocker Tallulah Bankhead. We'll never know for sure, because seldom do the stump microphones capture the inter-ball hilarity.

However, now and again a sledge is picked up. It may give a flavour of this nourishing comedic form to quote this citation, offered by New Zealand blogger Michael Ellis as his candidate for history's greatest sledge: 'And of course you can't forget Ian Healy's legendary comment that was picked up by the Channel 9 microphones when Arjuna Ranatunga called for a runner on a particularly hot night during a one-dayer in Sydney. "You don't get a runner for being an overweight, unfit, fat cunt."' It is not known whether the Sri Lankan felt it beneath him to offer the mandatory reply to a portliness-related sledge ('Yeah, mate. Well, it's yer missus's fault for giving me a biscuit every time I fuck her').

The oppressively limited range of subject matter qualifies the sledge as sport's closest equivalent to the haiku. If the batsman isn't fat or a cuckold in the imagination of the Oscar Wildes of the slips, he must be gay. 'So,' Glenn McGrath once enquired of Ramnaresh Sarwan, 'what does Brian Lara's dick taste like?' 'I don't know,' responded the West Indian, preparing a foray into virgin sledging territory. 'Ask your wife.' If anything encapsulates the exquisite subtlety of the two-way sledge, it is McGrath's counterstrike to that. 'If you ever mention my wife again,' he said, expecting a degree of sensitivity (his wife, now deceased, had been diagnosed with cancer) his reference to the fellating of Mr Lara might be seen to have sacrificed, 'I'll fucking rip your fucking throat out.' Whether or not Mr Sarwan is indeed a friend of Dorothy, who would deny that Mr McGrath, in common with all the legends of Australian sledging, is a spiritual friend of Dorothy Parker?

86

Graham Poll

The public laundering of dirty washing is never a savoury sight. Every family has its private embarrassments, and the sane ones do what they can to keep them private. None of us wants the neighbours to learn our grubby little secrets. The same goes for companies, in which a specially acute strain of loathing is reserved for the whistle-blower.

So too it is with countries. You and I know that secondary education in Britain is a disaster, that scandalous numbers leave school barely literate, and that the innumeracy statistics are equally shameful. We know that the developed world's educative dunce's cap rests upon the British head, and it anguishes us. Government after government tries, or pretends to try, to sort it out, and through the lack of funds, will and courage, fails. These things we know, and these things we naturally prefer to keep to ourselves.

Yet in every family there appears to be someone who can't avoid spilling the beans, and in the case of our national family the blabbermouth is Graham Poll.

In front of the several hundred millions watching Croatia play Australia in the 2006 World Cup, our leading referee revealed that the British education system produces adults who, let alone struggling with their twelve-times table, cannot count to two.

Late in a game of mesmerising fractiousness, Mr Poll had sent off a brace of players when he showed Croatia's Josip Šimunić a second yellow card. The ensuing calculation was not, on the *prima facie* evidence, a demanding one. This was not an equation to have the average ref whispering, 'Get me Vorderman on the phone NOW' at the Fifa fourth official through his little microphone. Put simply, the equation was as follows: 1 yellow + 1 yellow = 2 yellows = 1 red.

On *Sesame Street*, Big Bird would have cracked it like a nut with a diseased and brittle shell. Yet it tantalisingly eluded Mr Poll. He allowed Šimunić to remain on the field for several minutes before ploughing virgin territory by making the Croat football history's first recipient of a third yellow card. Then, and only then, possibly concluding he'd gone as far along Revolution Road as seemed decent in one night, did Mr Poll fish into his back pocket for the red card.

Along with the mischievous pleasure at the pricking of a bumptiously over-inflated ego went a dash of sympathy. A reputation built over many years had been obliterated by one moment of inexplicable daftness, and that, as Gerald Ratner would confirm, is nothing to be relished.

Mr Poll retired from international football the next day, in the manner of the cabinet minister who elects to resign to spend more time with his family the night before he appears on the front page of the *Sun*.

The damage had already been done, of course. The dirty secret about British education had been broadcast to the planet. The subtle irony that this unwitting act of whistle-blowing ensured Mr Poll would never blow a whistle again on the international stage may have been little consolation to the man who cannot count to two.

85

Pat Cash

How fitting that Cash recently became tennis's youngest grand-father. The whiny tone to his tennis punditry, the classical ocker sexism and the sub-Blairite attempts to cling to his youth by playing electric guitar suggest a man at least three decades older than his forty-five years.

Plagued by the confusions that causing mild offence is a substitute for wit and grinning cockiness is indiscernible from winsome charm, Cash's specialist impertinence is ignorantly dismissing tennis players of infinitely greater talent and spirit than he ever showed. Allied to this is a rare talent for being wrong. To take one memorable example, early in 2007 Cash wrote a piece, headlined 'Serena is Lost Cause', in *The Times*, attempting to nudge the younger Williams sister towards retire-ment and describing her as 'deluded' for imagining she had a future at the top of the game. 'When Serena Williams arrives in Australia on her first foreign playing trip in a year,' began the world-weary elder statesman, 'and announces that it is only a matter of time before she is again dominating the sport, it's time to tell her to get real.' Two weeks later, as you will already perhaps have guessed, Serena annihilated Maria Sharapova 6–1 6–2 in the Australian Open final

Getting real seems a habitual problem for Cash. His own journey into retirement was not the gracious swansong he advo-cated for Serena. Far from it, the embittered grouch on annual display in the BBC's wretched Wimbledon coverage had an early run-out. He took deep umbrage at the failure of tournament directors and the ATP to give him wild cards late in his career, when the rigor mortis had set into his game. The therapy that followed did little to improve him.

There have been sporting pundits who endeared themselves by forever complaining that things ain't what they were (Freddie Trueman comes to mind) and scratching their heads until the scalp bled in mystification at modern ways. Cash is not among them. While he may choose to regard his vinegary carping about the venality and amorality of current tennis as the refreshing bluntness of a straight-shooter, it is in fact purely the self-pitying rancour of the nasty old geezer in the nursing home wash-clean plastic chair, muttering 'Dunno they're born' at anyone under sixty who appears on the telly. 'Nobody wanted anything to do with me,' he sniffled once of the indifference shown to him in the dog days of his playing career. You know just how they felt.

84

Richard Keys

Strictly speaking, this emblem of blazer-clad corporate loyalty – a man who would lay down his life, you suspect, in the cause of Sky Sports – should be of more interest to anthropologists than anyone else. In the latter days of his TV career, the advent of high-definition television that obliged him to shave his hands to spare the feelings of more squeamish viewers, rendered this less obvious than before. But there was a time when his fronting of broadcasts raised grave doubts about the professionalism of the Ape Recovery Squad at London Zoo.

His own professionalism was seldom in doubt before the heavily conflated and richly amusing scandal that cost him and Andy Gray, the Tweedledumb to Keys' Tweedledumber, their Sky berths. Until the release of off-air footage in which he made dismissive remarks about the capabilities of a female assistant referee, and the subsequently released off-air tape of him vainly trying to ingratiate himself with Jamie Redknapp by speculating that the latter had enjoyed coitus (smashed it!) with a young woman, he had anchored Premier League transmissions with a seldom-wavering dull competence unleavened by his slavish commitment to talking up what he routinely refers to, despite its transparent recent decline, as 'the best league in the world'. This rare example of a cliché without a shred of truth (Spain's La Liga has always had the edge in everything but the capacity to induce preposterous hype) was not, of course, his alone. The BBC propagates it with barely less fervour. The difference is that, where Gary Lineker is capable of admitting that a Premier League game was less than scintillating, Mr Keys was not. Supported by whichever permutation of pinhead pundits the afternoon or evening spews up, his devotion to his employer and the domestic competition that is its cash cow compelled him to talk up every match as if it were a classic.

Being easily entertained is an enviable gift, but there comes a point at which it becomes hard to distinguish from an illness. The reassuring news for any residual fans of Mr Keys, or new ones who have fallen in love with those dulcets as broadcast on the radio station TalkSport is that he was in fact perfectly well, and found much of the football as soporific as the rest of us, as his one, pre-smashed it, on-air cock-up established in 2007. 'Daft little ground, silly game, fuck off,' was his verdict, unwittingly broadcast, on a Scottish trip to the Faroe Islands, lending a piquancy to the many times he has prissily apologised, as Sky presenters must, for profanities uttered by interviewees or bolshy tennis players.

If he could have dredged up the same candour when aware that the microphone was live, and shown more respect for an audience that may be marginally less thick and pliable than he imagined than he did for the sensibilities of female colleagues and officials, it would have improved him no end. But then, honestly appraising football matches was never his function. Sky Sports is the public relations arm of the Premier League, and Richard Keys was, for almost twenty years, its regrettably missing link between a PG Tips primate and Max Clifford.

That his television career effectively ended because he was unearthed as a Neanderthal quarter-wit may constitute rough justice, as well as a blessed relief for subscribers. Yet this was less a startling revelation than a long-delayed official statement of the bleeding obvious, and to that extent nothing became Richard Keys like the manner of his sacking.

Harold 'Dickie' Bird

In the absence of an 'uncle' or schoolmaster showing undue interest in his development, the cricket-fixated boy of the 1970s knew no more unwanted an authority figure than the then doyen of Test match umpires.

It would be an exaggeration to claim that Dickie ruined my childhood and early adolescence, but his heightened fears about the weather condemned me to countless summer days of needless boredom. If he had an inkling in his bones that a raincloud drizzling over central Turkmenistan was contemplating a move in a westerly direction that might take it over Headingley by mid-November, he'd take them off. If the light dipped by one iota below the level required to read the bottom line of the optician's wall chart from forty paces, off he would take them.

Sweet-hearted as this eternal schoolboy seemed to be (even at seventy-seven years old you imagine him curling up under the bedclothes with his torch and a copy of *Wisden*), a searing pain in the bum he undeniably was. His morbid terror of making mistakes led to him routinely rejecting LBW shouts which Hawkeye today would show travelling like guided missiles towards the middle of middle stump. The surest method of avoiding mistakes, of course, was to avoid the playing of any cricket, which may explain why reports of a small shadow at deep fine leg at Sabina Park or the 'Gabba would have him taking them off at Edgbaston.

In retirement, alas, the endearing fussbucket nerviness of old mutated into something less lovable. Dickie Bird the umpire became Dickie Bird the National Character, and this dubious role he embraced without a shred of the neurosis he had lavished on unconfirmed reports of cloud movement in Chad. The success of his autobiography, imaginitively entitled *My Autobiography*, went to his head. The sweetness was replaced by a mild strain of egomania that persuaded him to keep raiding the same tiny storeroom of tales for the joy of a listening public that had perhaps been sated by hearing them the first time.

The Peter Ustinov of the bails appeared to have precisely three hilarious stories from his decades behind the stumps, which he recycled with identical stresses, timing and breathless delight in their drollness. There was the one, from his late career, when Alan Lamb ('Lamby') handed him a mobile phone to look after while he stood at square leg, and he was then side-splittingly rung mid-over by Ian Botham ('Beefy'). There was the one about turning up at the Palace to collect his MBE fourteen hours before the ceremony. And there was the one about being invited for lunch at Geoffrey Boycott's house, no one answering when he rang the bell by the gate, having to climb a wall to gain admittance, and then being palmed off with cheese on toast.

Perhaps there were others the mind has blanked out, much as it supposedly does the pain of childbirth. But it is Dickie Bird's most remarkable achievement that in his anecdotage he came to make you wistful for the days when he used his mouth for no other purpose than to mutter 'Not out' as a ball that pitched on middle stayed on middle, and to engage his fellow umpire in urgent consultations about the threat posed to the continuation of play by a sandstorm in the northern Sahara.

82

Mervyn King

If Mr King is the raging Caliban of darts, perhaps he has sound cause for his fury. The prospect of a footnote appearance in darting history as only the second-best arrowsman to come out of Ipswich can't be easy for so resentful and paranoid a man to bear.

In truth, that Suffolk town's finest chucker is no easy act to follow. No leisure pursuitist has had as powerful an impact on national life, cultural and political, as Keith Deller. His surge in 1983 from unknown qualifier to world champion not only inspired Martin Amis to write *London Fields*, the lairy yet engaging anti-hero of which, Keith Talent, was modelled directly on Mr Deller, but also shaped British politics. According to the Channel 4 docu-drama *When Boris Met Dave*, watching Deller beat Bristow by taking out a legendary 138 inspired the undergraduate David Cameron. Apparently this shock victory taught him never to give up in the face of daunting odds – a lesson from which he profited twenty-two years later when coming from nowhere to steal the Tory leadership from the prohibitive favourite David Davis. Who is to deny that but for Deller there would be no coalition today, and that a right-wing Tory Party led by Mr Davis would be languishing on the opposition benches? Here, as the likes of Vernon Bogdanor and Anthony Howard would agree, is one of the great what-ifs of post-war British history.

Set against all that, Mr King's claims to immortality rest precariously on three achievements. He has the worst nickname even in darts, in which the myopic former Kwik-Fit fitter James Wade flirted with 'Specstacular' before settling on 'The Machine'.

If, like Mr King, you share your name with the man in charge of the Bank of England, on what conceivable grounds would you not choose for your sobriquet 'The Governor'? Or even, going that extra mile down the Kray-esque path trampled half to death by Bobby George, 'The Guv'nor'? By way of a dramatic lurch into lateral thinking, Mervyn King prefers Mervyn 'The King' King, a nickname as stultifyingly obvious as it is, with Phil 'The Power' Taylor showing no ambition to abdicate this side of Doomsday, impertinently preumptious.

Secondly, this bristling ball of East Anglian resentment has forged such a close bond with darts crowds that he now wears earplugs on the oche to cocoon himself from their appreciation. They loathe him, and without the panto-villain tone to the barracking that attended 'One Dart' Peter Manley before he flipped his reputation by cunningly adopting 'Is This the Way to Amarillo?' as his walk-on tune. When Mr King strides to the stage to Motörhead's metallic dirge 'Bow Down to the King', his attempts to feign unconcern serve only to highlight his discomfort.

And thirdly, he has a stylistic affectation even more irksome than Eric Bristow's raising of the little finger (see no. 64). Mr King's trademark is a pre-throw twiddle of the dart between thumb and index finger seemingly designed to suggest D'Artagnan nonchalantly caressing his sword before leaping to the defence of Porthos and Aramis.

To his credit, it cannot be denied that Mr King is a man of principle. Livid at suggestions in January 2007 that he was poised to forsake one of darts' two sanctioning bodies for the other (see Tony Green, no. 94, for a brief account of the split), he threatened to quit the BDO world championships in their midst if the rumours persisted. It speaks to his integrity that he waited a full month before duly announcing his defection to the PDC.

Long after that is forgotten, perhaps, the thing for which this nightclub bouncer *manqué* will be remembered is an excuse plucked elegantly from the Spassky–Fischer era of insane chess paranoia. After losing a 2003 world semi-final to Raymond van Barneveld, Mr King showed customary grace in defeat by insisting that the air conditioning unit had blown his darts off-course.

Every sport, game or leisure pursuit requires its hate figures. Darts is regally blessed to have Mervyn 'the King' King.

81
Virtual Racing

Few entries in this book pain me more than this one, because for twenty-five years the high street bookie was a second home. At times, not least when supposedly revising (more correctly vising) for law exams failed by record margins, it was in fact my first, and in daylight hours only, home.

I adored everything about these shabby, seedy, grubby, putrid rooms: the sullen, speechless camaraderie with fellow losers, the fug of fag smoke mingled with clothes that long ago yielded their Lenor freshness, the proximity to other lives being lived in quiet despair, the thrill of occasional victory (no money tastes half as good as that unearned), and the addictive anguish of near-perpetual defeat.

Real gamblers, as Dostoevsky knew, gamble not to win but to lose. It's a whipless form of sadomasochism, with its cathartic cocktail of pain and self-disgust, and the bookie's in the old days was as skilled a dominatrix as you could desire.

Elegance was always in short supply. Until very recently, a local William Hill in west London retained an ancient blue sign asking customers to avoid urinating in the street on the way out. The bookmaking firms treated us as scum, denying us access to toilets until not long ago, the staff seldom bothering to disguise their contempt; and as scum is precisely how we wanted to be treated.

It started going wrong some twenty years ago, with the introduction of banks of TV screens churning out live satellite feeds (so much less atmospheric and tension-inducing than garbled commentaries over the blower, when a half-length win required a nerve-shredding five-minute study of the photo-finish print to confirm). Then they started cleaning the places, a gross breach of etiquette, and installing such ponceries as vending machines and even, God help us, loos. The public smoking ban was another blow, although not their fault. Gradually, these shops became sanitised, and their peculiar charm vanished.

Nothing was as brutal a turn-off, however, as the advent of virtual racing – appallingly unconvincing computerised horse and dog races presumably created by the dunce-cap wearer at the back of the remedial class at Pixar College. It was hardly as if Ladbrokes, Hills and the rest needed something with which to fill the vast temporal chasm between actual races. The real ones come along every few minutes, and for those who can't hold on there are 'fixed odds' slot machines offering roulette, blackjack, poker and other games to plug the gap. We were never short of things to bet on in a betting shop.

Yet the rapacity of the high street chains knows no bounds. So it was that a few years ago, the screens began to feature these simulations – their results pre-determined by random-number generators in the three- or four-minute gaps between the real versions.

What is particularly tragic about virtual races is that they are enlivened by in-house commentaries identically as involved, dramatic and hysterical as those that attend the Derby and Grand National. Somewhere in a London office, in other words, an employee of William Hill is sitting at a screen watching the virtual race unfold and becoming unhinged by simulated action involving animated animals at an imaginary racetrack.

'Going behind Elysian Fields, going behind. Hare's running at Elysian Fields,' it begins. 'And they're away. Trap 2 Fellatio Flyer gets out best, ahead of Hashimoto's Thyroiditis in 4. There's trouble behind, with 1 baulking 5, and off the first bend it's 2 leading 4 and 6. Down the back straight, and 6, John McCririck's Codpiece, takes it up just ahead of 4, 2 and 3. Round the second-last bend, and 5, Aortic Aneurysm, joins 6. Off the final bend, and there's nothing to choose. It's 5 and 6, 6 and 5 [screaming now], 5 and 6, and here's 3 finishing like a train up the outside to join them. Coming to the line and it's 6, 5 and 3 in a line, they've gone past together. Very close, Elysian Fields.' A short, tension-heightening hiatus. 'Result, Elysian Fields. Trap 5, Aortic Aneurysm, has beaten 6, John McCririck's Codpiece.'

For the committed gambler such as myself, telling fantasy from reality is hard enough. Virtual racing is an animated hoof or paw step too far. Every sensible dealer knows that when you have an addict in your power, you don't actively encourage the overdose that will either kill him or persuade him to seek professional help.

That, in a sensationally loose manner of speaking, is what virtual racing forced me to do. After that quarter of a century of dismal love, it proved the tipping point, and I turned to internet poker instead. There was a time, truth be told, when that threatened to turn nasty too. But I'm pleased to report that I have learned to control the appetite, and have it down to no more than fourteen hours a day.

80
Alastair Campbell

The possibility must be acknowledged, before we go on, that whatever this psychotic dry drunk is remembered for when tomorrow's historians do their work, it won't be his contribution to British sport. They may prefer to focus on his role in preparing the 'intelligence' dossiers that helped take us to war in Iraq; his mutually destructive persecution of the BBC for reporting that role in a way that seemed entirely accurate to all but himself, the judicial buffoon Lord Hutton and a few Blairite ultras; and his part in the exposure of Dr David Kelly as the source for that report which led directly to the weapons inspector's death in the woods. Next to all that, the degradation of the civil service's integrity and independence and so much else besides, Mr Campbell's sporting persona is a purely humorous one.

The one-time writer of soft pornography and devoted fan of Burnley FC became the Comical Ali of British sport in 2005, when for reasons that pay credit to the eccentricity not just of himself but also of Sir Clive Woodward (see no. 62), he became 'media manager' on the calamitous British Lions tour to New Zealand.

As so often in this book, the questions raised – by both the offer of the job and its acceptance – seem better suited to a month-long annual convention of psychoanalysts in Zürich than to a sports hack. Who, without relevant professional qualifications, would feel confident in positing a theory as to why Woodward thought it wise to place media relations in the grubby hands of a character with half the credibility of Pinocchio's longer-nosed brother Whopperio? Why Campbell agreed to this lunacy is slightly easier to guess. Sitting in the kitchen of his Tufnell Park home staring longingly at the dormant red phone directly connected to Downing Street cannot have been much fun. Even so, boredom alone hardly explains in full why this delicate flower was blithely prepared to expose himself to the ridicule that must, it seemed at the time, ensue.

So it did. Not since his namesake role model in Baghdad looked out of his ministry window at the American tanks rolling into town, and rushed to a press conference to inform the world that the Republican Guard was doing a bang-up job in driving the infidels into chaotic retreat, had anything rivalled what followed.

The Lions were thrashed in all three Tests, and as the on-field débâcle unfolded the media's attention was diverted to a spat between Woodward and Gavin Henson, whom the coach had curiously omitted from the squad for the first match against the All Blacks. It was at this point that Campbell's gift for managing the media was unshackled. In order to persuade a British public bemused and livid at Mr Henson's exclusion that reports of a bust-up were nonsense, he staged a photograph of Woodward and the father-to-be of Charlotte Church's children walking together after a training session. It was taken by an agency photographer from a hidden position, with a long lens and possibly without Mr Henson's knowledge, and Mr Campbell then distributed it to national newspapers in Britain. Mr Henson's subsequent amnesia, as expressed in a book, led him to forget the agreement between them about this picture to which Mr Campbell has always laid claim.

Not content with that morale-repairing masterstroke, Mr Campbell then underlined the humility for which he is loved by taking it upon himself to give a pre-match team talk. Why several members of the side, most vocally Ben Kay, were aston- ished by this, what with Mr Campbell placing rugby union as high as fourth in his list of sporting preferences (after football, athletics and cricket), who can say? As to the notion that he dipped a toe into the foetid pond of bad taste by invoking the exploits of the SAS in Bosnia to stir their blood, well, some people just live to take offence. Personally, I'd have been even happier had he referred to the work of British troops in Basra, in the war he played a small but crucial part in facilitating, but perhaps that's just me. And to think Martin Johnson had contented himself with Agincourt before some of those same players beat Australia to win the World Cup for England two years earlier.

Sir Clive, quite a spinner himself, declared himself delighted with Mr Campbell when the tour was over, explaining that the fault lay entirely with the media, and not one iota with its manager. 'The media has missed an opportunity,' he said. 'If they had spoken to Alastair, he would have given them ideas on how they could have written more creative stuff.' Indeed he would. He'd have persuaded them that the trio of savage Test defeats were thumping wins, the confusion emanating from a series of faulty electronic scoreboards. 'That's why I brought him along,' Woodward went on, 'to try to move everything with the media on to a whole new level, but unfortunately the media have not taken up the challenge.' Idiot media. Sir Clive concluded by describing Mr Campbell's contribution as 'outstanding'.

So it was. It stood out then, as it stands out now, as the most breathtakingly cack-handed display of media mismanagement in the annals of even British sport.

79

The Vuvuzela

The one-note plastic horn that played its selfless part in producing the worst World Cup thus far was, so Fifa assured us when the global outrage was at its zenith in the tournament's early days, too deeply embedded in South African football culture to be banished. Once, you could hardly help reflect, pissing in the pocket of the person in front of you was deeply embedded in England's football culture, but if the tournament had come here in the early 1980s, would Fifa prissily have refused to discourage that for fear of treading on effete cultural feet? I don't believe so.

Before we go on, let me say this. I love South Africa and its people. One of the happier weeks of my life was spent there covering the story of the Lemba, a tribe who believe themselves to be Jewish, insist that the Ark of the Covenant (*Ngundry Llogoma* in their language) was once in their possession, and have the coolest flag known to humanity (an elephant inside a Star of David). Another was passed in a Johannesburg hospital attached to a weird, bubbling machine re-inflating the lung punctured by a burglar, in the home of old family friends, who had the impertinence to stick a bread knife into my chest. It's an incident about which I never speak, though I will show the chest X-rays to anyone to whom I'm refusing to speak about it, pointing out the 1/12th-inch gap between the blade and the heart and the 1/18th-inch *cordon sanitaire* between steel and aorta.

For all the literal and psychic scar tissue the incident left behind, hand on nearly-pierced heart, I'd rather relive that lively dawn encounter than listen again to that drone of *basso profundo* killer bees trapped in a drum. If what my wife, whose finishing school was bombed in the war, refers to as the 'vulva labia' is indeed a central panel in the tapestry of South African national life, so too are Aids and carjacking, and you don't hear anyone slapping metaphorical preservation orders on them.

78

The Charlton Brothers

Are Jackie and Bobby Charlton Jewish? I wouldn't normally ask, because the fact that they were respectively decent and exceptional at football would seem to offer a definitive answer to that question. And even if it doesn't, the existence of coalminers among their north-east forebears surely settles the point.

However, there is something so immutably Jewish about their decades-long feud that you have to wonder. From Cain and Abel to Mike and Bernie Winters, and possibly (at the time of writing it remains too soon to be sure) David and Ed Miliband, the fraternal fallout has been a defining sub-strand in my people's troubled history.

Whatever their genetic roots, the Charltons have been pests for almost as long as they have been *broigus*, to use that Yiddish term for non-speakers. One intriguing thing about them … but no, that's too fanciful a thought even for this book. One mildly interesting thing they represent is an apparent paradox that is in fact no such thing. It is often commented, in mystification, that the greatest players tend to make the lousiest managers, and vice versa. The truth is that gifted individuals fixate on themselves, which is not a recipe for successful leadership, while the more mediocre need to think more about the team and their role within it to survive, which clearly is.

So it has been with the Charltons. Bobby, a magnificent midfielder for Manchester United and England, had one foray into management, wasting no time in easing Preston North End to relegation. Jackie, an effective clumper of a centre half for Leeds United and England, took both Middlesbrough and Sheffield Wednesday in the other direction before leading the

Republic of Ireland to an unlikely World Cup quarter-final in 1990.

Forced to choose the Charlton with whom to be trapped in a lift, it would probably come down to the toss of a coin. Jackie has a slightly cruel, laconic wit, putting you in mind of the Duke of Edinburgh he facially resembles, but might drive you mad with the didacticism and unpalatability of his opinions about the state of the world and who is to blame for it (see Prince Philip, above). His inability in press conferences to remember the names of players he selected for Ireland minutes earlier further suggests a man who might, in that faulty elevator, thrice entertain you with the same anecdote within the same quarter-hour.

Bobby, on the other hand, would bore you close to a coma far quicker than the lack of oxygen. A drearier old fart English sport has never known. His monotone could be used by riot police who left their CS gas back at the station, while added to the stubbornness that saw him retain the combover for thirty years is a sullen taciturnity to chill the blood.

There is an excuse for Bobby's failure to scintillate off the pitch as he once did on it, of course, and it pays credit to his elder brother's fraternal sensibilities that despite acknowledging how the Munich air crash of 1958 affected the younger's personality, Jackie disdains the making of any allowances.

The precise cause of the feud has fascinated scholars for decades, yet despite tireless research and the publication of both men's autobiographies, it remains a source of mystery. All that is known beyond doubt is that it centred around their mother Cissie, an apparently domineering matriarchal figure whom Bobby resented for disrespecting his wife, Jackie in turn resenting Bobby for ignoring Cissie as a result. Jackie also resented Cissie, in his case for favouring the more talented Bobby when they were children, but expressed that by showering money and time upon her. Oddly for an older brother of such seemingly limitless self-confidence, he seems much the more sensitive of the two.

The most admirable thing about both, meanwhile, and the one and only thing that binds them, is their adamant refusal to acknowledge the other. Here they show unwonted good taste, and set an example the rest of us will, in the absence of a broken lift, be happy to follow.

77

The Charity Fun Runner

Were the pen truly mightier than the sword, the penchant for marathon runners wearing fancy dress in the alleged interests of charity would not have survived that glorious scene in *The Office* in which, on Comic Relief day, David Brent is sacked while dressed as a comedy ostrich. Scything though it was, Ricky Gervais's satire of the exhibitionist dullard claiming to be motivated by the plight of starving Africans when driven solely by the craving for attention had no effect. Every year several thousand people continue to run the London Marathon dressed as superheroes, cuddly animals, ballerinas, vampires, and in one memorable instance a Rubik's Cube.

This is by no means an event screaming out for additional reasons to ignore it. As one of Gervais's own comedy heroes, Jerry Seinfeld, put it in his eponymous sitcom about nothing, when invited to a friend's friend's apartment to watch the New York version, 'What's to see? A woman from Norway, a guy from Kenya, and 20,000 losers.'

The particularly pernicious thing about fun runners, more even than how they plunder the event of its inherent nobility, is the hint their costumes offer about the callousness of their sponsors – the implicit suggestion that had they asked for donations to run in shorts and a vest, they would have been brusquely dismissed. Can it really be that, as the determinedly zany do the rounds of their locals, they often hear the words 'I'll give you 50p per mile, and gladly so, but only if you dress as Virgil Tracy. If you won't do it dressed as the pilot of *Thunderbird 2*, the local hospice can go hang'?

76

Rhona Martin

The Mrs Mop of the Winter Olympics (it's being so cheerful as keeps her going) is honoured with an entry very little for herself, and even less as a representative of a peculiarly nonsensical 'sport'. Primarily Rhona is honoured here as the catalyst for despair and self-disgust induced by her finest hour.

She seems a dour sort, to be truthful, does the captain of the Great Britain squad that won gold in Utah in 2002, and the doleful sheepdog haircut has its part to play there. But wouldn't you be miserable if you devoted your waking life to such a vocation? Many Olympic minority events are lent charm by their nihilistic pointlessness, and those of us afflicted with the obsessive interest in numbers and rankings that almost defines the Aspergers end of the spautistic spectrum can pass untold hours fascinated by the scoring systems of diving, archery, showjumping and even weightlifting.

Curling, on the other hand, is what that late and deeply lamented comic giantess Linda Smith wisely identified as 'housework on ice'. What it says about this country that millions of us were driven to emotional involvement in Martin's triumph is too obvious to say at all. But we'll say it anyway. What a preposterous sporting land this must be when the endeavours of four slow-skating charladies buffing up a sheet of ice for no apparent purpose is the cause of feverish national excitement.

This outbreak of proxy Henmania – the succumbing of otherwise normal people to patriotic impulses that overwhelm all rationale to cause more revulsion than pleasure – was as fierce as any in modern history. To care desperately, even for a few hours, about which stone has been ice-buffed to which part of 'the house' (the scoring section) was a shaming experience, and hers as depressing a gold medal as was ever placed around the neck of a Scottish housekeeper misrouted from overseeing the polishing of baronial floors to standing on a podium, moist-eyed, making a choral request to the Lord for the survival of our Queen. Shame on you, Rhona Martin, and infinitely more shame on us for watching you.

75

Arjen Robben

It pays rich testament to this gifted Dutchman that the fans of Chelsea FC, seldom saluted as the least partisan of supporters, cannot stand the man who contributed so much to the winning of their first Premier League title in 2005–06.

It was Robben's miraculous achievement to relegate Didier Drogba, sublime as he was at the reverse triple somersault with tuck, to the team's silver medallist for high-board diving. The Ivorian *über*-narcissist is a perhaps surprising omission from this book, due to a fondness I cannot quite explain other than to say that his histrionics are much reduced now, and that what remains has become endearing. The sight of him being hauled to his feet by John Terry with a brusque 'Come on, love, up you get, you'll live,' is one of the league's more touching rituals.

There is nothing engaging about the precociously bald Netherlander, however, and there never will be. A narky, arrogant, unceasingly petulant little bleeder, Robben may or may not be world football's most talented winger, but there's no doubting his status as its pre-eminent whinger. Any uncertainty concerning his status was removed by his spiteful moaning about Howard Webb's refereeing of the 2010 World Cup final. The Dutch performance, which raised the image of the infamous Uruguayan scythers of 1986 as coached by Bruce Lee, was, it goes without saying, an utter disgrace. As a betrayal of Holland's football tradition, the premeditated attempt to kick Spain out of their rhythm in a first half of unmitigated cynical violence will sooner be forgotten than Mr Webb's leniency towards the Dutch. One appreciated the Yorkshire copper's aversion to showing a red card in this particular game, yet in a different context the match would have ended before half time, with Holland forfeiting a technical 3–0 victory to Spain due to having fewer than seven men on the pitch. As Johan Cruyff succinctly put it, his successors in the orange shirts were 'anti-football' in Soccer City that night.

And yet, when it was over Robben somehow found the *chutzpah* to accuse Mr Webb of favouring the Spanish, his bleatings centring on one incident of sledgehammer irony. Having spent his entire career falling melodramatically and rolling for twenty yards in feigned excruciation for no physically explicable reason, he broke the habit of a lifetime by staying on his feet when clearly tugged back late in the game by the ageing carthorse Carlos Puyol. If he had gone down then, being through on goal, even Mr Webb might have shown Puyol a straight red, although that's far from certain, given that Mark van Bommel might have removed a scimitar from his sock and sliced Andrés Iniesta's head off without being offered first bash at the soap by Mr Webb.

Whatever, the lure of scoring the goal that won the World Cup kept Robben from the traditional collapse. Once Iker Casillas had safely collected the ball, Robben raced towards Mr Webb in the traditional moansome-aggressive style, screaming like the face in Edvard Munch's painting at the injustice. The outrage was rooted in his belief that he should have been rewarded for staying upright for the first time in his career. The rules of advantage, as correctly applied by Mr Webb, were an irrelevance. He had eaten his cake, and now he wanted to have it. It was a wretched vignette of a wretched man, and caught the essence of the unlovely Arjen Robben to gruesome perfection.

74

David O'Leary

No entry in this book has caused me as much grief as that for this oiliest of rags on the managerial bonfire. Acknowledging that Mr O'Leary evokes fierce distaste is the easy bit. Pinning down precisely why has proved the problem.

A portion of it, having said that, is easily explained. The former Ireland and Arsenal central defender memorably disgraced himself as manager of Leeds United. I refer here not to the grandiose £100 million transfer-market splurge that contributed to the club's flirtation with bankruptcy a few short years after it had come within a game of the Champions League final. As detached analysts of Leeds United will agree, that was greatly to the credit of O'Leary and his anagrammatic chairman Peter Ridsdale (dire Leeds prat), the sadness being that they so narrowly failed to pull it off.

The incident that best illuminates Mr O'Leary's odiousness was the publication of his book *Leeds United: A Season on Trial* within days of an assault case involving two of his players, Jonathan Woodgate (convicted) and Lee Bowyer (acquitted), being concluded. When he denied intending to profit from the beating up of an Asian man by insisting that the book's title was a hapless coincidence, he mixed the defining twin traits of arch hypocrisy and rampant self-righteousness into a lethal cocktail. Blithely continuing to select Mr Woodgate added a needlessly bitter twist.

More than anything, however, I suspect that the violent reaction to O'Leary is visceral. The sight of that overly smooth face and those shifty cow eyes, and the sound of that creepy, unctuous voice rouse subliminal memories of *Jungle Book* python

Kaa, or possibly early-era *Celebrity Squares* Bob Monkhouse, and the guts respond by piping acid up towards the oesophagus.

You don't see or hear much of him any more. Either he weaned himself off the addiction to linking his name with managerial vacancies he had less chance of being invited to fill than the late Professor Stanley Unwin, or football hacks finally tired of giving credence to these fantasies. But it pays tribute to the enduring influence of David O'Leary, from whom insincerity oozes like toxic treacle, that the thought of him retains the power to send you scurrying for the anti-emetics to this day.

73

Lleyton Hewitt

When it comes to mellowing arguably the least charming sports-man even Australia has yet produced, nothing has succeeded like failure. Now that he has been reduced to a journeyman, tinkering about in the lower reaches of the world's top thirty, and occasionally making a Grand Slam quarter-final, Lleyton Hewitt is little more than a minor irritant, where once he was a pustulating, septic boil on the buttock of professional tennis.

It seems almost surreal today that this cocky ball of ocker bumptiousness was the tour's leading player in the early nough-ties. Yet, inexplicable as it now appears, in the thankfully brief interregnum between Pete Sampras and Roger Federer he twice ended the year as world number one, and snaffled two Grand Slam titles (Wimbledon in 2002, and the US Open the following year). The mortifying prospect then was that he would domi-nate for years, and perhaps he might have done so, but for one poignantly minuscule slice of bad luck. He had exceedingly little talent, judged by the standards of those who so quickly sup-planted him, for playing tennis.

What he did have in spades was speed, footwork, energy and reliable passing shots off both wings, and for a little while that amalgam of the lower-range attributes was enough to take out less dependable baseliners, and serve-volleyers such as Tim Henman (whom he ritually slaughtered whenever they met) and Sampras, whom he dismantled in that US Open final.

And then, the Lord be praised, the quality of men's tennis surged with such startling rapidity that Hewitt went swiftly from number one to also-ran. It was no longer enough to be a latterday Jimmy Connors, all effort and sweat and what George

Galloway knows as indefatigability. To have a prayer of coping with the Fed, Rafael Nadal, Novak Djokovic and Andy Murray, you needed variety, cleverness and a nuclear weapon – an A-bomb serve like Andy Roddick's, for example, or an intercontinental ballistic missile of a flat forehand in the style of Juan Martín del Potro.

Hewitt had nothing of the sort. What he had, and has still, is what I would call typically self-conscious Aussie cussedness, but he would boastfully identify as 'heart'. Hence that endlessly repeated gesture of the fist banging his chest, en route to losing another love or 'bagel' set to the Fed, as he looks up to his box screeching 'Come awn!'

Heart's fine, if that's what it is, but brain is better, and a combination of both best of all. Cerebrally, alas, Hewitt is the amoeba of the tennis world, the personification of the classically Australian conviction that it doesn't matter a jot if a nine-year-old can't tell the time so long as he shows promise at Aussie Rules football or she is in the right swimming team.

Thus it was, during the US Open of 2001, that he told a press conference that there wasn't a *soupçon* of racist intent in the incident for which he will be remembered. He was playing James Blake, the Harlem-born black American, when a black line judge had the impudence to foot-fault him twice at important moments in the third set. Hewitt approached the umpire's chair, and the microphone captured the following remark: 'Look at him,' said Hewitt, gesturing towards the line judge, 'and tell me what the similarity is [gesturing now towards Mr Blake]. I want him [line judge again] off the court.' The umpire, the Swiss Andreas Egli, didn't oblige Hewitt there, but nor did he announce: 'Code violation, paranoiac racist idiocy, warning Mr Hewitt.' Perhaps Mr Egli figured that, what with coming from a land down under where Abo babies were plundered, to borrow from Men at Work, allowances must be made. In the pool halls of the outback, after all, Hewitt's remark would have struck the regulars as restrained and studiously polite, if not political correctness gone mad.

So it says something important about Hewitt's personality that even in Australia he was loathed and regarded as an embarrassment by the media and a fair chunk of the population long before he disgraced himself in New York.

Still, to his lasting credit, let no one claim that the fury of the US Open crowd, which booed him off court, and the condemnation of the wider world didn't teach him a lesson. Not only did he come to see how repugnant the accusation of racially-motivated collusion between a player and an official might appear, he made dramatic strides in mastering the wider lexicon of non-offence. At the following year's French Open in Paris, he addressed that same Mr Egli as a 'spastic'. His apology the following day to the Spastics Society of Australia, which curiously took umbrage, showed yet again that, while he had very little else to offer, there was never any doubting Lleyton Hewitt's heart.

72

Ken Bailey

Even during the glory days of football hooliganism, the reliably miserable experience of following England's progress offered no more depressing sight than this unnervingly strange old boy. For decades Ken Bailey's presence in his John Bull uniform – red militia tailcoat, blue top hat with Union Jack front centre – was a fixture at just about every international sporting event, broadcasting a stale aroma of Empire and long-anachronistic presumptions about English superiority across the planet. Wherever and whatever a national team played, the TV cameras would pick him out in the crowd. Eventually he bacame such a familiar character that Subbuteo honoured him not only by putting his image on the exterior of a five-a-side box, but including a Bailey figurine in its 1974 Munich World Series set.

I've no idea what foreigners made of the strange, angular figure with the passing resemblance to 'Genial' Harry Grout from *Porridge*. But by God, to borrow from the Duke of Wellington, he embarrassed the hell out of us. Affected English eccentricity, a barely remembered plague in an ever more homogenised world, was never a pretty thing, but it was seldom uglier than in this manifestation. Long before Forrest Gump set a mark for pointless running that would remain unbroken until Dwain Chambers (see no. 43), this simpleton was acclaimed for 'running all the way to America': a miracle of preternatural aimlessness achieved by jogging round and round the deck of a boat while it crossed the Atlantic Ocean.

He would later outstrip even this idiocy. In 1982, a decade before he was laid to rest in Bournemouth, the splendid Erica Roe streaked over the Twickenham turf during a rugby international. From the crowd rushed a scandalised Bailey to cover Ms Roe's proud breasts with his Union Jack. The joyless old scrote.

He once flew to Sydney for no other purpose than to stand in a crowd while the Queen did a walkabout. 'What are you doing here?' asked Her Maj, doubtless as spooked by the sight as anyone else. 'I'd go anywhere for you, ma'am,' replied Bailey. According to no less an authority on regal sycophancy than Lord St John of Fawsley, this made him Sir Jackie Stewart's most dangerous rival for the coveted court title of Most Egregious Royal Crawler Known to Sport.

71

Alan Sugar

Long before the Fauntleroy of commerce donned the ermine, and even before he thrilled a swooning nation with *The Apprentice*, the then Mr Sugar inflicted himself on Tottenham Hotspur as its chairman. Precisely why he did so remains a source of mystery. We know that it wasn't in search of further enrichment, because he has been impressively clear on this point, winning a libel trial during which he wept at the agony caused him by the *Daily Mail*'s suggestion that his motivation was financial. According to one rumour, he liked to put it about that he took on the club, struggling then with its debts, to honour a deathbed pledge to his father, a lifelong fan. While this has the flavour of what's known to Yiddish as a *bubba meise* (a self-servingly sentimental tall story you tell your granny), it may even be true.

What's in no doubt is that he was clueless. For all the shining altruism driving him on, he could never grasp that a football club is more a religious entity than a conventional business, and that players cannot be piled high and sold cheap like primitive though functional computers.

His great strategic error was falling out with Terry Venables (over allegations of financial irregularities yet decisively to be proved) at the precise moment when the lairy then Spurs manager was poised to realise the rich potential of the team he had created.

Curiously, given the innate sweetness of his nature, Sugar thereafter contrived to aggravate everybody involved with the club with the ignorant, Little Englander invention of the catch-all foreign-import archetype Carlos Kickaball, and the typical warthog rage he lavished on Jürgen Klinsmann. When *der Stuka* (the dive-bomber) left the club in accordance with the get-out clause in the contract Sugar had offered him, his little lordship went on the telly to wave Klinsmann's shirt at the camera, you may recall, and insist that he would not use the garment to wash his Rolls-Royce.

The Sugar years were marked not only by the appointment of a stream of inadequate managers. His hiring of the Arsenal stalwart George Graham (see no. 65) seemed a deliberate attempt to gauge the tensile strength of supporters' endurance for his disrespect for the club's traditions (he made his uncertainty about the year in which Spurs won the double a matter of record). If he noticed the irony inherent in bringing in one manager proven to be bent not so long after a fit of stern morality led him to oust another merely suspected of being so, he showed no sign of it. Doubtless Messrs Graham and Venables, best friends for decades, still chuckle over that paradox whenever they swap affectionate anecdotes about their erstwhile boss.

Twice have I had the pleasure of Sugar's company, once at a dinner party at the American Embassy when he refused to acknowledge me (fair enough; he was trying to sue me at the time), and once at a columnists' Christmas lunch presided over by an editor who, well aware of the rumbling tensions between us, deemed it a hilarious jape to seat us side by side at his table. Much the more pleasurable encounter, needless to say, was the first. The second was dominated by the flow of opinions of such blistering obviousness that it felt like sitting next to a peculiarly talentless parodist attempting to satirise the archetypal only-language-they-understand London cabbie. 'Have you ever considered seeking work as a leader writer at the *Guardian*?' I interrupted him during rant no 73(b), regarding unchecked immigration. 'Nah,' said the then Sir Alan, doing me the honour of taking the suggestion seriously, 'not my cup of tea at all.'

Yet, against all the odds, it seems that hidden deep within that sternly humourless façade a gifted self-ironist fights for freedom. Not so long ago, Lord Sugar bashfully offered his services as chairman of the Football Association in succession to his fellow New Labour peer Lord Triesman. Recalling his own record in football, this had to be a mischievous tease at his own expense. Surely?

70

John McEnroe

Does the adult human being have the capacity to change? It's a weighty question possibly best left to psychological and behavioural academics, but for what it's worth (a little less than zero, in truth), I can't see it myself. While we can learn to modify our behaviour and to mask our grubbier characteristics, fundamentally we remain whatever we were as small children.

Those who disagree might cite John McEnroe as a pardigm of personality transformation. Even people who loathed the curly-haired post-adolescent in his Disgrace to Humanity era have bought into the metamorphosis. The Irish-American rage has subsided in middle age, the received wisdom holds, and McEnroe is now beloved as commentary sage, cultivated art dealer and self-parodic sitcom cameo player in shows such as *Curb Your Enthusiasm.*

My own McEnroe journey has been in reverse. I worshipped the lip-curling punk in his late-seventies persona as tennis's Johnny Rotten, when he scandalised that gruesomely giggle-some, determinedly censorious bastion of Home Counties priss-iness the Centre Court crowd (see no. 40) just as the Sex Pistols outraged the rest of Middle England

What was not to love about him then? He was magnificent in panto-villain mode, hilarious in his deployment of hyperbolic insult and expressions of scandalised disbelief at the incompe-tence of others of the sort that gave this book its title. And he played, of course, the tennis of the gods. If that legendary 1980 tie-break against Bjorn Borg remains the high point of his career, his 6–1 6–1 6–2 demolition of Jimmy Connors in the 1984 Wimbledon final – a display of grass-court perfection unmatched even by Roger Federer – illustrated how even the most embarrassingly one-sided of matches can also be compelling.

However, so far as commentating on the sport goes – and I suspect this is very much a minority opinion – Connors beats him hands down. At moments of maximum drama, when the tension focuses his mind on the play, McEnroe is crisp and illuminating. But at all other times, the monomania that helped elevate him to such heights as a player renders him a little Geoffrey Boycottian for my tastes. Fawned on by those sharing the commentary box, towards whom he is reported to be curt and aloof off-air, he incessantly makes everything about him.

He bosses that box absolutely, implicitly demanding sycophancy from colleagues all too willing to oblige him. He accepts the puppyish obeisance of John Lloyd, Andrew Castle and the rest with the born-to-rule ease of a US president welcoming the leaders of Belgium and New Zealand to the Oval Office for a photocall. He never disguises his knowledge that he is an alpha male among gammas.

If he has a commentary *leitmotif*, it's choking. Seldom does a match pass without him dwelling on mental frailty, and with such condescension that you would naturally assume that it never happened to him. This was the thought that occurred to me the night in 2003 when happenstance placed us at the same dinner table.

Tim Henman had just been crushed in a semi-final by eventual champion Lleyton Hewitt, and McEnroe had not been impressed. If drink played its part in what followed, so too did a sense of patriotic propriety. Henman might very well be a choker, I thought, but he's *our* choker, and it's for us to kick him half to death for it, rather than you. This is much how liberal Jews feel about criticising Israel for her maltreatment of the Palestinians. It's fine for us to do it, and all too often a moral obligation. But when we hear the *goyim* laying in, the hackles soar.

Eventually, after a vat of wine, I raised the matter of the 1984 French Open final. A crackling hush fell over the table like a static-charged nylon blanket, though not for long. 'What,' bellowed McEnroe, the ashen hue to his face displaced by a rising tide of crimson, 'Is. Your. Point?' My point, I said, is that in Paris that day you led Ivan Lendl by two sets and a break, yet lost. 'WHAT,' yelled McEnroe, the decibels approaching pits-of-the-earth levels, 'ARE YOU TRYING TO SAY?' It's hardly opaque, I went on. You had Lendl by the balls, and yet on the verge of winning the one Grand Slam title you wanted most, you choked. There's no disgrace there – it has happened to Federer in finals too. It's just a little odd that you never use such an instructive personal experience to illuminate the sufferings of others.

Once my wife's left shoe had connected impressively with my right shin, I decided against pursuing this line of enquiry, and the full eruption never came. To the extent that John McEnroe has learned to prevent the toddler tantrums exploding to the max, he has certainly modified himself in middle age. But the rage, the monomania and the lip-curling charmlessness – the sources of such riotous merriment when he was twenty – are about as appealing in a man now in his sixth decade as were his calamitous forays into presenting game shows.

As he was leaving, in a wildly misguided attempt at eleventh-hour bridge-building, I asked which of the Williams sisters he thought would win the following day's women's final. 'How the hell should I know?' said Johnny Mac. 'You know more about tennis than I do, why don't you ask yourself?' It was a good and well-merited putdown, delivered with the venomous petulance of a man who has not, for all the affected *bonhomie* he husbands for the airwaves, changed a bit.

69

David Bryant

Readers under thirty-five may find this impossible to compute, but there was a time when crown green bowling – unnervingly odd folk apparently misrouted from parish council meetings and writing letters of complaint about litter standing about in history's worst garments contemplating how best to send a ball on a curvaceous journey towards the jack – was barely off the television. How darts fails to be recognised as a sport when bowling has long been a Commonwealth Games event is a mystery, although less so than how we managed to watch bowls for hours on end without the assistance of psychotropic medication. Somehow we did, and the best defence I can offer is that in the dog days of British deference, about halfway between the industrial chaos of the three-day week and the birth of alternative comedy, there wasn't much on telly and this was a most peculiar country.

Nothing illuminated the oddity more clearly than 1986 Pipeman of the Year David Bryant's rise to household namehood. Although records state that Mr Bryant was a Somerset schoolteacher, presumably of geography, at the remove of several decades I think of him less as a real person than as the template for a Harry Enfield character. Whether Mr Enfield wasted a chunk of his adolescence watching bowls, as I did, I cannot say for sure. But I'd bet the mortgage he did, and that he later modelled Mr You-Don't-Wanna-Do-It-Like-That, the imbecile busybody with the catchphrase 'Only meeeeeee', on David Bryant.

A ringer for the Enfield archetype right down to the foolish cap and prissy expression, Mr Bryant's trademark was one of those staggeringly irritating pipes – the easy-to-clean type with the transparent stem – smoking wispily away during outdoor events, and yet more irritatingly clamped unlit between his teeth during indoor ones. It was the type of pipe that shrieks 'Get off my lawn!', bespeaks Sunday-morning drives through the Cotswolds at 23 mph causing a five-mile tailback on a road with a speed limit of sixty, and looks primed to offer advice on how best to rainproof a garden fence at the first opportunity.

Frankly, I do not believe Mr Bryant wanted to do it like that. No one in their right mind would wish to heap humiliation on country and sovereign by winning world and Commonwealth titles clad in the bingo-night garb of the Florida condo-dwelling octogenarian, and with that uniquely pernicious pipe in his mouth. Do it like that he did, however, and for that David Bryant and crown green bowling will forever be twinned in infamy.

68

Badge-Kissing

In poker, the subconscious revelation of the strength or weakness of a hand is known as a tell, and some are more easily read than others. Homer Simpson's response to being dealt four jacks was to race round the baize table whooping with joy, for example, while in the movie *Rounders* John Malkovich's character Teddy KGB, a Russian mafioso, gave himself away to Matt Damon by twiddling an Oreo biscuit until the two halves separated.

Yet nothing in poker – not even Le Chiffre bleeding from an eye in *Casino Royale* – has ever been so obvious a tell as the footballer kissing his badge. Generally it means one of three things: a) The player is about to leave the club whose insignia he is snogging; b) He has spent several months using the threat of departure to bully an even more obscene salary out of the club at which he is now reluctantly compelled to remain; or c) He wants to advertise his wares on the open market, but wisely regards wearing a placard around his neck reading: 'For sale. Six previous careful owners: £130,000 per week ONO' as too constrictive.

Whichever it might be, with all but the very few survivors of that threatened species the one-club player (Ryan Giggs, Paul Scholes, Steven Gerrard, Gary Neville), this is the equivalent of Judas Iscariot reassuring Christ of his deathless love in the Garden of Gethsemane while nervily jiggling silver coinage in whatever passed, in first-century AD Judaea, for a pocket.

At the zenith of the honours board of hypocrites stand: Wayne Rooney, who celebrated his Manchester United afterlife by kissing the badge in front of the Everton fans he had so recently assured that he was 'Blue until I die'; Frank Lampard Jnr tonguing the Chelsea emblem half to death while the entire Stamford Bridge crowd well knew he was talking to Barcelona; and, legendarily, Emmanuel Adebayor, whose lips seemed welded to the Arsenal cannon on his left pectoral during the months he was so transparently flogging his services to every major club in Europe.

The peculiar idiocy here is that the very last thing the fan with an IQ over thirty-seven expects from a footballer today is emotional attachment to the club. In any institution, loyalty is a one-way conceit, created by the employer to pressurise the employee into obeisance but seldom reciprocated. We all know and accept that, in the age of the plutocratic foreign owner, the footballer is a mercenary, and has every right to be so in the knowledge that his club will treat him like toxic waste the moment he ceases to be of use.

So what's so offensive about the kissing of the badge isn't the cheapness of the gesture, or the blatant hypocrisy it represents, but the unthinking contempt it shows for the intelligence of the fans.

Parents of three-year olds – generally the default developmental reference point with the professional footballer – who are still addicted to their dummies sometimes resort to coating them with a substance so repulsive to the taste that the child has no choice but to kick the habit. With the club badge, my substance of choice would be hemlock.

67

In da Hole!

On one very limited level, there is something almost life-affirming about this Tourette's-like imprecation, so often conjoined with its soulmate 'You da man!', as screeched by American golf crowds whenever home favourites, but especially Phil Mickelson and Tiger Woods, hit any shot. Sport has known no more stirring an expression of the triumph of hope over experience since Graham Taylor picked Carlton Palmer a second time for the England midfield.

In certain contexts it even makes sense. If, for example, Woods has just putted, played out of a bunker or chipped from the side of the green, or even hit a wedge from within a hundred yards, there is a quantifiable chance that in da hole is where the ball will go.

When the cry goes up in the immediate aftermath of a drive on a 595-yard par five, however, what is it, do you imagine, that the tee-side optimist anticipates? That, unknown to USPGA officials, the player has secreted a nuclear-powered magnet at the bottom of the hole and then drilled a magnetised iron ball bearing into the core of the dimpled sphere? That gravity will suspend itself for the twelve seconds required for the ball to fly those near-600 yards, re-exerting itself at the very moment it is over the hole, so that it drops vertically onto the flagstick and slips in? Or, least outlandish of all, that an eagle with a large ante-post bet on Phil or Tiger to win the US PGA will swoop as the ball is in flight, Quidditch-fashion, scoop it up in a talon, fly it to the green and release it into da hole?

Or is it, unlikely as this may seem, that chunks of American golf crowds are plain and simple imbeciles, desperate to ingratiate themselves with golfers who regard them as an irksome amorphous mass to be sullenly tolerated and occasionally patronised with the odd raised arm, doffed cap and false smile?

Either way, at least until a golfer does achieves that elusive hole in one on a par five, every scream should be met, in accordance with presidential edict, with a single bullet fired from a long-range rifle operated by FBI Golf SWAT teams strategically placed around the course. In da head! You da corpse!

Sir Geoffrey
Charles Hurst

In his defence, Sir Geoff cannot be blamed for the facts that the match official known to all as The Russian Linesman was a homer, and that his eagerness to please a Wembley crowd would oblige a country to devote the rest of its existence to: a) debating a question to which it knew the answer all along; and b) confusing itself with a major footballing power, with the inevitable grief this self-delusion has entailed.

If it wasn't technically Hurst's fault that human error one sunny June afternoon in 1966 fossilised him in the amber of a heroism to which he was not entitled, however, he had no business turning himself into a single-issue human as a result. You'd have thought the time would have come, no later than 1972, when he'd have snapped and said, 'It happened, the flag was raised, I scored my third, we won, enough.'

Not a bit of it. While some low-rent celebs are said to go to the opening of an envelope or a fridge, if it offered the prospect of wittering on about 1966 Sir Geoff would show up for the opening of a bowel. For a moment in 2010, it seemed he had finally found closure. Eschewing the usual nudge-nudge, wink-winkery about that goal, he candidly admitted that the ball did not cross the line. Alas, as a glance at the date of the relevant edition of the *Sun* confirmed, this was the first, and with luck the last, time a newspaper chose to confuse a simple statement of fact with an April Fool's joke.

Although Hurst may not be the sharpest stud on the boot, and could bore for earth in any interplanetary contest, the saving grace about his coy little reflections as to whether the ball crossed the line was that England's World Cup victory naturally meant the world to him. Who wouldn't treasure the memories and venerate the artefacts that represent that glorious victory? If he sits up night after night polishing his medal and gazing lovingly at his shirt, you thought, well, who would begrudge him the pride in his central role in what will always remain the high point of our football history?

Imagine the visceral shock to the system, then, on coming across a newspaper questionnaire in 2002 which had the insolence to ask Geoff Hurst whether he would consider selling that medal – the thought of it! You might as well ask the Queen if she'd flog the jewels she was crowned in – should he ever fall on hard times. The answer was as chilling as 'Quid pro quo, Clarice,' hissing forth from the mouth of Hannibal Lecter. 'It wouldn't depend on falling on hard times,' replied Sir Geoff smuggly. 'I'm not in hard times and recently sold the medal to West Ham United for a substantial sum.' It then emerged that this Laureate of 1966 nostalgism, though perfectly well off, had also auctioned the shirt – the red shirt, you may recall, with the number 10 on its back – at Christie's for £80,000.

The consolation, so it seemed, was that having voluntarily revealed himself to be as clinical about 1966 as he affects to be sentimental – by contrast, his team-mate Nobby Stiles seemed heartbroken when forced to sell his medal recently after suffering a stroke – his dignity would not permit him ever again to play the part of Vera Lynn singing 'We'll Meet Again' at a war veterans' convention. As if. Every five minutes to this day, out he is wheeled to reprise the blisteringly tiresome tale, replete with knowing grin when asked the ritual Russian Linesman question, for any media outlet that will bung him a few hundred quid.

If tomorrow I were made totalitarian dictator of Great Britain, which seems unlikely, the third thing I would do (after scrapping Trident and giving up the permanent seat on the UN

Security Council) would be to make it a statutory criminal offence, carrying a mandatory twelve-year sentence, for any sporting star to speak in public after retirement. After-dinner engagements and motivational talks would be expressly excluded (if people want to pay to hear them, that's their funeral), while dispensation could be sought on the basis of wit, charm, intellect and articulacy. Those like Michael Atherton, Steve Cram, the tennis player Sam Smith and others with a discernible talent for illuminating the sport they used to play would be granted it. Dictators can and should, where possible, be benign.

In the absence of such dispensation, however, no former sports person would be allowed a public platform from which to ruin sacred memories of their former splendour. The name of this essential legislation, you may have guessed, would be the Sir Geoffrey Hurst (Sporting Tranquillisers, Fake Nostalgists and Assorted Dullard Hypocrites) Act, 2010.

65

George Graham

Someone appears to have been tampering with the Wikipedia entry of a drill sergeant major disciplinarian type so charmless in every regard that I find myself resenting him for besmirching Winston Churchill's memory by entering the world on the wartime leader's seventieth birthday.

Mr Graham 'is best remembered', states that online encyclopedia, 'for his success at Arsenal, as a player in the 1970s and then as manager from 1986 until 1995'. No he is not. He is best remembered, and outside Arsenal perhaps only remembered, as the first and so far only top-flight manager to be done for taking those illicit payments euphemised in the argot of the game as 'bungs'. The elegant midfield style that won him the nickname 'Stroller', and the paradoxically sterile football he teased from Arsenal in the pre-Wenger era of offside traps and the semi-ironic celebratory chant of 'One–nil to the Arse-en-all', have long since faded from the memory.

What will never be forgotten about Graham, who in his post-Arsenal manifestation had the indecency to accept the offer to manage Spurs (see Alan Sugar, no. 71), is the £425,000 he graciously accepted, in cash, from the Norwegian football agent Rune Hauge – and this back in 1995 when almost half a million quid was widely viewed as a decent wedge. Why he did so remains the source of contention. Mr Graham has never failed to insist that the cash was 'an unsolicited gift', a token thank-you from Mr Hauge for buying a couple of his Scandinavian clients of the sort that the most basic good manners demand – and all the better finishing schools on the banks of Lake Geneva include this in their first-year syllabus – be stuffed, in treasury notes, into carrier bags.

Others of the breed known to Mr Tony Blair as the cynics and sneerers chose not to see things in quite that way. However, it is not, and never has been, my way to encourage the doubting of a man's word. So let us merrily accept Mr Graham's own version of events, and luxuriate in the warm glow that comes from learning that within every decent, Godfearing football agent, a committed philanthropist fights valiantly for self-expression.

64

Eric Bristow

Petty crime's loss was televised darts' great gain the day the Crafty Cockney chose arrows over housebreaking. Until then, the young Bristow's life had seemed to involve trips into and out of jug for the sort of naughtiness for which, as he confided in his autobiography, he routinely went tooled up with a claw hammer as a junior member of a north London gang. Perhaps, with hindsight, he should have stuck to the stealing. For where at the height of his chucking powers he was struck down by dartitis (the oche's version of the yips), so far as I'm aware there is no such psychological disorder as nickitis.

Long since denuded of his talent by a psychological flaw hinting that the cockiness may be transferred insecurity, these days he earns a crust as a 'spotter' (advising the TV director where a player will aim next) on Sky Sports. Such is his popularity with colleagues that, while he is now and again allowed out of the technical truck to sit in the studio, he is never permitted near the commentary box.

As a panto villain in the eighties golden era of Jocky Wilson, John Lowe and Bobby George, when he dominated darts much as Steve Davis did snooker, Bristow was undeniably a decent turn. With the abrasive, sneering persona of a man whose world view, as also expressed in that elegiac memoir, is that everybody but him is 'a wally', he was less the man you loved to hate than the man you were morally obliged to despise. Alongside the lairy, fake hard-man persona designed to suggest the imminence of low-level gratuitous violence, there was the affectation known to him as 'me perked-up right pinkie' – the little finger extended vertically after the fashion of an Edwardian Hyacinth Bucket wrongly imagining how Queen Mary would drink her tea. Had the young Bristow come across someone holding a pint glass in that manner dahn the boozer, he would doubtless have been tempted to administer an instant slap, and been well within his rights to do so.

What brushes with the law Bristow has lately enjoyed have been limited to an arrest on suspicion of punching his then wife in the face, of which he was subsequently cleared, and an encounter with a Gateshead copper recorded, by pleasing happenstance, for the cerebral ITV show *Street Crime UK*, and worth a glance on YouTube for his comedy drunk insistence that 'I did not threaten nobody' (arguably a rare instance of the double negative used correctly).

Whether the braggadocio stems from genuine cockiness or, as so often, its polar opposite is a question far from worth the effort of exploring on grounds connected with the shortness of life. Simply put, Bristow is the wally's wally, in his 1980s *Only Fools and Horses* argot, and the man who put the cock in Crafty Cockney.

63

Jonathan Pearce

During a 2010 World Cup match screened on the BBC, a friend emailed a question to which I've since given a great deal of thought, in the way you do with finely balanced philosophical conundra.

'Which Pearcey do you prefer?' it ran. 'The man who enjoys shouting, or the supposedly more mature, sub-Alan Green, wannabe Barry Davies sophisticate version?'

It isn't easy. Deciding which of Jonathan Pearce's guises is the less irksome is much like being asked whether you'd rather be stuck in a broken lift for six hours with Cherie Blair or Esther Rantzen, or being forced at gunpoint to choose between sex with a syphilitic rhinoceros or with Andrew Neil. Screaming 'Neither' isn't an option in that game. Nor is suicide. But they should be.

Mr Pearce announced himself to the football-following public in the early 1990s as the London radio station Capital Gold's resident foghorn. He screamed without pause, possibly in the belief that the volume of the commentator's voice would be mistaken by listeners for an accurate reflection of the excitement of the game.

Worse than the shouting itself was its indiscriminateness. He conjured up equal decibel levels whether the goal won an FA Cup final or turned a 4–2 League Cup lead for West Ham over Brentford into one of 5–2, or indeed if it wasn't a goal at all. He shouted when a corner was conceded, and now and then for a throw-in. He would have shouted, you felt, at a pigeon landing on a penalty spot during the half-time interval.

Even more agonising, arguably, than the shouting was what might charitably be described as his wordplay. When Ian Dowie scored for Crystal Palace in an FA Cup semi-final, he screamed, 'Wowie, it's Dowie!' the tone of self-delight hinting at this Birmingham University history graduate's satisfaction at giving the *Oxford Book of English Verse* selection committee something to think about.

'Never mind your José Carreras, never mind your *Don Quixote!*' was how he greeted England's ill-deserved victory over Spain, on penalties, in the Euro 2006 quarter-final. 'Your boys are out! So you can stick it up your Julio Iglesias! England are heading for the biggest, biggest prize!' This was so wrong in so many ways, and on so many levels, that we have little choice but to let it pass. We will also gloss lightly over his status, when he doubled up as Capital Gold's sports editor, as on-air humiliater of junior colleagues – a petard of his own on which he would later be hoisted, at Radio 5 Live, by the aforementioned Alan Green (see no. 4).

What cannot be allowed to pass is the lurch into unintended hilarity with which Pearcey greeted latecomers to a World Cup qualifier in 1993. 'Welcome to Bologna on Capital Gold for England versus San Marino!' he shouted. 'With Tennent's Pilsner, brewed with Czechoslovakian yeast for that extra Pilsner taste, and England are one down.'

How a man capable of that sentence could entertain the ambition to be a respected football commentator pays testament to the limitless human capacity for self-delusion. Nonetheless, via stints on various telly channels and that brief and unsuccessful tilt at Mr Green's supremacy on 5 Live, he landed up on *Match of the Day*, where he remains to this day.

In his reinvented persona, the shouting has been jettisoned, as have the hideous puns and rhymes. In their place, alas, is a pompous, sonorous, would-be professorial tone that may be at least as excruciating as what it has replaced. These days Pearcey is a temperate, judicial figure in the commentary box, weighing his words with ponderous intensity, and delivering them in a tone that one would take, were it anyone else, for a savage pastiche – possibly discovered on a long-lost tape made for friends by Peter Cook – of a man of little brain affecting to be clever.

The thing about Barry Davies is that he was clever. He was a touch bombastic, and now and again a little mannered, but by and large he was a brilliant commentator, who read a game beautifully and occasionally came up with snippets that branded themselves on the football lover's memory: 'Look at his face, look at his face' (of Franny Lee); 'And Lineker used him by not using him' (of Vinny Samways' decoy run in the FA Cup semi-final of 1991); and, best of all for its honesty and simplicity, 'Oh, you have to say that's magnificent,' of Maradona's astonishing second goal in the Hand of God game of 1986.

Mr Davies's Oxbridge cleverness went out of vogue at the BBC long ago, sad to say, in the cause of 'inclusivity' (appealing to the lowest-common denominator, or dunce demographic), which may explain the hiring of Mr Pearce. The irony, if that's the case, is that he then elected to model himself on the man who had been dropped for being too intelligent. On balance, I think he should have stuck to the 'Wowie, it's Dowie!' persona, which at least had the benefit of being true to himself. As a statesmanlike pontificator, he doesn't cut it – though he has found his perfect level as the commentator on *Robot Wars* – and never will.

Even the people in charge of BBC sport appear to be realising this. When the 2010 World Cup final gig had to be filled in the wake of John Motson's semi-retirement, Mr Pearce, the pre-tournament hot favourite for the honour, was passed over in favour of the faintly anonymous but quietly competent Guy Mowbray. For those of us obliged to sample his work, if not for the man himself, this was and will forever remain the zenith of Jonathan Pearce's career.

62

Sir Clive Woodward

For a man besotted with the McVerities that stream from the mouths of motivational speakers – how easily one imagines him telling his charges, 'Never assume: it makes an ass out of you and me,' with no parodic intent – the irony is that Woodward ignored one of the very few that makes sense. Had he only accepted the wisdom of always leaving the crowd wanting more, he might still be regarded as a masterly sporting thinker, rather than an unnervingly odd megalomaniac.

His time to leave the stage was late in 2003, in the roseate afterglow of coaching England to the rugby union World Cup in Australia. At the time, he seemed a genuine coaching talent. With the hindsight provided by his subsequent failures, the suspicion is that England won thanks to Martin Johnson's captaincy, Jonny Wilkinson's flawless kicking and the odd slice of luck, and if anything in spite of Woodward rather than because of him.

No genius, after all, could have presided over the subsequent British Lions tour to New Zealand in 2005, in which Woodward first hinted at something close to madness by hiring Alastair Campbell (see no. 80) as media supremo, showed blatant favouritism to the squad's English players, and tried to disguise his falling out with Gavin Henson with such cack-handed idiocy that the only philosopher-guru brought to mind was David Brent.

His Olympian arrogance unaffected, Woodward concluded, hilariously, that his gifts for painstaking organisation and management-speak gibberish deserved a fresh outlet. The time had come, he decided, to sprinkle the Woodwardian magic on association football, which he claimed he had always favoured over the chasing of the egg.

Happily for nemesis fans, the hubristic fantasist alighted upon the only other living creature who agreed with him that experience of one sport could be directly transplanted to another. His friend Rupert Lowe, the chairman of Southampton FC, hired him first as the club's 'performance director'; and then, when a palpably bemused Harry Redknapp soon moved on, as 'director of football'. Alas, like a kidney given in error to a recipient with a different blood type from the donor's, the transplant had no chance of taking. The lunacy eventually penetrated even Mr Lowe's lead-lined skull, and Woodward departed.

Having made the seamless progression from coaching doyen of British sport to its top-ranked standing joke, the next step was inevitable. In 2006 Woodward was appointed 'Director of Elite Performance' by the British Olympic Association – a role of such studied vagueness that he is thought unlikely to do much damage in it.

Thus far, with the London Games a year away at the time of writing, his most notable contribution to 'Team GB' (a styling which probably deserves an entry of its own) has been to issue a fifteen-point declaration of the 'bare minimum standards' he expects of UK athletes in 2012 – a document of such breathtaking condescension and inanity that you would, were the author anyone else on the planet, automatically take it for crude satire. To take but one of those points, 1), in its entirety, reads 'Hygiene'. There is no word yet that Woodward will institute a mandatory morning fingernail inspection in the British section of the Olympic Village, but no level of patronising idiocy should be placed beyond his reach.

After the 2012 London Games, assuming he doesn't try his luck in another area that requires no experience or knowledge – Elite Performance Director at NASA might suit him – you assume that Woodward will fall into the traditional safety net for sport's unemployable. Henceforth he should confine himself to talking motivational tosh – a bit of Sun Tzu here, a smidgen of David Brent there – to mid-management nebbishes in hotel conference suites on the outskirts of Northampton.

In the increasingly unlikely event of a biopic being made Steve Buscemi would be the natural first choice for the lead – and a finer testament to the disturbing weirdness of Sir Clive Woodward than that there could not be.

61

The Japanese Racing Driver

On the outskirts of Bath this Sunday, should you be there and take the trouble to look, you will see an eighty-seven-year-old at the wheel of a 1957 Morris Minor – cloth cap on head, pipe in mouth, reaction time to change of traffic light from amber to green: 4 minutes, 29 seconds – with more driving ability in the little finger of his begloved right hand than any Japanese ever to spin a Formula One car into a tyre wall for no apparent reason.

Sixteen Japanese have driven Grand Prix cars (which of us has forgotten Masahiro Hasemi and Naoki Hattori?), without a single win between them and the tiniest handful of finishes in the points. Every one was hired either for teams using Japanese-made engines and therefore under pressure from a manufacturer thinking more of the domestic commercial possibilities than of anything so *recherché* as driving ability; or because the driver came with sponsorship money from Japan. Had the financially troubled Larousse team had a free choice between the two in 1994, it would have gone for my late grandmother Bessie Norman, who celebrated passing her test at the age of seventy-seven by driving her Austin Princess into my grandfather's knee, over a certain Hideki Noda.

It's not their fault. Very few are capable of following Dirty Harry's injunction that 'A man's just gotta known his limitations,' and how many of us would find the strength to reject the offer of being paid a fortune to drive a very fast car, albeit very slowly? I know I wouldn't, even though it often takes me half an hour to park the little Audi A3 in a space thrice the size of Finland.

As a spectator, however, only so many times can you hear Martin Brundle shriek 'And Takumo Sate's spun off! We won't know till we've seen the telemetry, but it looked like driver error to me,' without having the bad taste to compare Japanese F1 drivers with Pearl Harbor. The Japanese Imperial Air Force hardly covered its country in glory that day, but it did bring the United States into the war, which wasn't such a bad thing. What have Tora Takagi and Ukyo Jatayama ever done to safeguard the democratic world?

Japanese efforts at the wheels of F1 cars having developed not necessarily to anyone's advantage, it's time for the raising of the white flag. One thing's for sure: none of them is ever going to see a chequered one.

60

Jonathan Edwards

The honours board of ostentatious sporting religiosity has had few more pernicious names stencilled upon it than that of the Creeping Jesus of the Sandpit.

There is an irony here, as Richard Dawkins would swiftly note. Mr Edwards's own field event, the triple jump, ranks alongside famine, war and Sarah Palin as powerful anecdotal evidence against the existence of God. When Evander Holyfield thanked his maker for enabling him to win a fight, you took the point: you'd want a powerful imaginary friend on hand with Mike Tyson nibbling your earlobe. Besides, the Old Testament has at least as much smiting as begetting, so it seems fitting for those keen on scripture to view the big-fight game as doing the Lord's work.

The triple jump, on the other hand, is an innately preposterous event that no benign deity could have created even half-asleep on His rest day – the very Sabbath on which, for many years, Mr Edwards refused to jump, once missing a World Championship final in the process. Yet the whole Eric Liddell shtick might have worked better had he spent his retirement as a missionary in the developing world. Becoming the presenter of *Songs of Praise* never quite cut it.

Looking back on his career in retirement, Edwards would describe it as 'always a means to an end: glorifying God' – as though his rendition of the hop, skip and jump was right up there, alongside the Sistine Chapel and Mozart's *Requiem*, among the more spectacular examples of divinely inspired iconography. This outlandish claim carried the morally superior tone of the would-be martyr. He wasn't doing it for the joy, the money or the medals. Far too spiritual and high-minded for that, he jumped in self-sacrifice.

Soon enough, however, Edwards came to mislay the faith that had propelled him down the runway and launched him to the world record he set in 1995 which stands to this day. Revealingly, when he spoke about the belief he had lost it was as if it had never been more than a legal performance-enhancing drug, a way of inducing psychochemical energy and confidence detectable in the holy heart but not the bloodstream. 'Believing in something beyond the self can have a hugely beneficial psychological impact, even if the belief is fallacious,' he told the excellent Matthew Syed of *The Times* long after giving the Creator His marching orders. 'It provided a profound sense of reassurance for me because I took the view that the result was in God's hands. He would love me, win, lose or draw. The tin of sardines I took to the Olympic final in Sydney was a tangible reminder of that.'

When Eric Cantona gave his famously opaque press conference, who could have dreamed that a sportsman would one day unleash a more irksome sardine reference than the Frenchman's gnomic thought about seagulls following the trawlers?

Seven years after John West had joined with the deity in helping Edwards to his Olympic gold in Australia, now retired and needing no more supernatural Stanozolol to drive him down the runway, the smug little ingrate had decided that God was 'incredibly improbable'. As if coming to that conclusion was any sort of barrier to becoming an archbishop, even of Canterbury, in the Church of England. The air of the tambourine-wielding, truism-spouting rural vicar, who ministers to the spinsters of the parish in their more blushworthy dreams and is the apple of his bishop's eye, clings to Jonathan Edwards still, regardless of his alleged loss of faith, and always will.

59

Sven-Göran Eriksson

For his failure to breach the top fifty in this book, Sven must do what may not come easier to him these days than to anyone else. He must thank the England football team. In performing at least as abysmally under Fabio Capello in 2010 as under him four years earlier, the 'golden generation' conclusively established that the identity of a coach is purely incidental, and that England will stink the tournament up regardless of who is nominally in charge. He can no more be blamed for the surreal fiasco of 2006 than can Don Fabio for the catastrophe of 2010. The inevitable humiliation of the national side is dictated by forces far deeper and more powerful than those of personnel (see the England Football Team, no. 2), and Eriksson's record as England coach remains statistically the best after Alf Ramsey's.

Nor should we hold his amorous adventures against the ponderous Swede. Far from it, all the stuff about the platform shoes left outside compatriot Ulrika Jonsson's bedroom door was a delight, and barely less thrillingly unexpected a revelation than that of John Major's affair with Edwina Currie. What with Nancy Del'Ollio and his brief fling with FA secretary Faria Alam, he offered infinitely more entertainment off the pitch, and of much higher quality, than his England teams managed in all the aggregated games that followed the astonishing 5–1 win in Munich in September 2001. Who'd have believed that the tradi-tional light-comedy-of-manners enquiry 'Anyone for Svennis?' would be answered in the affirmative by so many women? He is living proof that looks and personality are no barrier to erotic triumph, and thus has pin-up status for middle-aged schlubs everywhere.

The solitary reason for his presence here is the greed and lack of discernment that fuel his employment choices. However far beneath his professional dignity, there is no job he will refuse if the money is right. This is the Michael Caine of coaches, and for every *Alfie* (his time at Lazio, when he earned the epithet 'the successful failure') there are several *Miss Congenialitys*. Where Sven's time as Director of Football Affairs at Notts County falls into the filmic *oeuvre* is hard to say. It could be that even Caine has never approved a script as laughably incoherent as that one, though *Blame it on Rio* makes that a hard call.

There is no post he wouldn't accept if a Thai human rights abuser or a bunch of sheikhs held out the promise of a fat cheque on his dismissal, and the jobs come and go with such bewildering rapidity that he might as well be on the books of a temping agency. The only salient difference, speaking as one who was once sacked from fourteen temp typing jobs in a fortnight for no more solid reason than the inability to type, is that when you're sent home after two hours of a week-long booking at the Deciduous Fruits Board in The Strand, one thing you don't take with you is a seven-figure pay-off.

58

Sir Allen Stanford

It's all too easy to sneer at others for what has come, with hindsight, to look foolish. So no snarky nonsense here, thanking you, about the *Sunday Times* headline on an article of 27 April 2008 which audaciously ran: 'Sir Allen Stanford, England's Saviour'. The sub-header – 'The Billionaire Behind Plans for a New Twenty20 English Premier League has a History of Seeing Plans Though to Fruition' – wasn't half bad either.

That the only plans to bear sweet fruit in the Stanfordian grove thus far have been those of the FBI to bang him up while awaiting charges of massive fraud adds to the sense of wistfulness invoked by this tale of grandiose ambition narrowly unrealised.

Then again, how could anyone have been suspicious about a man described, in every article of that time, as 'billionaire philanthropist Sir Allen Stanford'? Admittedly, the billions belonged to other people, and the only anthrop he was philing was himself. But it is not my purpose to encourage pedantic quibbling.

No, it seemed the most natural thing in the world, in the summer of 2008, for a six-foot-four-inch Texan with a strikingly un-American title (awarded to this dual passport-holder for services to the Caribbean islands of Antigua and Barbuda) to land his helicopter on the Lord's grass in order to finalise his rescue mission for English cricket. What on earth could have seemed suspicious about that?

Well, perhaps a slightly dim boy of seven might have heard the distant ringing of alarm bells, and asked himself what in the name of all the saints such a character would want with a game that has remained so stubbornly out of vogue in Houston and Dallas ever since the 1982 scandal that rocked Southfork, when Cliff Barnes gave Miss Ellie out LBW off a JR googly that was missing leg stump by a good six inches.

Happily, it isn't a faintly dim seven-year-old boy who runs English cricket, but Giles Clark, an intelligent fifty-seven-year-old whose business résumé includes the foundation of that excellent chain Majestic Wine Warehouse. Deploying the keen antennae for dodginess that helped to make him a leading quango-crat, the chairman of the England and Wales Cricket Board welcomed Sir Allen with capaciously open arms and giant dollar signs flashing in his eyes. What followed was as embarrassing for him as it was hilarious to those of us who regard Twenty20 as a McCricket excrescence worthy of the humiliation the Texan suspected felon wasted little time in visiting upon it.

Sir Allen's masterplan to match a West Indies invitational team, modestly named the Stanford Superstars, against England in Antigua in 2008 was bedecked in fiasco from start to finish. The players took umbrage at his appearances in their dressing rooms before games (see Alastair Campbell's team talk to the British Lions, no. 80), and even more umbrage at his alleged playful groping of their wives and girlfriends. You can't imagine Douglas Jardine or Gubby Allen going a bundle on Twenty20, to be honest, but if you are going to introduce the glitzy Eurotrash values of football's Premier League to cricket, I suppose you might as well go the extra mile by selling it to the drollest vulgarian in view.

When the Stanford Superstars duly trounced England by ten wickets, we looked forward to many years of English cricketers flying to the West Indies to massage the outsize ego of a professional exhibitionist by competing haplessly for a multi-million-dollar winner-takes-all bounty.

And then, with heart-rending suddenness, the dream died. In June 2009, after spiritedly evading the authorities for several months, Sir Allen was nicked and charged with defrauding investors of several billion dollars in a Ponzi scheme of a scope and ambition second only to dear old Bernie Madoff's. All very W.G. Grace.

The trial is scheduled for January 2011, and we all wish him well with that. If, God forbid, it goes wrong, and he gets one of those 345-year sentences the ironists of the US judicial community like to dole out to sixty-year-olds, there will be a silver lining. Is there anyone on this earth better suited by nature and inclination than the erstwhile saviour of English cricket to having all the time in the world to spend poring over his collection of first-edition *Wisdens*?

57

The Jockey Club

Even Britain, beacon of clueless sporting administration to the planet, has never known an overseer as smug and incompetent as this one.

Whether it was ever an administrative body at all is an intriguing point of debate. It would insist that it was, and is. I would posit that it was always a glorified residential care home for inbred, quarter-witted, aristos, allowed by one another to run a medium-sized industry as an alternative to other, more conventional therapeutic pastimes such as weaving macramé pot-plant holders and gazing catatonically into the far distance while claiming to be Napoleon on Elba.

The Jockey Club, in other words, was the most eccentric bespoke form of occupational therapy known to humanity until Mr Tony Blair brought David Blunkett back into his cabinet in 2005, as Work and Pensions Secretary, in the midst of a peculiarly grave pensions crisis, 'to help sort his head out'. The lunatics didn't so much take over this asylum as create it for themselves. They built it in 1750, to adapt the line from *Field of Dreams*, and have kept coming for more than 250 years.

In the middle of the eighteenth century, during the reign of George II, the notion of a private members' club running a sport for the amusement and aggrandisement of its members was hardly odd. Even in the mid-twentieth century, it was not out of place. By the mid-1970s, however, the vista of a few dozen titled gentleman, several reportedly blessed with chins, controlling horseracing had acquired an anachronistic patina.

Hats off to them for guarding Britain's last rigid caste system – one enforced primarily by the wearing of various hats – so jealously. In an ever more bemusing world, there's comfort in knowing that jockeys called before the stewards for using the whip too liberally are still addressed in the manner of medieval peasants being rebuked by a manorial lord, and that there remains a solitary haven in which hereditary titles still hold sway.

Yet there is a problem. The intellects of sporting administrators are supposed at least to match, and preferably to exceed, those of the creatures under their control. With the Jockey Club, the difficulty isn't so much that their brains are smaller than those of the trainers and jockeys they oversee. It's that their brains appear to be smaller than those of the horses. And the equine brain, in relation to its body mass, is among the smallest in the animal kingdom. In fact, the cerebral powers of Jockey Club members seem modelled on the ostrich kingdom, their primary skill being the burial of noble heads in the sand whenever claims of corruption are made.

Precisely how dodgy horseracing is we cannot know, but cash-rich businesses built on gambling tend inevitably to be beset by villainy. For those of us whose love of racing lies partly in its Runyonesque richness this is as it should be. The conspiracy of silence that binds the entire racing press – which is effectively part of the sport's public relations wing, and thus honour-bound to keep anything of interest for gossipy evenings in Newmarket pubs – forbids any mention of this, but some of the most celebrated riders in history have also been the most bent.

One reportedly regularly accepted a carrier bag full of treasury notes from a major bookmaker to throw the big Saturday handicap. Another was so skilled at the dark arts that eventually his trainer sacked him on the grounds that 'Even I don't know when you're pulling a horse [deliberately slowing it] any more.' So hard is it to make a living at the margins of the sport, meanwhile, that some of the more obscure trainers can only survive by landing the odd touch, by deliberately nobbling a horse until the odds are right for a touch, or by getting friends or surrogates to lay horses they know will lose on the betting exchanges.

All this and more goes on, and everyone involved in racing knows it and turns a blind eye. When, however, champion jockey Kieren Fallon was secretly recorded by the *News of the World* bragging to a supposed Arab visitor (in fact that paper's 'Fake Sheikh') of his ability to influence races hours before dropping his hands and being caught on the line, the ritualistic Jockey Club bleatings about the integrity and cleanliness of the sport did sound a little misplaced. Although a subsequent criminal case against Mr Fallon collapsed due to lack of evidence, when later it fell to the French racing authorities to find cocaine in his bloodstream, you asked yourself whether the stated commitment of their British counterparts to policing the sport rigorously might be fanciful.

Eventually, the embarrassment occasioned by their continual and often hilarious failure to unearth the tiniest portion of the villainy known to everyone outside HQ at Portman Square gave way to a typically English solution. Rather than change its *modus operandi* or, God forbid, its personnel, it changed its name.

A few years ago, its regulatory arm was merged with something else to become what is now known as the British Horseracing Authority. It was a cunning ruse, and it very nearly worked. Had the Jockey Club gone that extra mile for the transparency it claims it promotes in racing, by renaming itself Aristocratic Dimwits Swanking Around in Top Hats Betraying the Interests of the Betting Shop Punters Who Fund Their Sport But Are Far Beneath Their Contempt, it would have been better. But that wouldn't have fitted on the letterhead, and since the *raison d'être* of what we will always know as the Jockey Club is appearances, and the keeping up thereof, that would not have done at all.

56

Daniel Levy

Since assuming the chairmanship of Tottenham Hotspur in 2001, the pixie-like Levy has failed to forge a harmonious relationship with the author – and this despite what my wife identifies as the clear advantage of never having met me. If anything, indeed, relations have been even cooler than with his predecessor, the noble Lord Sugar (see no. 71), who is quoted in Piers Morgan's memoir *The Insider* referring to myself, with some reason, as 'that fucking idiot'.

The source of friction with Daniel, as with his thin-skinned little lordship, has been the stewardship of the club to which all three of us claim to be shackled by unflinching bonds of loyalty. It's a tragic verdict on the emotional range of the football fan that while he (he standing here for 'he or she') is capable of changing religions, political world views and spouses, the one thing he cannot change is allegiance to his club. At the age of six or seven you make the choice, or have it made for you by family and/or geography, and that's that. It is a life sentence from which very few are paroled.

If the porridge has lately become gentler for Tottenham inmates, with Champions League qualification representing a transfer to a south coast open prison, this cannot excuse all the years in HMP Belmarsh under the capricious rule of Governor Levy. Like Morgan Freeman in *The Shawshank Redemption*, we became not so much inured to the despair as addicted to it and the gratifying self-pity it produced.

Enough of the institutionalised lifer metaphor, and on to the facts. For a man who takes such pride in his educational record, Daniel is an astoundingly slow learner. Even if his degree was in

Land Economy, the thick sportsman's special, the pre-Harry Redknapp era at White Hart Lane obliges us to wonder which hallucinogen the Cambridge examiners were overdosing on the day they awarded him a First.

Daniel's stylistic calling card has been a genius for replicating the same transparent error of judgement. He was, pre-Redknapp, hooked on the 'creative tension' (a transparent mode of ego-inflation, in that it weakens the power and prestige of all but himself) between a manager and a director of football, or 'sporting director'. First Glenn Hoddle and David Pleat, then Jacques Santini and Frank Arnesen, then Martin Jol and the enigmatic Frenchman Damien Comolli, finally the hapless Juande Ramos and that same Comolli ... the moment these relationships collapsed, as they inevitably do under the artificial divide-and-rule strain, Daniel unleashed another. Eventually, after the departure of Ramos and Comolli and with Spurs marooned at the bottom of the table, he buckled. He put Redknapp in sole charge of the team, and by one of those astounding coincidences that verge on Jungian synchronicity, the improvement was instant, dramatic and, so far, sustained.

And yet, from the adorably pointy-headed Daniel, not a case of champagne, a note, or even a word of thanks. This rankles. Time and again I patiently explained his error to him in the *Evening Standard*. Eventually, his response was to ban me, and the newspaper, from White Hart Lane, rescinding the ban when this public relations masterstroke received a widespread gentle ribbing.

Over so many fiascos has Daniel presided that selecting a couple to give the flavour seems invidious. But this brace must suffice. The calamitous start to the 2008–09 season that led to Ramos' and Comolli's sacking stemmed from Tottenham's novel jettisoning of the convention about having strikers in the squad. Dan delayed the sale of the effete Bulgarian Dimitar Berbatov so long, to chisel a few extra million out of Manchester United, that the transfer window closed with no time to buy a replacement.

As for the firing of the engaging Dutchman Martin Jol, the only competent manager in Levy's pre-Redknapp period, the handling of this was memorably unconventional. Why Jol, who had led Spurs to two fifth-place league finishes, had to go after an incredibly brief run of poor form at the start of a season was unclear. But having decided that he did, Daniel amateurishly managed to have himself photographed flying off to Seville to hire Signor Ramos, while denying any intent to do so; and then, having apparently informed Jol of his decision, exposed the engaging Netherlander to humiliation as a White Hart Lane Uefa Cup crowd learned the news mid-game from their mobile phones and BlackBerries.

Meanwhile, after almost a decade at the helm as placeman for the Caribbean-based currency trader Joe Lewis, Daniel has made no progress in the development of the existing ground, or a move to another with less anarchic transport links. In a fraction of that time, Arsenal built the Emirates and moved in.

Spurs, it pains me to admit, have always been the lesser of the north London clubs, and probably always will be. Dan's crime, despite the recent revival, has been to leave us without the room to fantasise that fact away and cleave to the fanciful pretensions of old.

55

Joe Bugner

Younger readers acquainted with this peculiar character only from his eccentric appearance in the Aussie jungle on *I'm a Celebrity ... Get Me Out of Here* will be startled to learn that he was once a far greater irritant to the British public.

Such an arrogant braggart was Bugner in his days as one of the world's more talented white heavyweights, indeed, that he is the source of the solitary complaint about the Soviet Union of a friend who becomes tearful even now at its fall. This unapologetic Stalinist will brook no criticism of the gulags, state murders or other elegances of totalitarian brutality. The solitary mistake the USSR ever made, to his mind, was invading Hungary in 1956, and then purely because that act of imperialist might loosed Joe Bugner on Britain. A child then, he fled the country with his family after the tanks rolled into Budapest, and grew to manhood in Buckinghamshire before eventually tiring of his adoptive land and adopting another.

For his initial success in infuriating the boxing public, he cannot be blamed. If referee Harry Gibbs was the only spectator who believed that he beat Henry Cooper, by a dementedly precise quarter-point, to take Our Enery's British title belt and send the lovable Brut-splasher into retirement, that was hardly Bugner's fault. What followed was entirely his fault, however, as he treated us to an intoxicating cocktail of Olympian conceit, offputting weirdness, an air of misplaced intellectual superiority and Edwardian-shopgirl refinement, and a fighting style better designed to have viewers slumping back in their seats snoring than fidgeting excitedly on their edges.

In 1975, when he fought Muhammad Ali for the world heavy-weight crown, he produced what remains widely regarded as the most crabbily defensive display in title history. In fifteen rounds he barely took a punch, for one simple reason: he never threw one. The contrast with Cooper, who downed the then Cassius Clay with his left hook (his 'Hammer'), and was all guts and honest effort where Bugner had the talent but none of the fighting heart, was poignant.

Eventually, after coming out of retirement almost as often as Liza Minnelli, though without ever selling out Madison Square Garden, the Magyar nomad resurfaced in a former dominion across the seas with a reinvention of exquisite subtlety. By the artful device of adopting a hat strung with corks, he recreated himself as 'Aussie Joe', and embarked on yet another boxing career in front of fans yet to discover the thrill of watching him stand statuesque in the middle of the ring with his gloves covering his face.

It seems that even this sparkling renaissance failed to resolve his financial problems. And so it was that in 2009 Ant & Dec wheeled him into the jungle camp as a late substitute for a madly neurotic ballroom dancer who could take no more than a couple of days.

What the audience never heard from Aussie Joe, ITV being too prissy to broadcast this theory, was his insistence that Aids was created by the CIA. This claim nearly destroyed Barack Obama's candidacy for the Democratic presidential nomination when a tape of the Revd Jeremiah Wright making it in church emerged during the campaign. From Bugner's lips it caused no worse than the affected distress of two gay contestants who had spent enough time in his company to know better than to rise to this bait.

More offensive than that infantile wind-up have been the various final acts to his career in the ring. Eventually, as is inevitable if a fighter carries on long enough in the age of so many meaningless belts, he won what calls itself a 'world heavyweight title'. In 1998, pushing fifty, he huffed and puffed his senescent way to a title sanctioned by something called the WBF, by beating fellow geriatric James 'Bonecrusher' Smith on points.

For almost thirty years, this magnificent physical specimen had played the part of boxing's smartest cynic. Yet he ended up risking his health by continuing in the ring long after his reflexes had deserted him. Many others who have done so at least had the excuse of punchiness from taking too many blows. He palpably did not. In the end, as he confirmed on *I'm a Celeb*, the great pseudo-intellectual of the ring proved to be the dumbest of them all.

54

Flavio Briatore

Nothing in recent years – not the twenty-year-olds driving convertible Bentleys, not the £14,000 nightclub splurges on the Kristal, not even the twin thrones on which bride and groom greeted their subjects at the Beckham wedding – has captured English football's descent into the Eurotrash inferno like the mysterious involvement in the game of this Italian beauty.

'Eurotrash', having said that, doesn't do Signor Briatore justice. 'Eurofilth' seems more fitting for a creature who somehow progressed from owning a restaurant that went bust, via a four-and-a-half-year prison sentence for gambling-related fraud (dodgy cards) he avoided by fleeing Italy, to managing Grand Prix drivers and running the Benetton and Renault Formula One teams.

It is in the latter capacity that this pastiche of the yacht-swanking 1970s playboy earned his chapter in the Compendium of Sporting Rogues, though again 'rogue' feels inadequate for one who jeopardised the lives not only of his own driver but also of stewards and spectators in the incident known, with all the fearsome originality of scandal nomenclature, as 'Crashgate'.

'A manager is supposed to encourage you,' as the driver involved, Nelson Piquet Jnr, later put it. 'In my case it was the opposite. Flavio Briatore was my executioner.' Given that Briatore ordered Piquet to crash his Renault early in the Singapore Grand Prix of 2008, this is closer to the literal truth than Piquet's reference to his subsequent sacking was intended to suggest.

The crash, into a tyre wall at high speed during the fourteenth lap, was engineered for reasons too tedious (this is, after all Formula One) to dwell on, but connected with stopping the race and restarting it under the safety car for the benefit of lead Renault driver Fernando Alonso.

Briatore professed himself 'distraught' at being banned from the sport for life, stoically adding that he was 'just trying to save the team', and describing the FIA investigation that led to his ban as 'a tool of vengeance'. That life ban was revoked, and he was awarded a token €15,000 compensation. In the magical kingdom of Max Mosley and Bernie Ecclestone (see no. 7), such turns of events long ago lost their power to amaze. Theirs is a parallel universe, governed by a moral code outsiders cannot hope to comprehend.

More curious than Signor Briatore's moral outrage at being punished, however briefly and inadequately, for an offence to which he tacitly confessed, was his involvement with Queens Park Rangers Football Club. The oddity isn't that a creature like Briatore would wish to jump on the football bandwagon, but that he chose to do so at a genteel club such as QPR. I live a five-minute walk from Loftus Road, and watch them now and again, and there is no sweeter or more homely club known to man. I was warned about my future conduct once for muttering the word 'Wanker', at around the time that a steward at Stamford Bridge saw no cause for a stern word with the man in the nearby seat who pledged, on his late father's life, to stab me to death at half time for revealing an allegiance to Spurs.

QPR didn't deserve Briatore, any more than it deserves the involvement of his friend Little Bern and the steel magnate Lakshmi Mittal. Billionaires have no place at this homeliest of clubs (although, with Rangers seemingly heading back to the Premier League at the time of writing, perhaps its fans would disagree).

Thankfully, Signor Briatore, its erstwhile chairman, has no place there now. He resigned in the aftermath of Crashgate, sparing the fearless administrators of the Football League and its chairman Lord Mawhinney (that nasty old git from the dog days of the Major government) the trouble of deciding whether or not he passed the 'fit and proper person' test. Quite a fearsome conundrum that would have been.

53
John Motson

In British public life, perseverance is king. However scorned and disliked, even hated, a public figure may be, they will come into vogue eventually if they just stick at it long enough. As Alan Bennett said, in England you need only live to ninety and be able to eat a boiled egg to be thought worthy of a Nobel Prize. Football boasts two obvious beneficiaries of the British public's reverence for tenacity in its least well-loved personalities. One is the life president of Hartlepool United, the noble Lord Mandelson. The other is John Motson.

In 1994, it seemed the game was up for Motson, whose career had taken off vertically some twenty years earlier when he was blessed with Hereford's legendary FA Cup defeat of Newcastle (Ronnie Radford and all) for his debut *Match of the Day* commentary.

For perhaps a decade, he was more than adequate. The spautistic fixation on statistics neatly recorded in his notebook was held in check, the sheepskin coat chimed with the bleak sartorial times, no one even knew that clichés were clichés back then, and in all fairness – or, put another way, to be fair – he had the right voice and overgrown schoolboy persona to enhance moments of high drama. Very much so. He never had an iota of David Coleman's authority, of course, or Barry Davies' Oxbridge smarts, but he was fine. He was, at his best, more than fine.

By 1994, the appeal had faded. The coalescence of Gazza's tears, Nick Hornby's *Fever Pitch* and post-Hillsborough and -Heysel traumatic shock had dragged football out of its Neanderthal era, and made it trendy for the university-educated middle class. Davies' erudition chimed with the moment, and he was given the World Cup final in place of Motty.

This was a relief. In a previous World Cup, one of Motty's over-rehearsed spontaneous witticisms had identified Socrates as 'summing up the philosophy of Brazilian football'. Had he been at the microphone for the atrocious final of 2004, in which Brazil beat Italy on penalties after 120 minutes of stultifying goalless inaction, he would have greeted the introduction of a second-half substitute with, 'And on comes Viola. Now then, is this the man to pull the strings for Brazil?'

Mr Davies was also handed the following year's FA Cup final, another atrociously dull game, and blew it in studiedly ironic fashion by unleashing a torrent of Motsonian pre-prepared *aperçus*. Motty was reprieved, and another decade and a half on, although retired from international duties, he remains a constant presence on *Match of the Day*. The very qualities that had made him the source of ridicule – the clunkingly hackneyed language, the nerdsome reliance on meaningless facts and figures – had transformed him, by way of the alchemical agent that is survival, into that dread creature, the National Character. He became, quite simply, Motty.

In the dog days of his commentary career, a new trait has come to dominate his work. Generally with individual sports-people, the first thing to go is not the body but the mind. You see it most clearly in snooker. There is no physical reason why a forty-year-old man is less able than a twenty-two-year-old to sit in a chair, walk two yards to a table, and bend an arm. But whether it's the damage done by accumulated stress or the ebbing of testosterone, the concentration and the nerve evaporate.

So it is with some commentators. It happened to Brian Moore, a fine and forceful presence on ITV in the 1970s but by the mid-1980s so fearful of mistakes that he qualified everything to death.

Motty is worse. Almost nothing can happen on a football pitch about which he will not equivocate. If a goalbound shot hits a defender on the head and changes trajectory by ninety degrees en route to going behind for a corner, he will ask, 'Now then, did that one possibly take a subtle deflection?' If a replay transparently reveals one player bringing another down in the box with a move borrowed from Greco-Roman wrestling, he will enquire, 'Well, was there enough contact there for a penalty? I'm not sure, but you've seen 'em given.' If a player stood in the centre circle, took out a Kalashnikov, stuck the nozzle in his mouth and pressed the trigger, Motty would say, 'Well, he's gone down and he's not moving much. Will he be able to continue, or might Sam Allardyce have to make a substitution?'

In Britain even today, the instinct to relish what richly belongs in the coffin of history remains potent, as the enduring commercial success of the *Daily Mail* confirms (see also Peter Alliss, no. 1). A *sine qua non* about nostalgia is, or should be, that its objects are no longer with us, and the day Motty finally retires will be the day to bash out the mandatory quote from Joni Mitchell's 'Big Yellow Taxi'. So long as he survives – indulged by Gary Lineker and the gang as a sage, and treated on Radio 5 with a veneration once reserved on the BBC for the octogenarian Churchill – you know exactly what we've got before it's gone. Red and blotchy (likes a drop, he does), endlessly irritating, forever obliging the hand to scratch the head, Motty is football's psoriasis, and twice as hard to shift.

52

Willie Carson

If the magnificent Clare Balding performs one more miracle, she will become the first TV sports presenter in history to become a candidate for sanctification by the Holy See of Rome.

She already has two to her name. Of the first, I wish to say little. Suffice it to report that, in 1998 at the Wimbledon greyhound racing track, at a dog meeting sponsored by the newspaper for which we were then both columnists, she cajoled me into betting £4,000 to her £6,000 that she would, within the next decade, have a baby. The day a Sunday tabloid revealed the sexual preference that made such a nativity less likely, she emailed sheepishly to ask if the bet was still on. Piously, I replied that the secret of successful betting is having the edge in inside knowledge, so the bet was entirely legitimate, and stood. She eventually accepted £1,000 in full settlement, which was exceedingly gracious.

If that act of charity struck this impoverished mug punter as a minor miracle, her other one belongs on the biblical honours board with the parting of the Red Sea. Somehow she has contrived to appear on the BBC for many years alongside Willie Carson without once attempting to strangle him, as any minimal sense of public duty appears to demand.

Her forbearance as they stand beside one another facing the camera – him on his upturned soapbox, the pair playing the parts in this viewer's mind of 'love' and 'hate' tattoos on adjacent knuckles – is astonishing. At times, stretching saintliness to the precipice of madness itself, she seems actively fond of the little bleeder.

Others are less so. Carson is regarded as one of the most unlovable characters in a sport hardly known for a famine of those. Short-tempered, hysterical, watchful to the edge of paranoia, like so many men who laugh far too loud and too easily his eyes seldom reflect the mirth. By looks, demeanour and nature, he is designed to understudy the psychotic and murderous ventriloquist's dummy Chucky if and when Tim Rice decides to make a West End musical out of the *Child's Play* movies.

The ceaseless cackling, at a pitch to shatter glass and possibly tungsten, invariably lacks any identifiable cause other than the urge to ingratiate. (In the lamented screen absence of Anthea Turner, is there a more gratingly winsome telly presence?) As much for its blatant insincerity as for the soul-piercing visceral horror, it is a sensationally monstrous noise.

To experience the sight and sound of Willie Carson and his demented giggle is to be reminded why a fear of clowns is among the more common phobias. There is something acutely menacing about synthesised good humour worn as a mask, and with him the coiled rage is almost tangible.

That said, it's hard to be desperately scary at four feet eleven inches. All Clare need do is reach out a hand and take his throat to silence the cackling for good. One day surely she will snap. I'd bet £4,000 to her £6,000, in fact, that she strangles this ghoulish munchkin within the next ten years.

51
Mike Gatting

In that skinny leaf-shaped Venn intersect between ignorance and unpleasantness, there once lived Fat Gatt. How the most perfectly spherical character known even to cricket, which always welcomed the stouter gentleman to its bosom, squeezed himself into so tiny a space defied the earthly laws of physics to a degree unknown outside the Tardis itself.

With good reason is Gatting remembered more for a talent for wandering bemusedly into scrapes than as a pulverising top-order batsman, barely adequate occasional change bowler, and one of the better England captains of the modern era. Although less able than his brother Mikes Brearley, Atherton and Vaughan, he led his country with bluff yeoman competence, and at the time of writing remains the last captain to win an Ashes series in Australia.

Whether it was the contretemps with Pakistani umpire Shakoor Rana that saw him become the first person in media history to be quoted using the 'c' word on the front page of a British newspaper (the *Independent*), or the suicidal reverse sweep that cost England the 1987 World Cup final, or his astonished reaction to Shane Warne's first ball in Ashes cricket, the mental image his name conjures is that of a cavernous mouth gaping in disbelief above a goatee beard. If Edvard Munch had lived to follow *The Scream* with *The Schtick Fleisch Mit Oigen* ('lump of meat with eyes' in Yiddish), Gatting would have been his muse.

All the above are, to varying degrees, forgivable. Mr Rana, no sweetheart himself, had called Gatting a cheat. Admittedly, the response lacked a certain *politesse*, as he and the even more corpulent umpire stood toe to toe pointing reciprocal fingers like cricketing sumos having a pre-bout hissy fit, while Gatting serenaded Rana with the memorable chorus, 'You fucking cheating cunt.' Yet you can appreciate how being accused of gamesmanship in Pakistan in the era of Javed Miandad must have been an ironic affront too far. Anyway, we all love the hilarious queeniness of the sports-induced diplomatic incident of the kind that saw that match briefly abandoned. Gatting paid the price soon enough, when the captaincy was taken from him, and since that constitutes him discharging his debt to cricketing society, we'll hear not another word about it.

The reverse sweep was a shocker, it's true, and a gross abrogation of his duties as a senior middle-order batsman. England were heading, if not cruising, to victory at the time, but lost momentum when the lardbucket chose to show his contempt for the gentle off-breaks of Alan Border, hardly a proto-Muralitharan, by top-edging him to the keeper. Still, at least it showed aggressive intent unseen again against the Aussies until Kevin Pietersen decided (however briefly; see no. 15) he was English.

As for the Warne dismissal, not for nothing is the leg break that pitched way outside leg stump and spun back to take Gatting's off stump known as 'the ball of the century'. The miracle, as the writer Martin Johnson sagely observed at the time, was that any delivery could have spun the width of Gatting himself. Frankly – I speak admiringly, as a portly fellow myself – you'd have thought traversing that vast range would have tested the fuel tank of a light aircraft, Gatting's buttocks having separate postcodes at the time.

Perhaps it was a little unfair that the frequency with which bamboozlement hijacked those lumpen features made him appear tuppence farthing short of the shilling. Those who know him insist he's nothing like as dim as he seems – a claim he subtly reinforced when asked once at a post-England-victory press conference if he felt that 'the selectors and yourself have been vindicated by the result'. 'I don't think the press are vindictive,' he replied. 'They can write what they want.'

This ringing endorsement of freedom of speech would come back to bite him when a free press took grave umbrage over the one incident, in a career laden with controversy, that can never be forgiven. Gatting's leadership of the last rebel tour to South Africa in 1990 remains a high water mark in sporting infamy, almost as much for the disdainful ignorance to which he laid claim as for its mercenary grubbiness.

'I don't know much about how apartheid works,' he declared before departing, as if the racial laws of South Africa were up there with the bicameral constitution of post-Warsaw Pact Hungary among the more arcane political matters known to the globe, 'but one way to find out is by going there.'

This portrait of the tour as a field study was weakened by the fact that he took his money not from a corporate sponsor, as all previous rebel tourists had, but directly from the apartheid government itself. At an intensely delicate political moment, with apartheid tottering but still in place, and Nelson Mandela still in prison, it caused unrest that might have proved catastrophic. After the most violent of the demonstrations held outside the tourists' hotels, in Pietermaritzburg, Gatting underscored a burgeoning reputation for diplomacy by dismissing the protest as 'just a bit of singing and dancing'. Maybe he thought he was being treated to the kind of ethnic entertainment more usually reserved in Africa for a visit by the Queen. Perhaps this successor to Basil D'Oliveira as a middle-order batsman and occasional bowler really did have no clue why taking cash from the South African government to circumvent sporting sanctions drew from the pen of Frank Keating the judgement: 'No more inglorious, downright disgraced and discredited team of sportsmen wearing the badge of "England" can ever have returned through customs with such nothingness to declare.'

With Gatting, as I said, the borderline between idiocy and malevolence has always been treacherously difficult to identify.

50

Footballers in Gloves and Tights

Although splendid in their ways – not least for the alluring wartime whiff they offer of begloved young women trading coitus with US airmen for a pair of nylons – tights have no place on an English football pitch. Nor, by any means, do gloves. That seems too obvious to be worth stating. But thanks to the influence of that Premier League archetype the Posturing Gallic Ponce, more gloves are now on display in an early spring Premier League game than at the Annual Convention of Sufferers from Raynaud's Phenomenon (a circulatory disorder that turns the extremities white with cold, to which my mother has long been a stoical martyr).

Thierry Henry (see no. 30) was an early proselytiser of this effeminacy, which long ago spread like herpes not only to other nationalities but even the odd native as well. As for the fad for Lycra tights, although this has ebbed for reasons more closely connected with fashion than climate change, these remain on occasional view.

The wearing of such garments on an April afternoon is every bit as off-putting as its direct corollary, the obese Geordie going shirtless in February (see no. 26). In a properly administered sport, gloves and tights would earn their wearer a first yellow card during the warm-up – an activity opaquely named after its knack for warming people up, so that nothing Mrs Slocombe sold at her Grace Brothers counter could conceivably be required – with the second to follow if they were undiscarded by kick-off.

49

Paula Radcliffe

The long-distance runner's entry comes more heavily cloaked in sorrow than anger, and even imbued with poignant reflectiveness on a love affair that fizzled out.

Once, and for so long, there was no more adorable athlete. Modest, approachable and charming, she showed the same raw courage in grinding out wins as in her public attacks on the tolerance of drug cheats. She was always excruciating to watch, but you could even see (were you auditioning for Pseuds Corner) a kind of savage beauty in that hideous running style. With the head oscillating wildly in the style of Katharine Hepburn accepting her twenty-ninth lifetime achievement award, the eyes rolling maniacally like a seizure victim, the symbiosis between the agony of runner and viewer meant that she inspired empathy like no one else. Her suffering instilled a sense of awe that she would endure literally anything, within the rules, to win.

Then she proved it, and everything changed. It is Radcliffe's tragedy that, after all the thousands of hours spent enduring intense agony on the road, she will be remembered primarily for yielding to discomfort for a few seconds off it. Mention her name now, and the only topic of interest will be that unscheduled rest break during the 2005 London Marathon. Every sport throws up its feverish debates. Did Geoff Hurst's shot bounce over the goal line in 1966? What made Devon Loch do the splits within sight of the Grand National winning post a decade earlier? Were the judges right to give Sugar Ray Leonard that contentious split decision over Marvelous Marvin Hagler in 1987?

The Radcliffe Debate is at least more easily answered. She crapped. To this day the majority view holds that she peed, even though she resolved the conundrum on the day, and with a treasonously unEnglish lack of embarrassment. 'I was losing time because I was having stomach cramps and I thought, "I just need to go and I'll be fine," ' she explained, having gone on to win the race. 'I didn't really want to resort to that in front of hundreds of thousands of people. Basically I needed to go. I started feeling it between fifteen and sixteen miles, and probably carried on too long before stopping. I must have eaten too much beforehand'.

If the incident did her Public Toileting: How to Void Your Bowels Without Showing Your Knickers diploma from Lucie Clayton's little credit, which of us hasn't been caught short and toyed in desperation with the horrors of roadside evacuation? You can hardly expect an athlete to set world records in defiance of the limitations of a butt plug or an outsize Pamper. It wasn't pretty, but so what? Only the British would fixate on something so natural and trivial, and debate for years which orifice was in play. That at least is the case for the defence.

Less easy to forgive, if less memorable in so scatologically-minded a country, was the lachrymal incontinence a year earlier in Athens when she retired from the marathon when well beaten, a few miles from the finish. Physical excuses (the stomach again, the broiling heat) were made for her, but palpably she cracked under the intense pressure of Olympic favouritism, and preferred to quit than to trundle home out of the medals. The interminable sobbing jag that followed must have horrified previous hard women such as Norway's Grete Waitz, who I seem to remember running the last nine miles of a marathon dilated to ten centimetres, and refusing a Nurofen when the baby's head became visible through the front of her shorts.

Somehow, you couldn't help feeling a year later as she squatted beside the road, Paula Radcliffe's priorities had become confused. The goddess of our misestimation would have quit a lucrative annual marathon to evacuate herself in private, and finished the Olympic one, however far out of the medals, dry-eyed and proud. She showed rank disrespect towards Baron de Coubertin's dictum ('It's not the shitting that matters,' as the creator of the modern Olympics famously put it, 'but the quaking fart'), and in so doing sacrificed our love.

48
Tony Blair

Judged against other of his contributions to national and international life, the former Prime Minister's sporting calumnies may strike some as trivial, and there is not even a tantalising prospect that he will ever stand in a dock in The Hague to answer allegations of crimes against sport. Relatively minor as they are, however, the charges must be laid.

The first is that he lied about the timing and passion of his support for Newcastle United. Whether or not he ever claimed to have seen Wor Jackie Milburn, who retired when Mr Tony Blair was four, from a St James' Park stand that had yet to be built, remains unclear. But since Alastair Campbell has repeatedly and categorically denied this, the assumption is that he did.

The cynical use of football as a shortcut to popularity with the C2 and D demographics was barely less irksome than the glottal stops and Estuarine twang. The contrast between his pretend love of the game and John Major's genuine and rather sweet obsession with cricket speaks for itself. That keepy-uppy heading session with Kevin Keegan before the 1997 general election was nauseatingly smug, and the 1999 knighting of Alex Ferguson before Ole Gunnar Solskjær's treble-winning goal had bounced out of the Bayern Munich net was typically cheap and opportunistic. As for his admission, in his recently published memoir *A Journey*, that he sought advice from Sir Alex as to whether he should sack Gordon Brown as Chancellor, here words begin to lose their efficacy. Sometimes incoherent spluttering seems the most eloquent response.

A more serious charge, meanwhile, is besmirching the good name of tennis. With his friend and chief fundraiser Lord Levy, he worked the scam technically known as The Old Tennis One-Two. Levy would lure potential donors over for a Sunday-morning game at his Totteridge home with the bait that that the PM might join them for doubles. Mr Blair would duly show up and throw a set or two, before rushing off to invade a country or join Silvio Berlusconi on his yacht. Ego duly inflated, the victim – or 'mark', in the argot of grifting – would joyously unbelt. To think people got aerated over the unusual betting patterns in tennis matches involving Nikolay Davydenko.

The worst of Blair's sporting crimes, needless to state, was using the legendarily persuasive charm that came so heart-rendingly close to producing that second UN resolution to win the 2012 Olympic Games for the city of London. For a fuller account, see Sebastian Coe (no. 3), but in terms of inexcusable profligacy with public funds in the futile quest to sate the demands of his ego, Mr Tony Blair might as well have commissioned another twenty-five Millennium Domes.

47

BBC Sports Personality of the Year

Regarding the inbuilt paradox that defines this celebration of British mediocrity, no more need be observed than that an award with the word 'personality' in its title has twice gone to Nigel Mansell, the charismatic figure whose most glamorous advertising contract as Formula One world champion was spearheading a recruitment campaign for drivers of London buses. Knowing this, what purpose could there be in adding that the honours board also boasts the names of Torvill and Dean, Michael Owen and Steve Redgrave, the least engaging hoarder of a certain precious metal humanity has known since Auric Goldfinger?

None of this, of course, is the fault of the sportsmen and women concerned. They cannot be blamed if the BBC devotes ninety minutes – I know, I know, it feels like a fortnight, but in fact it's only an hour and a half – to reflecting on twelve months of national sporting triumph which could, in a good year, be compressed into seven minutes.

It is at this point that we are obliged to thank the inventor of the Sky+ remote for allowing us to rattle through the nonsense at thirty times normal speed in the search for the two or three pieces of footage worth reviewing. This way one is at least spared the excruciation of Sue Barker and Gary Lineker picking on stage-struck paeans to inarticulacy for those stultifyingly point-less thirty-second set-piece interviews.

'So, Dame Kelly, quite a year for athletics.'

'It certainly was, Sue.'

'And especially for Jessica Ennis.'

'Absolutely. Jess was awesome at the Europeans.'

'And every chance for her at London 2012?'

'Definitely, Sue.'

'Ladies and gentlemen, Dame Kelly Holmes!'

In olden times, the one consolation was the programme's magnificent naffness. In the presentational eras of David Coleman, Frank Bough, Harry Carpenter and Des Lynam, there was an artless allure to the tongue-tied goalkeeper being invited to save a penalty kick, the wheeling on of the Grand Prix car, and Frank Bruno shambling out for some sparkling vaudevillian repartee with Mr Carpenter. It was silly, pointless, mildly embarrassing and, in its amateur-hour way, incredibly sweet.

What has replaced the endearing foolishness is a style that clashes assonantly with the paucity of global success on display. The greater the failure of British sport in the previous twelve months, the more portentous the tone and the more melodramatic the build-up to the revelation of which human narcotic from a *recherché* minority sport has been selected to remind us all that, by wealth and population, there is no less successful sporting nation upon God's bounteous earth than ours.

46

Colin Montgomerie

This rotund ball of peevishness has always had his knockers, which may go some way to explaining why he is known to US golfing crowds as Mrs Doubtfire. The sadness for Monty is that ultimately there was too little fire and too much self-doubt, hence he heads towards retirement as a player with no more lustrous title under his belt than 'Best Golfer Never to Win a Major'.

How can the 2010 European Ryder Cup captain, whose preparations for the biannual clash with the United States were interrupted by a trip to the High Court for reasons into which it would be indelicate to trespass, be included in this book, you may ask, when the sensationally unlovable Nick Faldo is not? The answer is that the latter is by several light years the greatest individual sportsman Britain has produced. The chippy, monomaniacal arrogance that once led to him thanking the press 'from the heart of my bottom' after an Open victory must be excused because without it he would have been yet another British choker. Another Monty, in other words, whose own irritability and lack of grace stem not from Olympian self-belief but the opposite.

If Faldo always suggested the over-indulged mummy's boy who tells Basil Fawlty 'These eggs look like you laid them,' Monty hints at the fat, whiny kid being taunted by the bullying gym teacher (see Mick McCarthy, no. 31) as he quivers pitiably halfway up the climbing rope. Sporting crowds have finely attuned antennae for weakness, and the teasing that ensued when his petulance became apparent seemed less a capitulation to base instinct than obedience to a moral imperative.

The signs were there from the earliest days of his career in the late 1980s, when the young Monty was eager to state his adoration of Mrs Thatcher. That he would develop into a shouty, fair-haired character with nice breasts and a shrill intolerance for being questioned by the media seemed several steps too far in the cause of paying homage to a role model.

Had he taken the final step and discovered Thatcher's ruthless killer instinct, he'd have been fine. Millions voted for Thatcher time and again because, fear and loathe her though they might, she was palpably a winner. Despite topping the European Order of Merit 129 times, collecting a plethora of minor titles and punishing those insolent American crowds by performing brilliantly in Ryder Cups, Monty, by the highest of golfing standards, was not.

The moment that enshrined his status as golf's perennial bridesmaid came on Sunday, 18 June 2006, when he stood in the centre of the eighteenth fairway in the final round of the US Open, with 172 yards to the flag and a seven iron in his hands. All he needed to win his first major at his fifty-eighth attempt, it would soon transpire, was to take another four shots from this blessed position.

A friend once reported abandoning a Sunday-morning round at a Hertfordshire course due to uncontrollable giggling induced by watching an octogenarian Jewish grandmother press the wrong button on the remote control, thereby guiding her buggy into an ornamental lake. Even that dear old bubba would have won that US Open from that position

Monty, revered for the excellence of his iron play, virtually shanked the shot to find the deep rough thirty yards short of the green. If the ensuing chip technically qualified as a 'recovery shot', it did so solely in the manner of a heart-attack victim shooting himself in the head to recover from the pain.

There are blind double amputees in late-stage Parkinson's who'd have played that chip with more control. It rolled and rolled past the hole, stopping for a root beer and a pastrami on rye on the suburban outskirts of Oklahoma City before coming to rest some twenty feet from the hole. Yet even then Doubtfire had two putts for the title. He took three.

For the patriotic armchair viewer, there is something particularly brutal about golfing disappointment, and that thing is the sense of wasted time. Eighteen hours over four evenings had been invested in watching him break his major duck at last, and every moment of it had been wasted

Whenever a disaster of this kind befalls Lee Westwood, who is closing in fast on Monty's 'Best Golfer Never …' title, human sympathy leavens the self-pity that goes hand in hand with emotional involvement in the progress of British sporting stars, because Westwood is a sweetie. But Monty's own inexhaustible supplies of self-pity brought out the worst in people. He turned too many of us into honorary PE teachers as he dangled corpulently up the rope, and, despite the partial redemption offered by his Ryder Cup captaincy in 2010, that remains very hard to forgive.

45

Glenn Hoddle

For anyone planning to teach a sports-psychology-course module entitled, in the traditionally dry academic style, Why Great Individual Footballers Make Crap Managers, Glenn Hoddle would do nicely for the paradigm.

You could spend an entire term dwelling on why he could not translate his brilliance as a player into a successful career as a manager, though the answer might be stated in a few words. Two parts egomaniac to three parts dunce, with a heavy twist of infuriating self-righteousness and a cherry of mild lunacy on top.

For a while, it seemed that dear old Glenda might join Johann Cruyff as the exception to the rule that lavishly gifted players make poor coaches. His managerial career started well at Swindon and then Chelsea, and for a tantalising while he even flattered to deceive with England. The performance he drew from the national side in 1997, when they went to Rome needing a draw to qualify for the World Cup and imperiously outplayed Italy in a scoreless match, was inspired, while his refusal to include an increasingly wild Paul Gascoigne in his squad for the finals was both brave and correct. He looked, for about two seconds, like a winner.

And then it began to unravel, as history teaches that it must. The feeling that Hoddle was as much a halfwit off the pitch as he had been a genius on it had already been stoked by his drafting onto his coaching staff of Eileen Drewery, the psychic healer, and his habit of taking centre stage at training sessions by showing off skills that the players, to his undisguised irritation, couldn't master. His appraisal of Michael Owen would solidify nagging suspicion into a certainty.

This Decca-and-the-Beatles misjudgement wasn't the worst of it. Admittedly, citing Owen not being 'a natural-born goal-scorer' as the reason for not picking him for the first World Cup game wasn't brilliant. If there is such a thing as the Aristotelian ideal of the natural-born goal-scorer, the seventeen-year-old Owen was it, as everyone else seemed to understand; and as Owen would swiftly confirm when he came on as substitute in the second game against Romania, and then in the last-sixteen game with that wondrous goal against Argentina.

However disturbing Hoddle's inability to see the bleeding obvious, it was his failure to acknowledge his howler that offered the clearest omen of what lay ahead. Monomaniacal arrogance and successful coaching are hardly unfamiliar bedfellows, as the careers of Brian Clough and José Mourinho make plain, but the pathological inability to admit and learn from mistakes is something else. Hoddle would underline this lethal flaw with his infamous book, rushed into print after the World Cup finals with all the rapacity of the New Labour ex-cabinet minister and twice as self-justificatory. In it he blamed everybody but himself for England's early exit (though in fact it wasn't so much early as inevitable. In World Cups on foreign soil, they always go precisely as far as it takes to meet a global giant of the game, and then go out – see the England Football Team, no. 2).

Having alienated the entire squad with that literary effort, the dropping of the other shoe was inevitable, if not the precise method of its descent. His identification of genetic disability as a punishment for offences committed in a previous life was itself quickly reincarnated as his P45. It took a little help from Mr Tony Blair (see no. 48), who took to Richard and Judy's sofa to express his disapproval with all the persuasive force of one who believes that the wafer he ingests each Sabbath is literally the body of Christ, and the communion wine physically His blood. Any faint paradox in that denunciation was overlooked by an FA desperate, with the qualification campaign for Euro

2000 not having started well, to be rid of a growing embarrassment.

Hoddle's subsequent managerial stints at Southampton, Spurs and Wolves left him no choice but to travel the well-trodden path of the failed coach by treating Sky Sports viewers to his witless opinions and anodyne analyses. His attempts at humour, thankfully sporadic though these are, do little to undermine an observation of an erstwhile Chelsea team-mate. 'When Glenn tried to be funny,' said the intelligent Tony Cascarino, the Irish striker turned poker professional, 'it was time to pass around the laughing gas because he was probably the unfunniest man I have ever known.' If that constitutes lavish praise from one who featured in Republic of Ireland squads alongside Mark Lawrenson (see no. 14), Cascarino's next words seem the perfect way in which to bid Glenn Hoddle a fond farewell. 'He was also completely besotted with himself. If he had been an ice cream he would have licked himself.'

44

Andre Agassi

If ostentatious cynicism is an essential quality in anyone who devotes much of their life to watching sport, it sits less well with those who earn their living from it. We the viewers know that they the players are often venal horrors, and the self-aware among them doubtless know this too. The relationship between watcher and watched only works, however, so long as they maintain the pretence that they see themselves as pristine souls devoted only to the purist quest for glory. If they jettison this façade, we lose that satisfying sense of cleverness that comes from having rumbled them. As soon as they metaphorically wink at the camera like a pantomime villain, it all breaks down.

The wink from Agassi came early in a career the length of which, in the light of his autobiographical claim to a pathological hatred of tennis, has come to seem a shade demented.

The snidest sportsman of modern times ignored Wimbledon as a very young player, reviving the habit of 1970s American clay-court specialists such as Harold Solomon and Eddie Dibbs who steered clear of the grass to avoid dropping ranking points with early exits on a surface they loathed. When eventually Agassi did deign to appear, by way of a droll irony it was Wimbledon that gave him his first Grand Slam victory when in 1992 he outlasted Goran Ivanisevic in five sets.

It was immediately after winning match point that he revealed himself to those paying close attention. Having instinctively reacted with admirable restraint, he glanced up at his entourage in the Players' Box, and when one of them made a hand gesture a little like an adult patting a small child's head, down to the turf he collapsed in feigned delirium. The fall was designed, needless to say, with nothing more in mind than the improved commercial possibilities available from this show of synthetic ecstasy.

We have since learned, thanks to his lively memoir *Open*, that this descent was not the only fake thing about Agassi that day. The brown hair that formed that hideous mullet, although real, had belonged to someone else before being weaved into his scalp. It seems a cloyingly cute metaphor for a man who for twenty years contrived an image at striking variance with the version in the book. Those who distrust his every word will wonder why Amazon didn't have the wit to market it in a two-for-one deal with a giant tube of Saxa. Large pinches of salt are the suggested seasoning for many of his assertions, although there is no questioning his veracity when it comes to the disdain for Pete Sampras (see no. 17) on which he dwells.

In the dog days of the greatest rivalry tennis has known, between Federer and Nadal, that between Agassi and Sampras has come to seem the Bizarro World version. The essential clash of styles – one the best serve-volleyer of his generation, the other its finest baseliner – was there, of course, as was the contrast between the personalities. It's just that, where Nadal and to a lesser extent Federer (faintly irksome as he has become; see no. 101) are positive archetypes, whose more titanic defeats have induced sympathy for the loser, the tragedy regarding the scraps between the arch poseur and the simian dullard was that there had to be a winner at all.

The mild preference for the winsome charms of Agassi over the mechanical power of Sampras might have been reversed had we known then what Agassi has told us since. 'I play tennis for a living, even though I hate tennis,' he wrote in his book, 'hate it with a dark and secret passion, and always have.' It is not abundantly clear why, in the light of that dark hatred, he extended the source of what Dan Maskell knew as his neo-Strindbergian *weltschmertz* by playing well beyond the normal age of retirement. Who can say whether going on until he was thirty-six was evidence of a fascinatingly masochistic character trait, or whether in fact he loved tennis and lied about his feelings to sell books and make himself seem deep and intriguing?

Blaming a domineering father for the grief tennis gave him added a note of self-pity to a memoirist mix already sated in that direction, while the most arresting thing about his belated confession to lying to a credulous ATP about how the Class-A drug crystal meth found its way into his bloodstream is that he introduces this passage with an unintentionally hilarious 'I've always been a truthful person.'

In fact, one thing and one alone is reliably certain about the preening cynic with the pigeon-toed walk and the self-effacing charitable instincts of Smashy and Nicey (whatever does the glorious Steffi Graf see in him?). If you asked Andre Agassi for the time, and he replied with a cheery 'Midday,' you'd thank him warmly and head off to hunt out your pyjamas.

43

Dwain Chambers

Not since Forrest Gump jogged across America has a man of such childlike naïvety become known for his running, nor run to such little purpose. So aimless has the lifetime Olympic ban rendered his resumed career that the best analysis as to why Chambers bothers may well be Mother Gump's imbecile saw: Stoopid is as stoopid does.

Stoopid he certainly was, at least by his own account of how he came to take an astounding array of banned substances without once asking the infamous Victor Conte of the Balco Nutrition Center in California about the contents of the many pills and unguents he doled out as if they were vitamin supplements. Nutritionally, as it transpired, they were not items you'd find on the shelves of your local Holland & Barrett.

Surviving a combination of drugs that would have killed a herd of elephants will prove the greatest of Chambers' achievements, although the competition for that laurel lacks intensity. He was never more than a fine European sprinter, which equates to an also-ran at world level, and the only gold medal he ever won had to be returned. So, more poignantly, did those of the other three members of the relevant 100-metre relay team.

With Chambers, it was not so much the cheating that irritated, but then it never is. If people are willing to risk their health for their sport, and in the case of Florence Griffith-Joyner her life, we should laud their commitment. In a less cant-ridden age, athletics would be split into two on Formula One lines, with medals for the athletes and a parallel podium for the pharmacologists.

What grates is that, after a host of failures in other fields, he returned to sprinting to launch futile legal challenges against that Olympic ban, and to play the part of ghost at the athletics circuit's less bounteous feasts. His presence embarrasses everybody but himself.

Life may or may not be like a box of chocolates, but with Mr Chambers you know exactly what you're gonna get: a dogged, respectable run in 10.13 seconds, some fifteen metres off the pace Usain Bolt would set if he was running with a Zimmer, followed by a display of Uriah Heepery in which no one believes other perhaps than himself.

If redemption of sorts came for Dwain Chambers on 28 July 2010, it was not as he would have wished. Finishing fifth in a European Championship 100-metre final was not a great achievement, but his reaction to missing out on a medal by a few thousandths of a second certainly was. The pre-disgrace Chambers was hardly a paragon of good grace in defeat, but his response to this one suggests that the bewildering variety of banned substances he ingested, while they did little for his running, worked wonders on his personality. Being there was contentment enough for him, said the Chauncey Gardiner of the track, and compatriot Mark Lewis-Francis's unexpected silver medal the icing on his cake.

In this, Dwain Chambers established himself as an immortal sporting purist, and it came as a relief to find him succeeding in a new role after all the failures. His foray into American football, confusingly with a team in Germany, was ended before it began by a stress fracture to the foot. His subsequent rebranding as a rugby league star endured longer (one reserve game for Castleford), and he lasted about the same time as one of Gordon Ramsay's punchbags in *Hell's Kitchen*, where his signature dish of Soufflé Stanozolol failed to rise. A subsequent bid to lend his career an extra protective layer of clownery ended when he was the first contestant ejected from reality show *Cirque du Célébrité*, a full eight weeks before Lady Isabella Hervey.

There had been rumours that he was contemplating yet another fresh start. However, as ill timing would have it, his trip to those European Championships in Barcelona coincided with the news that bullfighting is to be outlawed in Catalonia, although there had already been concerns about finding matadors willing to take him on.

So it is that he remains on the track, smiling blissfully at defeat, and as indifferent to the indifference he generates as he is to the resentment of those relay teammates obliged to return their gold medals by the blind faith he placed in Mr Conte.

More than merely the last of the Corinthians, his refusal to slink away despite that lifetime Olympic ban makes him the noblest manifestation of the Olympic ideal. For this latterday Baron de Coubertin, not only is it not the winning that counts. Uniquely for Dwain Chambers, it isn't even the taking part.

42

Sir Ian Botham

Choosing a lone representative of the Sky Sports cricket team has been an anguished process. Cases could be made for David Gower (on purely tedium grounds), David 'Bumble' Lloyd (overemphatic repetition of the bleedin' obvious), Bob Willis (sniffy disapproval, headmistressy pince nez), Paul Allott (narcolepsy) and Nasser Hussain (whiny, adenoidal tone). But for the excellence of the Michaels Atherton and Holding, the solution would be to nominate Sky cricket as a whole. Taking tough decisions is the hallmark of authoring important works of reference, however, and so the nod goes to the man to whom his colleagues religiously refer as 'Sir Ian'.

With such unceasing reverence is the title deployed that the keen diagnostician can hardly help sniff out a case of Ben Kingsley Disease, the disorder that obliges the recipient of a knighthood to insist on its use in print and speech (and in the actor's case, famously, on a movie poster). Even if he is not a sufferer, however, the plain fact that Botham didn't order them to drop the 'Sir Ian' rot long ago establishes that, like so many anti-establishment young firebrands, he has mutated in middle age into a *petit bourgeois* snob.

The irony about the overuse of the title is that the more you hear it, the more obvious becomes the paradox that this not atypical product of Yeovil (not a notably warm and friendly town) should have been given that emblem of gallantry in the first place. He may have cuckolded others himself, but only in the sub-Carry On double entendre sense is this a latterday Sir Lancelot.

Botham has worked ferociously to shrug off the image of boozy swordsman and professional narcissist (you may recall his hilariously brief attempt to crack Hollywood). The wine-buffery, though mildly pretentious, is excused in honour of his vinous mentor on Sark, the glorious John Arlott. But it has long been impossible to encounter tabloid accounts of his annual amble across the country without wishing he'd drop the Smashy & Nicey charidee exhibitionism, and raise the money for leukemia research by selling his house and wine cellar instead.

As a pundit, meanwhile, he suffers from a traditional delusion. Magnificent all rounder that he was, before the weight gain robbed him of his pace as a bowler, as England captain he was an unqualified disaster. Whether or not the amnesia stems from eschewing the spittoon at tastings down the years, this inadequacy has entirely slipped his mind. Never have I heard him preface his default sour criticism of a captaincy decision with, 'Look, everyone knows I was rubbish at it myself, so please don't take a shred of notice, but I do wonder if Andrew Strauss might think about a leg slip?'

Infernally cocky he always was, and so he remains. A friend who visited the Sky area at a Test reports that while all the others were charming, Botham lolled about with his feet up, imperious and aloof, reading a paper in preference to watching the action, although when his next stint began some osmotic process enabled him to sound remarkably *au fait* with what he had missed.

This is the most infuriating thing about the current Botham. He doesn't seem especially interested in cricket. Perhaps this is inevitable with someone who played it so well. It's often said that the greatest individual talents make the most indifferent spectators, and that describing a game is not so much a poor substitute for playing it as no substitute at all. But never does he communicate any insight or enthusiasm, and the grandiose sense of superiority can begin to grate.

Call Ian Botham 'Sir' until it sates even his appetite for deference, give him a grace-and-favour apartment in Clarence House, have the Queen invite him for deerstalking weekends at Balmoral, find some genealogical anomaly to make him heir to the Dukedom of Norfolk … do all that and more, and he will remain the same cocksure vulgarian with playground bully overtones he always was, and the very last chivalric hero at whom you'd care to be accused of looking the wrong way in a Yeovil car park – or indeed an Adelaide one (see introduction) – in the early hours of a Saturday morning.

41

Ron Atkinson

Shortly before it happened, a friend and I put together a proposal for a spoof football manager's autobiography. Our anti-hero, Big Len Gordon, was a bling-laden, permatanned, casually racist Scouser with a plethora of School of Hard Knocks opinions and a staggering store of nihilistically pointless showbiz anecdotes.

The mistake was with that 'casually'. Just as we were touching up the proposal, the inspiration for Big Len rendered the parody a shade less attractive to publishers with the most infamous unwittingly live broadcast since Ronald Reagan informed the American people that the nuclear obliteration of the USSR would commence in five minutes.

Atkinson would have made my top hundred regardless. Had he not referred to Marcel Desailly that April evening in 2004 as 'what is known in some schools as a fucking lazy, thick nigger' – had he in fact spent half his adult life running guns over the Namibian border to ANC compadres – he would be honoured here for his vicious vendetta against the English language.

His contribution to the lexicon of football cliché is immense and unrivalled. To hear him as sidekick to ITV commentator Clive Tyldesley was to yearn for an English–Recherché Cliché lexicon. Some of the terms he pioneered became popular ('early doors', of course, and 'lollipops' for dramatic step-overs). Others never caught on. All too seldom these days do we hear 'eyebrows' (a backward-glancing header) or 'nominated' (to indicate that an apparent cross that floated inside the post was in fact intended as an effort on goal).

His major linguistic contribution, however, was a tense now in common usage. The video historic is what football folk use when watching a replay of an incident. On one level they understand that it took place in the past (historic). However, watching it at normal speed on tape (video) leads them to believe, on another level, that it must be happening now. Hence the hybrid. 'We've come out strong for the second half, and the boy Smith's drifted over to the left, and he's looked up. He's seen the keeper off his line, and he's said, "Eh, I can do this." And he's chipped him. He's nominated that.'

Whether in the true Atkinsonian sense Big Ron nominated his racist rant, and meant every word to find its target, only he can know for sure. There are those, not exclusively white, who insisted then that he did not; that the choice of language, though infelicitous, just kind of slipped out. Such stout defenders supported this theory by pointing out that, by filling his West Bromwich Albion midfield with a trio of black players ('the Three Degrees') in the late 1970s, Mr Atkinson was a brave, lone pioneer of racial equality in the tradition of Rosa Parks.

Whether tolerating black people at work is invariably a fool-proof defence against the charge of racism, who can say? In the absence of any contemporary testimony from the plantation owners of the American South and the slaves they raped, beat and murdered, it's just too close to call.

Whatever the truth of it, Big Ron paid a fair price for his thoughts on Monsieur Desailly, and has barely been heard from again. We wish him well in the future, safe in the knowledge that he of all people will take not the slightest offence if we part company with the reflection that he is what is known in some schools as a bulbous-nosed, fucking thick, tangerine-hued grotesque.

40

The Centre Court Crowd

It took the Queen thirty-three years after watching Virginia Wade's Jubilee win in 1977 to return to Wimbledon's Centre Court, and it's testament to her commitment to her work as All England Club patron that she hurried back so soon.

It's the crowd that kept her away between 1977 and 2010, of course. Call Her Maj an inverted snob if you must, but the old girl just can't tolerate that gruesome congregation of Home Counties ninnies. Who can?

In that bashful English way, we like to bang on about Wimbledon being the greatest of the Grand Slams, and in terms of prestige (if not tennis quality) perhaps it is. Where it unquestionably leads the entire sporting world is in the irritation induced by its crowds.

Unlike audiences at Roland Garros, where French Open tennis-goers boo and hiss with capricious pantomime abandon, the Centre Court crowd is always impeccably polite, and therein lies a large chunk of its horror. It isn't really a sporting audience at all. It's the planet's largest flower-arranging tutorial, rounded up from village halls and Norman church altars from Devon to Norfolk, and for reasons never made entirely clear transposed to south-west London for a fortnight's holiday each summer.

In strict truth, it isn't quite as psychosis-inducing now as it was in the days when it treated Cliff Richard's impromptu rain-break recital with delight rather than the volley of snipers' bullets that seemed indicated, and worshipped Tim Henman. Being spared the sight of the maidens in the 'Come on Tim!' T-shirts, giggling with self-conscious glee at their audacity whenever the cameras dwelt on them, is a blessing. Not that their adoration of Henman (see no. 12) didn't make sense. He was their representative on grass, his genteel background and innate smugness a perfect mirror image of their own. It was in the suspicion that Tim invaded their erotic dreams that the core of the nightmare lay.

They can't be doing with Andy Murray, of course. They tolerate him with a courteous diffidence, but he's not their cup of Darjeeling at all, the uncouth boy from Dunblane. No breeding. He wouldn't have a clue how to eat asparagus. Don't laugh, but he'd only use his knife and fork.

They loved Virginia (a vicar's daughter), and Sue Barker (a lovely-looking gel, and such impeccable manners). Annabel Croft was a good sort too, but Jo Durie was a bit common, as was John Lloyd (though so good-looking). And if Buster Mottram had some rather trenchant views, well, I'm not a racist myself – there's that delightful Indian doctor in the village Giles and I have over for drinks now and then – and I'd never have voted for the National Front, but he did have a point about immigration, didn't he?

Barely less irksome, is the wilful twittishness. How often can the same human being hear an umpire tell a crowd not to use flash photography and still deem it worthy of wild applause, as if he had just taken to the Stockholm stage to accept the Nobel Prize for Literature on behalf of Doris Lessing? How many Hawkeye reviews can the same spinster watch without wondering whether the excitable whoooo-oooo-ing has run its course?

'Ladies and gentlemen, as a courtesy to the players, please switch off your mobile phones' – it must be twenty years since that one made its Centre Court debut, and still it excites them so much more than an impossible running forehand down the line from the racket of Rafa Nadal, or one of Roger Federer's preposterous half-volley pick-ups. Half of them might be Justices of the Peace, moaning incessantly about the fact that they can no longer bang up some local ruffian for six months for poaching a hare, but there comes a point when applauding the enforcement of an informal regulation becomes the sort of crime that even now, under the iron fist of the PC Brigade, should carry a custodial sentence.

It's no coincidence that the second most electrifying Wimbledon final ever, in which Goran Ivanisevic beat Patrick Rafter in 2001, was delayed by rain until the Monday, and was therefore watched by properly partisan Croats, Australians and locals without debentures or corporate hosts. For once this was a sports crowd, uninhibited and raucous, and it not so much got the match it deserved as made the match what it was.

Involved passion is what's needed from any sporting audience, and this, as much as the surface, is why the US Open in New York produces so much more melodrama than Wimbledon. This is also why, the minute I become Sports Minister, I intend to draw up legislation cancelling all debentures and corporate tickets at Wimbledon, and placing 90 per cent of all Centre Court tickets in a lottery which only season-ticket holders at Millwall, Leeds United and Cardiff City will be eligible to enter.

The monarch, I think, will back me up on this, announcing it in her Queen's Speech with special feeling. Who knows, with a bit of atmosphere on Centre Court, she might even pop back again before 2043.

39

Will Carling

Although little has been heard for several years from Old Bum Face, as the one-time England rugby captain was fondly known for reasons loosely connected to that arse-crack-impersonating cleft chin and other features, he deserves his entry partly as rugger-bugger paradigm, and partly for himself.

His sport has never known a more perfect archetype of the minor public schoolboy in whose tiresome punditry dialect a player's performance was never 'good' but 'awesome', and never 'great' but 'immense'.

In rugby union even today, in a manner that died out in cricket decades ago, the class system survives. The game remains run by the tiresome, reactionary East India Club buffers whom Carling dismissed as 'fifty-seven old farts' – a description for which he was sacked as captain, though hastily reinstated, despite firmly belonging to the officer class himself (literally so, having bought his way out of his commission as an army lieutenant to concentrate on the game). Me, insofar as it's possible to have a preference, I like the other ranks of the game slightly better. They at least have the capacity for idiotic hilarity, like the NCO member of Billy Beaumont's team who, presented with a complimentary bottle of cologne at a post-match dinner in Paris, unscrewed the cap, put the bottle to his lips, and drained every last drop in one go.

Rugby's officer class, on the other hand, melds innate dimness with pomposity and conceited intolerance. The Harry Enfield sketch in which he and Martin Clunes engage in a drinking game replete with rugby chants before nutting someone for looking like 'a weirdo' remains the most reliable reference guide to that.

What made Carling stand out in the officers' mess was, of course, his caddishness. In more recent interviews, since consulting John Cleese's psychotherapist ex-wife Alyce Faye Eichelberger, he has dropped the rugby lingo for low-grade psychocobblers, and admitted that he behaved poorly. Whether he means it or not, who can know? With the most literal truth, he has tended to enjoy a slightly hands-off relationship.

He has always denied an affair with Princess Diana, for example, whom he attended in Kensington Palace via the traditionally gangland conveyance of a car boot. Even after their liaison was one among those listed by witnesses at the inquest into her death, he continued to insist that they were Platonic friends. If this shows an admirable aversion to cashing in on cuckolding the Prince of Wales (technically treason, and still a capital offence), or to distressing Diana's sons, whose admiration for him was the catalyst for their friendship, it does him a level of credit not sustained in subsequent relationships.

Leaving his first wife, Julia, for Ali Cockayne, a minor royal of sorts herself as the then sister-in-law to Queen Mother of Football Gary Lineker, was one thing. It was how he then left Ms Cockayne, mother of their young baby, that explains his absence from the television screens, freeing up more time for his events-organising firm and – what else? – motivational speaking. Ms Cockayne had no notion of his imminent departure until reading the first paragraph of a press statement he was preparing on his computer screen. 'Will Carling is leaving his partner Ali Cockayne,' began this emotional *cri de coeur*, 'for a future with Lisa Cooke.' Ah well, better than reading about it in the papers. Well, quicker anyway.

If it can't have been enormous fun for Ms Cockayne, it was worse, so he would have us believe, for Mr Carling. 'It was incredibly traumatic,' he later confided to an interviewer after sharing a lot of moving chit-chat about looking to his childhood to make sense of his behaviour. 'My self-esteem plummeted and

I wondered if things would ever get better. But sometimes you need to go through something like that in order to see that there are more important things in life than rugby.' Indeed, indeed. And what a consolation to the abandoned mother of his son to learn, several years later, of her peripheral yet invaluable role in teaching Mr Carling how to prioritise. 'When the headlines were getting worse and worse,' he went on, 'there were times when I was not really sure who the real Will Carling was.' Ignorance is bliss.

38

Tiger Woods

So long and relentlessly has the cry of 'In da hole! In da hole!' followed Tiger Woods, whose chances of recovering his dominance of golf are dwindling quickly through a combination of poor form and accumulative damage to both body and mind, that it was perhaps inevitable that he would end up taking it too literally in a non-golfing context.

Yet it isn't the sinking of all those short, penile gimmes on his whirlwind tour through cocktail waitress America that earns Woods his entry. Those who look to sporting deities for moral guidance on matters uxorial have only themselves to blame when it goes wrong. If they find themselves shocked – shocked! – on discovering that Croesus-rich young sporting demigods tend to play around with rapacious, star-struck young women to whom they are unshackled by the bonds of holy wedlock, so was Captain Renault when he came across unlicensed gaming at Rick's Bar in *Casablanca*. The worst aspect of the revelations that followed Woods' unfortunate tripartite vehicular collision with a hedge, a fire hydrant and finally a tree in November 2009 was the subsequent public displays of a penitence he transparently didn't feel. How much more admirable had he simply insisted that, what with him being neither a televangelist nor a politician of the Christian right, it was no one's business but his and his wife's?

To the extent that one minor role for the globally fêted sportsman is to sate the curious Anglo-American cravings for synthetic moral outrage and a misplaced sense of superiority, Woods selflessly performed a public service. As for the chasm between his commercial image as a family man and the reality, which of us would blithely wave away hundreds of millions in sponsorship because of a silly little thing like rampant hypocrisy? If anyone genuinely saw in the pre-disgrace Woods a shining exemplar of fifties family values, that belongs between them and their therapists.

It isn't even the aloofness, arrogance and borderline rudeness that offends. The male ego is an emotionally retarded creature, wretchedly ill-designed to cope with fame. Countless men behave with a Woodsian lack of grace on the strength of a job presenting sixty-second news bulletins on unwatched cable channels. A man who becomes the planet's most recognisable face at twenty-one, and spends the ensuing decade being deified by a slavish public and a sycophantic media, will not emerge the same modest, approachable boy he was at nineteen. To this extent, Woods is at most as cocky and charmless as one would expect, and probably a little less.

The on-course spitting, cussing and angry club-thwacking may repel Peter Alliss and his prissy gang of G&T, ice-and-slice Corinthians, but most of us actively relish any overt sign of passion, however uncouth, in a game beset by standards of mannerliness that seem stiflingly anachronistic and artificial. As for the golfing press, though emboldened by Woods' downfall to express its resentment at his studiedly tedious press-conference persona, it gave up any right to show umbrage by jealously guarding its suspicions for so long.

All in all, there is more to admire about Tiger Woods than to denigrate, not least his magnificent storming of the Augusta National Golf Club, where not so long ago he would only have been allowed into the clubhouse to serve the drinks. If he was no Cassius Clay, and kept the studious distance from matters of race for which some have criticised him, it was his right to do so. There is no sovereign obligation for a sportsman, however rich his genetic pool, to take a political stance.

Besides, if Woods does appear a dullard incapable of a vaguely interesting thought, how else would a person who had devoted his entire being to the endless repetition of the same physical actions since infancy come across? His dedication is as bizarre as his raw talent, and even if he is in irreversible decline now, he inspired more visceral excitement and awe – winning the 2008 US Open on one leg will always live in the memory – in a relatively brief golfing career than Arnold Palmer and Jack Nicklaus together provoked in theirs.

The one thing for which Woods cannot be forgiven may strike some as a relatively minor offence on the charge sheet of his life, and perhaps it is. Yet it casts a dazzling, halogen spotlight on the incipient megalomania and inherent cynicism in a way the serial adulteries cannot. After all the false public shows of penance, all the transparently fake declarations of humility, all the claims to want to learn from his mistakes delivered through heavily gritted teeth, what was Tiger Woods thinking when he made a Nike TV commercial – in black and white as if that lent it gravitas and feeling – featuring the voice of his dead father, Earl?

In the advertisement, Earl wanted to know what was going on in his head too. 'Tiger, I am more prone to be inquisitive to promote discussion,' he intoned, a little pompously for a dead man. 'I want to find out what your thinking was. I want to find out what your feelings are, and did you learn anything?'

The very fact of making such a creepy, mawkish and manipulative commercial, on behalf of a loathed corporate giant and in the interests of rebuilding a devalued image, established that he had learned nothing about the futility of insulting the intelligence of his audience with sub-Oprah verities and crude appeals for sympathy.

If the intended subliminal message was that he went off the rails after the beloved father who shaped his life and career died, in the way Mike Tyson went crazy when his father figure Cus D'Amato popped his clogs, it didn't cut it. It did, however, offer an insight into Tiger Woods' abundant disloyalty in his personal relationships, and next to this betrayal of the person he had always claimed to love so deeply, the sexual infidelities that led to it seem very small beer indeed.

37

Sue Barker

Younger viewers who know Sue Barker solely as an effervescent laugh-machine on *A Question of Sport* would never guess that she was once best known for occupying the opposite end of the emotional range.

There was a time when you could tell the date, to within a few days, from her lachrymal eruptions. Anyone shipwrecked on an uninhabited Indian Ocean island in the early years of Mrs Thatcher's dominion, and informed by an insane pilot spelling out in jet-exhaust fumes the news that Sue Barker had been photographed sobbing on Cliff Richard's shoulder, would have instinctively muttered, 'Aha, the first Tuesday of Wimbledon. Must be the last week of June.'

Even British tennis has never known a choker quite like Sue, and that, you will agree, is saying something. Her tremulousness on court made Tim Henman look like Jason Bourne on beta-blockers.

She certainly had the talent. A magnificent forehand took her to number three in the world, briefly, and in 1976 she won the French Open, albeit that all the leading women (Chris Evert, Evonne Goolagong, Virginia Wade, etc.) gave it a miss that year, and that she contrived to drop the middle set of the final 0–6 to a certain Renata Tomanova from Romania.

The following year at Wimbledon, when poised to gladden Her Majesty's heart by … all right, that's going too far. Short of growing an extra pair of legs, a chestnut coat and fetlocks, and winning the Derby in the Queen's own regal colours, no sporting entity could manage that. But Sue was on the verge of making it an all-Brit Silver Jubilee final against Ms Wade when she somehow contrived to yield the semi-final to the stolid Dutch journeywoman Betty Stove.

Despite the necessarily curious romantic relationship with Cliff, con-grat-you-layay-shuns were seldom to be offered her again. Following a quarter-final defeat to Billie Jean King in 1978, there ensued a run of stupendously feckless Wimbledon failures at the hands of various world number 792s from Papua New Guinea.

The infuriating thing about her reinvention as a BBC star presenter is that it hints inescapably at the tungsten core that was so hard to discern on court. Where once her talent was betrayed by lack of nerve, this equation has been reversed. She lacks a shred of the talent of Clare Balding, and even Hazel Irvine, but her steeliness has seen her supplant both. That, of course, and the BBC's obsession with promoting retired sports-people over professional broadcasters, regardless of their respective abilities. Here we find Sue cast as the Gary Lineker to Clare's Adrian Chiles.

As a live presenter, it must be admitted, she scales heights of adequacy tantalisingly beyond the range of those unable to read an autocue or reiterate words hissed into an earpiece by the production team. It is on *A Question of Sport* that Sue, physically morphing into a Barbara Windsor doppelganger by the month but without hinting at the power to ping a bra across a field into Kenneth Williams's face, sends the hackles skyward. Being easily amused is among the greatest gifts that God and genetics can confer, I've always thought, but there must be limits.

Apologies if the problem is medical. Inappropriate laughter can be a symptom of pathological illness (in an episode of the medical drama *House*, a cop is reduced to helpless chortling by a gunshot wound to the chest). Alternatively, she might have picked up an undiagnosed viral brain infection after drinking from the same green-room wine glass as Kriss Akabusi (see no. 91). A dangerous addiction to nitrous oxide cannot, without invasive tests, be dismissed.

And yet the suspicion remains that succumbing to melodramatic mirth at every witless drollery of Matt Dawson's until the integrity of her knicker elastic is endangered is Sue's idea of winsome coquettishness. These are not words anyone sane would have envisaged appearing in print back in the late 1970s, but given the choice between the Tiny Tears of Centre Court and the gigglesome geisha of *A Question of Sport*, you'd take the soggy Cliff Richard shoulder every time.

36

Andy Gray

Impressive as the pundit's scoring record was as a striker with Aston Villa, Wolves and Everton, it has been more so off the pitch. To give the flavour not only of his sexual incontinence but also the Byzantine range of his imagination, let it suffice to recall that as a young man he fathered two sons by different women – one of them, in all fairness, his wife – within a few months, naming each of them Jamie.

His boorishness has matched his libido. This was evident long before the News International hackee was removed from Sky Sports, when in the aftermath of his sexist exchange with fellow pinhead Richard Keys (see no. 84) his employers conveniently located old footage of Gray inviting a production assistant to tuck a microphone pack down his pants. One notable incident that might have prepared the nation for this devastating revelation had occurred in La Manga in 2007, when he and his mates serenaded fellow hotel guests with obscene football chanting before he asked the concierge, as the *Sun* reported, 'Eh, senoreo, where is the fucking taxio?' Quite the cunning linguist, then, as he swiftly confirmed by approaching the first of the evening's targets and smooth-talking her with a lyrical 'You've got great fucking tits.'

Had Gray to transpose such admirable directness to his comments on Sky, it would have improved his work. Instead, when sat beside the human sleeping pill Martin Tyler or the excellent Ian Darke, he relied primarily on two stylistic elegances. One was the intransigent refusal to admit a mistake. Having declared on first viewing that a penalty should have been awarded, he would reiterate the judgement while seven different camera angles were establishing in the slowest of motion that you could have parked an aircraft carrier between the defender's leg and that of the supposedly fouled attacker. The other was inappropriate giggling (see the previous entry) at Mr Tyler's monumentally witless pre-prepared puns.

Unsurprisingly, then, given the face for radio, on which he has reformed his partnership with Mr Keys thanks to the beneficence of TalkSport, and the voice for Trappist vows, his best work has been on paper. Jealously as he hides the fact from Sky viewers, this is one of English football's more tactically astute and sophisticated analysts. *Flat Back Four*, his book on the modern history of tactics, is a masterpiece of clear expression and insightfulness. Why he struggled to transplant that gift to his broadcasting isn't easy to understand, although the technical difficulty of giggling relentlessly and for no identifiable cause on the printed page must have helped.

If the sycophantic chortling constituted a bold bid to persuade his audience that he is a cuddlier character than his vast accumulation of press cuttings suggests, it had the opposite effect. All it did was add the mistaken assumption of imbecility to the certainty that this, even by the impeccable standards of the modern footballer, is a particularly unlovable oaf.

35

Mark Nicholas

In the style of the Prime Minister at the dispatch box, I refer the honourable reader to the entry accorded to the Channel 5 cricket presenter's fellow narcissist John Inverdale some pages hence (see no. 24).

With Nicholas, as with Invers, the self-besottedness shines blindingly from every glance to camera. There are characters in Renaissance paintings gazing at their Saviour with less beatific intensity. It's as if he is in a constant state of traumatised disbelief that so much charm and gorgeousness could be contained within the one human form.

That Mr Nicholas is not wildly popular among his colleagues might go without saying. Workmates portray this cocky drawler as the sort of chap who struggles to talk to anyone for seven seconds at a party before his eyes start scanning the room for someone more interesting, famous or potentially useful.

This is by no means an endangered species in the jungle of television, and if all Mr Nicholas had against him was a shallow obsession with his own advancement and physical beauty, he could be written off as just another egomaniacal twit unable to distinguish between a glib knack for talking to camera and a precious vocation.

If there's one mantra all of us in the media might benefit from repeating *ad nauseam*, it is this: the most important thing we could ever do in our jobs is infinitely less important than the least important thing happening anywhere else in the world at the time. War reporters and investigative journalists are excused from this. The rest of us, be it in old media or new, print or broadcast, have a sovereign duty never to forget the transcendent banality and nihilistic pointlessness of what passes for our work.

In Mr Nicholas's case, two other offences, one general and one specific, must be considered. The first is a tone of crusty, lazy right-wingery better suited to an eighty-three-year-old clubland bore. After a harmless and good-natured pitch invasion by Pakistan supporters during a 2001 Test match at Trent Bridge, for example, he worked himself into a frightful lather. New laws to treat such calumnies were 'essential', he told viewers, in outraged mystification over the police's failure to treat these excitable fans' trespass with the crushing force it deserved. There had been, he harrumphed, 'not one dog, not one truncheon'. Although he restrained himself from ruing the absence of water cannon and rubber bullets, the regret was palpable. In more civilised times, you felt, when the sun never set on the Empire, he'd have ridden through the mêlée on an elephant, swishing imperiously at the natives with a cane.

His other crime against sport was as host of the most heart-rending interview ever broadcast. On the Saturday of the final 2005 Ashes Test at The Oval, he drew from our most beloved Richie Benaud, working on his last match for a British broadcaster, a tripartite series of revelations so excruciating that five years later I can barely mention them.

He asked Richie, a man I had worshipped for thirty years, about his taste in theatre, books and television. Richie reported a passion for the musical *Cats*, which he confessed to have seen twenty-six times; for the Harry Potter books written, by J.K. Rowling, for children; and, most distressingly, for the adolescent soap *Hollyoaks*. Another two minutes and he would have brought out his membership papers for the Celine Dion Appreciation Society.

It may appear harsh to blame Mr Nicholas for words that emitted from the mouth of a man adored, until that moment, for his austere good taste. But he should have checked with

Richie in advance, and so spared us the agony that invariably follows when a hero is encountered in any other context than the one in which he established his heroism. The good interviewer, in other words, does copious homework, on the grounds that he is more interested in the interviewee than in himself. In his defence, this is not is not a state Mark Nicholas could achieve without directing his questions to a mirror.

34

The Barmy Army

We are every one of us, concluded Andrew Marr in his splendid history of post-war Britain, the Children of Thatcher now, and the jug-eared smartypants was bang on the money there. Yet within that all-enveloping category lies a sub-strata of infantile society all the more paining for the paucity of its numbers.

I refer to the self-styled Barmy Army, that coalition of desperate and desperately unappealing saddoes who are not only the sons of Margaret Thatcher, but of Dave Lee Travis as well. As Richard Dawkins would agree, what an overpoweringly rich gene pool that one is. You'd have to be an even more Meldrovian curmudgeon than me to dispute that the Look-at-me-I'm-certifiably-off-my-chump-cuckoo-bananas contrived eccentricity of the erstwhile Radio 1 breakfast DJ has its rightful place in the national life. But you'd also have to be a genuine contender for sectioning under the Mental Health Act to deny that the rightful place in question is the Radio 1 breakfast show in 1979.

For this national humiliation, as with so many others in cricket, we must thank the Australians. The name was coined there during the 1994–95 tour, when our Ashes team was so unconscionably clueless that the local press concluded, with reason, that only the insane would voluntarily follow it. From the ensuing acorn of rhyming wit, which referrred to a small and noble bunch of decent sadomasochistic fans, would swiftly grow an oak to cast a brooding shadow over Test cricket. Soon enough it would become impossible to watch England without hearing that song sung on a loop, as lager-sodden regimental commanders rose relentlessly from their seats to lead their foot-soldiers in choral tribute to – who else? – themselves.

Everywhere we go/Everywhere we go
The people want to know/The people want to know
Who we are/Who we are
Where we come from/Where we come from
We are the Army/We are the Army
The Barmy, Barmy Army/The Barmy, Barmy Army
We are the England/We are the England
The mighty, mighty England/The mighty, mighty England.

Close analysis of the text seems futile. We might admire the dextrous use of repetition, and wonder what the choristers must think of the natives they encounter everywhere they go who, on coming across a bunch of men drunkenly bellowing 'Barmy Army, Barmy Army, Barmy Army, Barmy Army,' retain a need to ask them who they are. But literalism and textual analysis make no happier bedfellows than chanting and self-parody, and textual deconstruction of this kind seems more safely left to the F.R. Leavis school of literary criticism.

You might indeed posit that the words themselves are of less importance, to those who recite them, than the exhibitionism and misplaced jingoistic pride at which they subtly hint. All it's about with these self-styled warriors is them. They are the only faction of any sporting audience in history whose primary motivation for attending games is not to watch but to be watched.

What's especially offputting about the Barmy Army is how it induces a nostalgic fondness for the glory days of football hooliganism. Whatever their other failings, football thugs had integrity. Their desire was simple. They wanted a mash-up, and made no bones about it, and if it happened to lead to injury or death, so be it. The last thing they wanted was to be watched when indulging their hobby, which partly explains why the advent of CCTV surveillance ruined the merriment. They were always true to themselves.

The Barmy Army soldier is the opposite. His true self is the respectable, law-abiding IT operative in Swaffham, accountant from Wilmslow or stockbroker from Virginia Water, and not even turning up at the 'Gabba or Sabina Park in fancy dress – as Wonderwoman, Bertie Bassett, a Khmer Rouge death-camp guard, or whatever – can begin to disguise that. Quite the contrary, it serves only to highlight his conformity.

Now that the Barmy Army is so well established as a commercial organisation, with all the bargain travel and the merchandising, it's hard to imagine how we will ever be rid of it. But I do have one suggestion. If its conscripts really want the sense of purpose, belonging and discipline that military life provides, someone needs to round the lot of them up, press-gang them into signing enlistment papers and put them on the first RAF transport to Helmand province. It might not do a great deal to turn that futile war around, but it would be fun to watch an Afghan warlord asking who they are (who they are), and see whether the Taliban quake before the mighty, mighty England (the mighty, mighty England).

33

Ashley Cole

The most tediously obvious archetype of the instant-gratification Premier League age paradoxically contrived to present two of its least penetrable mysteries. What on earth did Cheryl ever see in him? And what in the name of all the saints did he fail to see in her? Given the near impossibility of seeing beyond the public façade of even a close friend's marriage, it is pointless and hubristic to attempt to unravel the wedlock of strangers. These, then, will remain rhetorical questions until Cheryl has her first autobiography ghostwritten for her, or until Ashley puts his name to his next. Since it's almost five years since his first effort, which with a restraint not always evident in other areas of his life he waited until he was fully twenty-five to publish, it shouldn't be too long.

The wittily titled *My Defence* was one of those memoirs, after the style of David Blunkett's self-piteous stream of semi-consciousness, that cause a public reaction in direct inverse proportion to the number of copies sold. All that anyone seems to remember of that poignant rite-of-passage memoir is the segment that passed instantly into football folklore thanks to its elliptical portrait of the modern Premier League diva's psyche. Whether he was driving the Bentley or the Aston Martin at the time is a detail most safely left to obsessives of the sort who fret to this day about the second man and the grassy knoll. What concerns us, as it concerned Ashley then, is why he came so close to departing the road in that vehicle.

Early in 2005, Ashley, then the Arsenal left back, was somewhere on the North Circular Road in one car or another when his agent Jonathan Barnett rang him with some very grave news.

Raising the gruesome spectre of the Victorian mill-owner condemning his workforce to starvation rations, David Dein, the vice-chairman of Arsenal, had refused to meet Ashley's pay demand for a weekly £60,000. We will now ask Ashley to take up the story.

'When I heard Jonathan repeat the figure of £55,000 I nearly swerved off the road. "He is taking the piss Jonathan!" I yelled down the phone. I was so incensed. I was trembling with anger. I couldn't believe what I'd heard.' And who in their right mind will fail to empathise with him over that? Hard to recall as it is in this age of plenty, back in 2005, £250,000 per annum was a fair sum of money to a man being asked to scrape by on a little under £3 million. Did Jimmy Hill fight his heroic war to scrap the maximum wage back in the 1960s in vain?

The ability to soak up pain without complaint is a quality we perhaps too rarely associate with the top-flight English footballer. Yet Ashley's response to this calculated insult was very much what Zeno had in mind in the Athens of the third century BC when he founded the stoic school of philosophy. Where most of us would have veered instantly into the central reservation, causing who knows how much mayhem and carnage, you will note that Ashley 'nearly swerved off the road'. Understandably, the effort of will required to keep the car within the white lines drained his reserves of self-control so completely that he would find himself unable to dredge up such iron discipline again.

He would, however, be consistent when it came to the demonstrating of loyalty. Having been caught cheating on Arsenal by way of a rendezvous with representatives of Chelsea in what he drolly termed 'a chance meeting', he would do the same to Cheryl with a regularity that even that most perplexingly forgiving of wives came to find monotonous. And this despite his discreet texting of those elegant photographic self-portraits of himself to various tabloid mercenaries in those tiny yet impressively billowing white pants.

At the time of initial writing, with the first of Cheryl's own memoirs about to be published, rumours that her dangerous bout of malaria had brought the two back together, and that they were contemplating a rapprochement, have been slightly undermined by the news that they have been granted a decree nisi. At the time of rewriting for the paperback edition, meanwhile, following Cheryl's humiliatingly brief career as a judge on the American X Factor, rumours of yet another reconciliation, and possible remarriage, have also been undermined by allegations that Ashley has been unfaithful once again. Mills & Boon devotees such as myself will grieve at the death of this romance, of course, at least until its next revival. But through the tears, all but the soppiest-hearted will have the residual realism to accept that even at her saintliest, Cheryl, having not so long ago survived a horrendous experience by way of one bloodsucking parasite, could hardly be expected to make a second trip down the aisle with another.

32

Olympic Race Walking

Even by the standards of the Olympics' more *recherché* minority pursuits, the notion that 'racing' and 'walking' are even vaguely compatible activities stands out as absurd. The primary defence for rhythmic gymnastics, synchronised swimming and the rest is their exoticism. Most of us could not do bizarre and pointless things with a ribbon, or regard an underwater suicide attempt as cause for death-rictus grinning. But the one thing anybody in possession of a working pair of legs, God-given or prosthetic, cannot avoid doing (and I write as one who has made it his life's mission to try) is walk.

One appreciates the IOC's desire, under its late Hispanic overlord Juan Antonio Samaranch, to nudge Mexico up the medals table by including these events. Why Mexicans have traditionally dominated this discipline remains obscure. My theory is that no substance on earth produces the requisite buttock-clenching stance better than the jalapeño pepper, but in the absence of detailed research I wouldn't wish to push it too hard.

For all that, not for one millisecond during a 20-kilometre or even a 50-kilometre race walk do any of the elbow-flapping, Chicken Tonight advert impersonators technically walk. However comical a version of this physical activity it may be, they are running.

That so many are disqualified for not having one foot in contact with the ground, by officials who leap out from nowhere to wave table tennis bats at them like deranged airport staff attempting to coax a Boeing 777 to plough into the terminal, confirms the obvious. The humane thing to do would be to send the officials to Mexico City airport, to wave the paddles at the medal favourites as they check in their bags for the flight to the Games. Instead, they permit these poor sods to cross the planet and compete for the pleasure of that elite corps of TV spectators with a sufficiently lavish boredom threshold to stick with it until the disqualifications and the weeping commence, when in its defence it does become a sadistic viewing delight.

The special wickedness here is the arbitrariness. How do they choose one slow runner out of so many to receive the paddles? Eye colour? Random computer generation of numbers on the runner's bib? Some form of Russian roulette?

Take Jane Saville. Jane was born in Sydney in 1974, on 5 November to be precise, and the calamity that befell her in her home town shall never be forgot. Not by me, at least. I was in Sydney for the 2000 Games, and stuck in a hotel bedroom with 'flu on the day of the women's 20-kilometre race – a captive audience for an event no free person would willingly watch. As the race developed, many competitors, not all Mexicans, were given the first warning by way of paddle for an 'illegal gait', and then arbitrarily disqualified in the usual manner – so many, indeed, that in the closing stages Jane found herself unchallenged in the lead. Can you imagine the ecstasy surging through her as she entered the tunnel into Olympic Park to the kind of deliriously visceral roar seldom heard since a Coliseum crowd rejoiced in their Emperor's downturned thumb?

And then, a few hundred metres from the finish line and a couple of minutes from the gold medal, out he jumped, the blazered IOC official, to wave the paddle of doom. What was he thinking? If ever there was an occasion for a race walker to defy the sport's convention by actually walking, this surely was it. What motivation could Jane have, unchallenged as she was and so close to the winning tape, to run slowly? She'd have taken gold by shuffling to the line on a Zimmer.

Needless to report, the poor creature fell to the ground sobbing pitiably. When a concerned observer later asked what she needed, she showed remarkable powers of mental recovery. 'A gun to shoot myself with,' she said. She recovered, as it happens, and ran slowly to the bronze four years later in Athens. But that gun should be pressed to the temple of every IOC board member who permits this cruellest of idiocies to persist, and followed by a click.

31

Mick McCarthy

Until the 2010 World Cup, this entry had been earmarked for an acquaintance of the Wolves manager. How can it be, you may wonder, that no place has been found in this book for Roy Keane and the eruption of psychotic rage (or so it seemed at the time) that led him to depart a previous World Cup before a ball was kicked?

Then Mr McCarthy was hired as a match summariser and studio bletherer for the BBC, presumably by a Trojan horse executive wheeled into White City under cover of darkness at the orders of the head of ITV sport. Within moments of his first broadcast, the disdain for that dressing-room explosion of 2002 metamorphosed, in a neo-Ovidian way, into respect, reverence and something close to love for Mr Keane. Suddenly, that foul-mouthed rant had come to seem restrained. The question was no longer why the Eire midfielder was willing to end his inter-national career by calling the international manager, among much else, an 'English cunt'. It was, what would anyone on speaking terms with sanity (not a demographic group, admit-tedly, into which Keano may casually be placed) not do to avoid the sound of Mr McCarthy's voice?

By half time of the game in question, this much had become crystal clear: were you in the final stages of congestive heart failure when a replacement heart was miraculously found, and were Mr McCarthy the transplant surgeon, on 'Death, where is thy sting?' lines you too would call him an English cunt to avoid hearing him describe the procedure in that sledgehammer Yorkshire brogue.

Bedside manner would be no more a McCarthyite strength, you suspect, than football punditry, though alighting on the job to which this didactic megabore is suited isn't easy. The best I can manage is a PE master in a Leeds grammar school in 1957, with a special talent for teasing the fat kid stuck up the rope.

It takes a brave man to escape the destiny to which nature has condemned him, and one with a higher intellect than a turtle to identify which boys are safest left unbullied. Mr McCarthy is neither. So it was, in that Irish World Cup camp, that he goaded Roy Keane into issuing the anatomically perplexing yet gloriously eloquent invitation 'You can stick it up your bollocks.'

Intransigent stupidity is a fine and even essential quality in its rightful place – the Penalty Fines Appeals Department of a metropolitan council, for instance, or in the case of Hazel Blears, the British Cabinet. An international team's dressing room beset by clashing egos is not the place for it, however, and nor is the commentary box. A degree of wilful idiocy is something to which long exposure to the work of David Pleat (see no. 28) seemed to have inured the armchair spectator. In adding to that an air of over-emphatic know-allery and a chronic case of Professional-Tyke-School-of-Hard-Knocks self-certainty, McCarthy raises the bar to heights unlikely to be scaled by anyone else this side of Doomsday. Stick it up his bollocks indeed.

30

Thierry Henry

The fact that we English would have worshipped him for it had he done it in an England shirt is not the point, though it is palpably the truth. Michael Owen cheated no less blatantly, and far more frequently, to win England penalties, and I recall few howls of outraged anguish on the back pages and phone-ins about that. I can recall, as perhaps you can too, the love I felt for him when he was felled by a gust of air against Argentina in northern Japan during the 2002 World Cup. That day he feigned contact with an Argentine with a virtuosity hinting at *summa cum laude* graduation from David Ginola University (formerly Jürgen Klinsmann Technical College). You had to be a magnificent diver to con Pierluigi Collina, greatest of all referees, into pointing spotward, and Owen certainly was.

What the moral distinction between diving for a penalty and handling the ball to facilitate a goal might be is, to borrow from President Obama on the question of when precisely an embryo becomes a human life form, above my pay grade. I suppose you could speculate that residual psychic scar tissue from the wound opened by Maradona in 1986 makes the English more sensitive to the wickedness of a handball, and that its rarity value compared to the dive for a penalty sharpens the critical antennae. But really, this area of moral equivocation is probably safer left to the late A.J. Ayer, a fanatical Spurs fan as well as among the leading philosophers of his day, or his intellectual heir Simon Barnes of *The Times* (see no. 98).

Yet however hypocritical the reaction to the Henry handball that won France their 2010 World Cup place at Ireland's expense, so be it. We are football fans, and double standards are in the bloodstream. You can't spend half a lifetime wishing an auto-immune disease such as lupus on referees for decisions you'd wildly applaud were they in your team's favour without a tiny shard of partisanship having pierced your soul. And would you want to if you could? We are, after all, British. We are not Canadian.

As British people, of course, we have a special footballing affection for our neighbours in our former possession to the west – the greatest fans in the world, as they like now and then to remind us, who will, win or lose, have a party. They were not, having said that, in party mood on the night of 19 November 2009, and with good reason.

What was doubly repellent about Henry's handball (and you do the maths) is that there were two of them: the first purely instinctive as his hand was driven towards the ball by reflex; the second gloriously cynical as he then stroked it towards his foot with a cunning glance. The cross that followed was simple, William Gallas's nodded header simpler still, and the Irish, who richly deserved to win that game, were gone.

In truth, Henry's disgrace came as less of a surprise than many thought. This notion of an angel suddenly and startlingly unveiled as a demon was plain false. Sweet and endearing as a very young, bit-part-playing winger in the World Cup-winning France team of 1998, and in his early years devastating Premier League defences in the Arsenal interest, Henry had been a nuisance long before the Ireland calumny.

Of his unearthing as a cheat with another part of his body (if only he'd used his hand more in that department of his life) we will not speak. His amorous adventures with women other than his wife and the mother of his tiny daughter are their business and theirs alone.

What concerns us is that several years into his Arsenal career, having established himself among the finest strikers in the world and scoring unforgettable goals with monotonous regularity, he was well down the road to insufferability. The pouting, the shrugging, the hands-on-hips disdain and other expressions of classical French *froideur* towards less gifted colleagues established the fact that he regarded himself as far above the team. Of course he was more talented than anyone else. Yet so is Lionel Messi, and you don't see sneering contempt from him.

He was also a perpetual disappointment on the grandest stages. His performances for France in World Cup finals have been mediocre by any standards, let alone his own, while for Arsenal against Barcelona in the 2006 Champions League final he was profligate and detached. Devastating when running at the defences of Leicester City and Bolton, but immutably average when offered the opportunity to embed himself in legend in a World Cup final, he may be the most talented flat-track bully the sport has known. Ultimately, you suspect, some psychological kink caused him to freeze under the most melting of spotlights. For this reason, he will never be ranked alongside Pelé, Maradona and his compatriot Zinedine Zidane on the top tier of the pantheon.

Not that many of us wouldn't have sacrificed a limb – preferably someone else's – to have had him born an Englishman. Had he used that hand to propel us to a World Cup final, he would be not a cheat but a national hero with a plinth in Trafalgar Square. Rampant hypocrisy is the very lifeblood of the fanatic, as I said, even when deployed in another nation's cause, and so it is that Thierry Henry takes his place in the history of English football as its one and only Va Va Twat.

29

Naseem Hamed

The all-night vigil awaiting Las Vegas world title fights beginning between 4 and 5 a.m. isn't easy. Time and again I've staggered through the dismal small hours all the way to the introductions, and dozed off the very moment Michael Buffer invited those in the arena and watching around the world to get ready to rumble.

Only one British fighter has made the vigil painless, and that was the arsehole formerly known as Prince Naseem Hamed. The prospect of seeing this preening puffball of swaggering self-regard lose his unbeaten record and featherweight belt negated any need for coffee, cold baths, middle-era Ann Widdecombe porn movies and any of the other traditional antidotes to the smooth functioning of the body clock.

When finally that glad day dawned, at the MGM Grand in April 2001, it felt a poor and anticlimactic return on all the previous nights devoted to this noble cause. Hamed had so sharpened the appetite that his unanimous points defeat to Marco Antonio Barrera seemed scant revenge. What the strutting narcissist deserved was an unscheduled catchweight contest with one of Siegfried and Roy's more myopic white Siberian tigers, escaped from the neighbouring Mirage hotel and bamboozled by Hamed's elegant leopard-print shorts into confusing him for its mate.

The little horror kept us waiting an entire extra hour that night to accommodate preparations for an entrance involving not just the usual fireworks, rock music and laser light-show, but a journey to the ring on a mechanical love seat suspended high above a catwalk. Even by the standards of this preposterous

British-Asian Jamaican gangsta wannabe with the self-aware-ness of a turnip – with hindsight he was always a malevolent prototype for Ali G – this procession to the ring was an act of hubris on a scale Nemesis could hardly ignore.

Nemesis, it would eventually become clear, had concluded that Hamed was a dish she preferred cold and rather fleshier than featherweight. After an unconvincing return to the ring, he retired to spend more time with his fridge (any further come-backs would have required a new division: Hattyjacquesweight); and possibly, though this may flatter his powers of introspection, the odd wistful reflection on immense promise unfulfilled.

Arguably the greatest raw talent British boxing has produced, with phenomenal hand speed and tremendous punching power, had been ruined by cockiness and egomania. He had long since fallen out with Brendan Ingle, the trainer who discovered him in Sheffield, surrounded himself with sycophants, and aban-doned such petty bourgeois orthodoxies for the would-be boxing immortal as proper training and the raising of hands to protect the chin.

After so nearly getting knocked out a little earlier by one Kevin Kelly, he must have seen the sucker punch coming, but he was too besotted with himself to take the most basic evasive action

It's a familiar boxing fable. Mike Tyson was one of countless greats to blaze the trail. Yet Tyson had the excuse of an unremit-tingly horrendous childhood, watching his mother die of cancer without medication, and carrying a gun for self-protection at the age of eight. As a Jewish boxing commentator who survived Auschwitz observed, the Brooklyn neighbourhood of Bedford-Stuyvesant was Tyson's concentration camp, and no one survives those intact.

Hamed's excuse was genetic rather than environmental. He was simply born – try to excuse the forthcoming vulgarity: I've had a fair old spin with the thesaurus, but sometimes elegant euphemism won't suffice – one of the most phenomenal twats ever to emerge from a birth canal.

Eventually, inevitably, he would become a pariah when the urge to show off to a businessman friend cajoled him into driving his £300,000 McLaren sports car across a solid white line at 90 mph and into an oncoming Volkswagen Golf. He broke every bone of the other driver's body and caused him brain injuries, emerging from his own car physically unscathed but ruined nonetheless. Needless to say, he showed not a drop of remorse.

Had the judge known of a previous ban for driving at 110 mph on the M1, and various other speeding convictions, Hamed might have gone down for four years. Instead, he was out after serving sixteen weeks of a fifteen-month sentence. Even if the additional loss of his MBE hardly made this a TKO for natural justice, the incident achieved what his endlessly repugnant personality had failed to do. It finished him for ever as a public figure, and for that inadvertent act of mercy, a certain Anthony Burgin, the driver of that VW Golf, should have been voted BBC Sports Personality of the Year for 2006.

28

David Pleat

Under our splendid coalition government, in which the economics of the right and the social policy of the liberal left mingle so joyously, William Ewart Gladstone is very much in vogue. But then, in at least one of that Victorian prime minister's guises, for David Pleat he always was.

It is more than twenty years since Mr Pleat was dismissed as Tottenham Hotspur manager after a second incident involving the police, and the injustice rankles still. Without wishing to rake up the details, let it suffice to say that Pleaty covered more ground in his legendary cream-suited, mad-uncle-distended-from-the-conga dance across the Maine Road turf, in celebration of his then club Luton Town avoiding relegation, than he did in the light-blue Mercedes that was his company car at Spurs. He was to that vehicle's engine as a maniacally over-protective mother. Fearful of exhausting the little darling, he never allowed it out of first gear as he crawled along the streets of King's Cross in his Gladstonian quest for young women to rescue from the kerb.

More than two decades later, Pleaty continues to earn an albeit reduced living (he has been dropped by ITV, which hired him as its big-match summariser in succession to Ron Atkinson) from a reputation for tactical astuteness he ridicules with almost every word. Long before the Italian press nicknamed Sven-Göran Eriksson 'the successful failure', Pleaty had blazed the trail with brio. With Tottenham, he almost won many trophies, but actually won not a carrot.

Ignoring his subsequent career in management and as a 'director of football' on intrusion-into-private-grief grounds, he sustained his form in his subsequent career. He is almost an effective pundit, in much the way that John Prescott is almost an impeccable grammarian, and Robert Mugabe so very nearly a role model for inflation-strangling fiscal discipline.

In his defence, Pleaty's summarising on ITV now and again released a shard of comprehensibility. Once or twice a season, he would say something that not only made sense, but came tantalisingly close to illuminating a game. He has his fans even now, among them curiously the sports section of the *Guardian*, where he again benefited from Mr Atkinson's sudden departure by inheriting Big Ron's weekly 'chalkboard' of tactical analysis.

His general form might itself be summarised, however, by his reflection on an unusually fiascoid evening in even Tottenham's history. On 4 February 2004, at White Hart Lane, Spurs led Manchester City 3–0 in an FA Cup replay at half time, with the additional safeguard that Joey Barton's red card had reduced the visitors to ten men. An hour later, Spurs departed the pitch as 3–4 losers.

Now, the thing about this is that it was, and remains, unprecedented. The yielding of a three-goal half-time lead at home, though unusual, is not unknown. To achieve it against a dispirited relegation-threatened side like the Man City of that night nudges us closer towards the borderline with the unimaginable. To lose from 3–0 up at home against ten men is, however, so far as my researches establish, entirely without a parallel.

Indeed, the one saving grace about this cataclysm, for those of us who relish our club playing any part in the making of history, however horrendous, was its singularity. But hark, how did Pleaty choose to précis the night? 'Ah well,' he observed sagely, having watched something perfectly unique, 'these things happen in football.' That neo-Gladstonian brain, much in the style of a certain luxury German motor car, is seldom out of first.

27

Sepp Blatter

Under the direction of its Swiss president, Fifa has achieved the seemingly impossible and become a more repugnant entity than the Petri dish for corruption and byword for laughable hypocrisy officially titled the International Olympic Committee. A year ago my publishers, reading the hardback edition of this book for libel, were mildly alarmed by that opening observation. Intervening events, notably those surrounding England's wondrously fiascoid bid for the 2018 World Cup, will have removed any residual concerns to the point at which it now has the flavour of an ironic understatement. The charge sheet against this emperor of bad taste is not, having said that, limited to bribery and corruption, which he has acknowledged in former Fifa colleagues but resolutely denies so far as he himself is concerned. The charge sheet is long enough to necessitate that we pass lightly over such matters as his suggestion that women footballers wear 'tighter shorts and low-cut shirts … to create a more female aesthetic'. However unconvincing his neo-feminist credentials, his oversight of the 2010 World Cup is of another offensive order. Not only did he preside over the dullest tournament ever held, thanks in part to his selection of the seemingly helium-filled Jabulani ball, but also he dealt with South Africa and its figurehead with the imperious disdain of a feudal overlord.

The creation of special 'Fifa courts' to try people – memorably, the women who attended one match wearing unauthorised advertising gear for a Dutch brewer – for what were not even offences under South African law gives the flavour. Fifa's limitless arrogance under Blatter was never better illustrated than by its treatment of Nelson Mandela, news of whose greatness has filtered through even to the likes of Alan Hansen: among the more memorable moments in a World Cup hardly overladen with them was hearing Mr Hansen greet a picture of Mandela with the words, as if to the *victor ludorum* at a public-school prize-giving, 'He can be really, really proud of what he's achieved.' High praise indeed.

Somehow, reports of Mandela's stature appear to have evaded Blatter, who took it on himself to treat the frail ninety-two-year-old, even as he was grieving for the thirteen-year-old great-granddaughter killed in a road accident on the eve of the tournament, with magisterial contempt. 'We've come under extreme pressure from Fifa requiring and wishing that he be at the final today,' said his grandson Mandla Mandela. 'They said that Sepp Blatter wished my grandfather comes out to the final. I think people ought to understand … we've had a loss in the family. Their focus is having this world icon in the stadium, not paying attention to our customs and traditions as a people and a family.'

Had Mr Mandela Jnr studied the works of Fifa over the past dozen years, he would have been spared the sense of bemusement, if not the moral outrage, he expressed with such dignified restraint. No customs, no traditions, no vestigial sense of decency could impinge on Sepp Blatter's self-importance and urge to self-glorification. Had he been in charge of the winter World Cup of 30 AD, he'd have sent a squadron of heavies for Christ, and had him carried to Gethsemane's Soccer City to bless the opening ceremony from the cross.

Yet he will be remembered less for his grandiosity than his blithe tolerance of a culture of corruption that would do credit to our own Metropolitan Police. We may never know the precise means by which the 2022 World Cup came, under his aegis, to be awarded to the ancient footballing stronghold of Qatar, with its furnace-like summer temperatures and poor human rights record. But then we don't need the detail of who paid how much or promised what to whom. The fact of it alone adequately reveals what Fifa has become under Sepp Blatter. Its transformation into virtually a personal fiefdom was confirmed by his unopposed re-election, for what he promises will be his final term as president, following the withdrawal of sole rival Mohammed bin Hammam.

Mr bin Hammam was subsequently banned for life from football-related activities by a body glorying in the oxymoronic title of Fifa's ethics committee. His home country of Qatar, however, on whose behalf he was accused of bribing, was allowed to keep the 2022 World Cup, while it was simultaneously announced that Mr Blatter would not be investigated for turning a blind eye to the bleeding obvious due to 'lack of evidence'. And all this, miraculously, without a shred of help from former Inspector Yates of the Yard. But then Fifa under Blatter requires no assistance from surreally indolent coppers to invoke wintry mirth at the clearing of its name. He has made it a law unto himself.

26

The Bare-Chested
Gargantuan Newcastle Fan

When the historians of tomorrow ponder the single greatest anomaly of the New Labour imperium, they will have two clear choices. One is the cringing support of an allegedly centre-left government for the deranged neo-colonial adventurism of George W. Bush. Mr Tony Blair's neo-colon adventure – his tenancy, to spell it out as elegantly as possible, of a holiday home two centimetres to the south of Mr Bush's large bowel – will intrigue geopolitical analysts and psychiatric conventions for decades to come.

The rival anomaly is this. During thirteen years in which thousands of new and by-and-large facetious 'crimes' were heaped on to the statute book, no one was ever arrested for one of our more ancient common law offences. I refer, of course, to the public indecency practised every fortnight, in the months between and including August and May, but especially between December and February, at St James' Park, whereby several hundred Newcastle fans remove their shirts and treat *Match of the Day* and Sky Sports viewers to the vista of their pendulous breasts.

For those historians, it will be a close call and no doubt a split decision – I have a hunch that Simon Schama will plump for Iraq, for example, while Dr David Starkey may opt for St James' Park – though there is a simple explanation for the police's failure to tazer the bare-chested of the Gallowgate End. Mr Blair (see no. 48) insisted he was a Newcastle supporter himself. Considering the alarmingly cosy relationship between

187

that Prime Minister and the forces of the law, it's no surprise that they showed his fellow fans a tolerance on the public order front they denied a young vegan woman arrested for quietly reciting the names of fallen troops in Iraq by the Cenotaph in Whitehall.

Before we go on, I should say that there is something refreshing about the monumentally fat advertising their girth in an age when morbid obesity is widely regarded as a sign of moral degeneracy. I'm a stout chap myself, to wander briefly through the plush meadow of euphemism, and admire these Geordies for their freedom from the self-disgust that greets every mirrorward glance on exiting the bath.

So much for the theory, and on to the practice. The belief of February's bare-chested Geordie that his apparent courage inspires shock and awe is misplaced. You need not be a world expert in calisthenics to know that imperviousness to cold is not decisive proof of hardness, or to believe that they are somehow insulated from the cold by being, to borrow their self-awarded Homeric epithet, 'the most passionate fans in the world'.

All you need to know is that overeating and overheating are more than rhyming brethren. If you weigh twenty-seven stone, and have breasts that could suckle both New Zealand islands simultaneously, you won't feel a thing even when the averagely weighted person clad head to toe in mohair is entering the later stages of hypothermia and calling wanly for the Bacofoil. Indeed, removing the black-and-white-striped shirt may, short of death, be the only way to avoid sweating. It isn't hard at all. Hard would be keeping it on. Taking it off is the coward's way out.

We all understand the genesis of this attention-seeking habit. By any formula comparing fan base and revenue to silverware, Newcastle United is historically the planet's least successful football club. Apart from headline-grabbing comic mismanagement of the sort so expertly provided by chairman Mike Ashley, fake eccentricity is the only means of retaining any interest from a media and a public that would otherwise have tired long ago of the club's grandiose claims to relevance.

If this is seen by Gallowgate End regulars as a sign of strength, I would respectfully suggest a more effective and less nauseating method of proving just how bastard hard they are. The next time the club is relegated from the Premier League (and the form book suggests that no one will be growing a ZZ Top beard in the interim), try to accept the teaching of Fergie. Not the one at Old Trafford, nor even the borderline bankrupt who used to earn a crust from US Weightwatchers, though she might also be a useful contact here. I refer to Fergie out of the Black Eyed Peas, who taught us, via the title of her 2006 single, that big girls – even those with penises – don't cry. When the Sky camera turns to you on the final day of the season, with another stint in the Championship assured, stare out with dry-eyed stoicism, you great soft northern jessie.

No one loves a crybaby, but if anyone was tempted, it wouldn't be a crybaby who could eat Nicholas Soames in a Cyril Smith–James Corden sandwich, and have room left over for a King of Tonga sundae.

25

Steve McClaren

In what remains known to the self-respecting football pundit as all fairness, nothing this hapless clown did as England coach should be held against him. The train of events that led to what was, even by England standards, a hyperfiasco was set in stone the moment Brian Barwick (see no. 88) gave him the job; for what followed you might as fairly castigate Vernon Kaye for struggling with any peculiarly challenging technical anomalies thrown up by the Large Hadron Collider.

What should be held against him, in the absence of a supercharged cattle prod, is taking the job in the first place. Refusing millions per annum to watch loads of football, suck up to the FA blazers at Soho Square and refer in star-struck tones to 'Lamps', 'JT' and 'Stevie G' can never be easy. But it's not impossible for those who follow the teachings of two of history's more gnomic life guides. 'Know thyself,' advised the oracle at Delphi, while Harold Callaghan of the Los Angeles Police Department wisely counselled a suspect, 'A man's just gotta know his limitations,' shortly before unloading the contents of a .44 Magnum into his head.

Old Beetroot Face (OBF) found himself in a minority of two along with Mr Barwick. Every other sentient being knew of his limitations intimately, because as Sven-Göran Eriksson's assistant and the man in charge of training the team that visited such global humiliation upon us at the 2006 World Cup, he'd advertised them in brightest neon for years. An exceedingly average club coach with Middlesbrough, his failure to grasp the tactical nuances of international football was plain long before he and that preposterous tuft of ginger hair at the front of his terracotta forehead succeeded the platform-shoed Swedish stud.

What ensued was so predictable that just about everyone other than Alan Hansen, who hailed the appointment as a masterstroke, predicted it; so transparently obvious that one unusually malevolent hack (your author) wrote an obituary to McClaren's England career the day it was announced. I append the following not to brag of my prescience, but to make the point that if I, well known within the trade as the least talented soothsayer since Comical Ali, could see it coming, it must have been devilishly hard to miss.

'Sympathy for Mr McClaren may be tempered by the £3 million per annum he is said to have been offered, and the enormous pay-off he will soon enough receive,' ran the last paragraph. 'Even so, he is in for a hellish time in the interim, so let us hope he is enjoying his moment of triumph to the full. From here, it will be downhill very fast and all the way.'

And so, with a couple of brief upward lurches in the middle, it was. There followed a sequence of shambolic performances in the vain attempt to qualify for Euro 2008 in which the alleged 'golden generation' seemed to be taking tactical instruction from a coalition of football strategists comprising former Vice-President Dan Quayle, the late Cyril Fletcher, Graham Taylor, one-time IRA bandstand bomb hero Sefton (a horse) and penalty-kick expert Diana Ross, who famously tutored Frank Lampard for his effort in the shootout against Portugal in 2006.

OBF, pitiably awed by his senior players, floundered in the optimistic belief that parroting jargon plagiarised from a 1985 course in vapid management speak at the University of Southern California more than compensates for the hideous results. And then somehow the team blundered into form, until miraculously it found itself on the verge of qualifying. All that was needed, at Wembley on 20 November 2007, was a draw against

Croatia – a side with nothing to play for, having already qualified, whose limitations Fabio Capello would soon unveil.

It was at this point that McClaren bucked the odds by transcending the gloomiest expectations that greeted his appointment. That he was a coach of unimpeachable mediocrity had never been in doubt. What few anticipated was that he would identify that match as the ideal competitive international debut for a young and nervy goalkeeper. It was, you will recall from OBF's touchline strolls beneath the brolly, by no means a dry evening in north-west London, and the pitch was treacherously greasy. Short of selecting his keeper from the multiple-limb amputation ward of the nearest hospital, he could not have made a more eccentric and suicidal decision.

What everyone else understood before kick-off only became apparent to Mr McClaren eight minutes after it, when poor Scott Carson allowed a weak shot to slip through his hands (and thank God that's the sort of catastrophe that only befalls even England once in a generation). Five minutes later, a stratagem cunningly lifted from *The Keystone Kops Official Guide to Defending in Association Football* saw the Croats double their lead.

Somehow, though, the match would come to mirror McClaren's career as England coach with exquisite accuracy. The cataclysmic start gave way to an inexplicable recovery, and with the match tied at 2–2 qualification seemed assured. With thirteen minutes remaining, however, Croatia scored the winner, and as McClaren fine-tuned his Gene Kelly act on the touchline, the betting markets on the identity of his successor were busier than the Croat goalie.

A tenure that had begun with the showboating foolishness whereby he relieved David Beckham of the captaincy, to affect the hard-man image he would undermine with relentless sycophancy towards the players, ended as it richly deserved to do. Off he went with his fat cheque.

At the time of writing, the process of historical revision is under way. Old Beetroot Face, having won the 2009–10 Dutch league with FC Twente, has been appointed the coach of Wolfsburg in Germany. His reputation is in the ascendant, and the day may yet dawn when amnesiacs posit that, having proved himself abroad, he deserves another crack at the England job.

In the unlikely event that he is, the one consolation will be that there is no risk of yet another run-out for that overquoted Marxist definition of history. It cannot repeat itself as farce, after all, when it was nothing but farce first time round.

24
John Inverdale

The old Yiddish saw (like there are any new ones) which translates as 'Of all his mother's children, he loves himself the best' cannot begin to capture this vulpine broadcaster's self-delight. If he could eat himself, you can't help thinking, he'd cultivate bulimia in the cause of bringing himself up and eating himself all over again.

Contemplating the rugger-bugger complacency, the onanistic drawl and the coquettish glances to camera, the barely credible thing about Inverdale is that he isn't a retired minor sportsman himself, like his twin preening peacock of the airwaves Mark Nicholas (see no. 35).

Among other irritations too numerous to catalogue is an interviewing manner by comparison with which the house style of *Hello!* magazine attains the savagery of Jeremy Paxman interrogating the late Pol Pot about the Killing Fields while suffering dyspepsia, gout and grievously impacted piles. At Wimbledon a few years ago, this gushing human oil slick contrived to ask Rita Wilson, an American actress who turned in a nice cameo in an Oedipal episode of *Frasier*: 'So, what's it like being married to someone of the stature of Tom Hanks?' Ms Wilson was excused the subsequent struggle for an answer. What on earth did he imagine she might say? 'Being married to someone of the stature of Tom Hanks is an experience of indescribable spiritual and physical richness. I cannot put into words the visceral thrill I get each morning when I wake and polish his Oscar'?

Even in an industry laden with Forrest Gumps, Mr Inverdale stands out as a fraud. His special trick – the classically English one known to an old teacher of mine as 'the words of command'

194

(see Alan Green, no. 4), is to project a sense of self-worth so impenetrable that others instinctively take him at his own estimation. It's worked so beautifully that he is given *carte blanche* to indulge himself by the BBC, bagging the most lustrous events, indulging his passion for rugby union, and latterly having a go as a current affairs anchor on Radio 5 Live. In this latter capacity, he swiftly sank. During coverage of the police hunt for his fellow narcissist Raoul Moat, the Northumbrian shooter, he dwelt with relish on the classic paradox that the north-eastern village at the centre of the story looked all tranquil and picturesque on his monitor. 'It's almost,' he said, 'like watching an episode of *Midsomer Murders*.' Although he had the minimal intelligence required to go to pieces when the insensitivity of this remark struck him – yeah, you really want the sports guy on the case with a gruesome breaking story like that one – within a couple of minutes the grin of self-adoration was audible once again.

Where life may indeed be like a box of chocolates, in that you never know what you're gonna get, John Inverdale is not. With him you know precisely what you're gonna get: a neo-Des Lynam lounge lizard but without the 'tache, the charm, the wit or the self-deprecating ironic detachment, looking into the lens with the one poignant regret that, although it may well be his second-favourite piece of glassware in all the world, the one thing it isn't is a mirror.

23
Kenneth Bates

All too seldom in this cruel world are we offered the heart-lifting public vista of perfect marital symbiosis. The union of Tony and Cherie Blair is one rare example, inasmuch as it restricts them to making two people miserable rather than four. The same goes for the unholy wedlock between Kenneth Bates, the country's least lovable football chairman, and its most charmless club, Leeds United.

If the fact that they deserve each other goes without saying, the question of how they came to jump the broom remains, like so many of Mr Bates's financial arrangements, the source of some intrigue. No one but Ken himself and his mystery backers knows who technically owns Leeds, just as no one has ever cracked the conundrum of who owned Chelsea during the lively Bates era at Stamford Bridge.

Quite how it is possible for the ownership of English football clubs to lack the kind of transparency expected of Soviet nuclear silo details under Mr Brezhnev is a matter more safely left to others. For now, suffice it to state the bleeding obvious: that English football is administered by various factions whose concerns for the game's welfare, as the recent fiasco at Portsmouth needlessly confirms, begin and end with the celebration of wealth (or in Portsmouth's case, the appearance of wealth).

The suggestion is not, of course, that the Captain Birdseye impersonator has ever indulged in any fiscal fishiness, let alone defied the law of the land or what might charitably be called football's financial regulations; merely that he and his enigmatic offshore chums, whomsoever they might be, have circumnavigated any financial rocks in their path with skill and élan.

Good grace has been harder to discern. Where other rough-diamond chairmen lay claim to no grander academic distinction than a First from the School of Tough Breaks, Kenneth is Professor Emeritus of Hard Knocks at the University of Life (formerly London Cabbie Polytechnic). He has taken W.C. Fields' famous dictum and raised it a notch. Here is a man who cannot meet a sucker without feeling the urge to give him an even break of at least one limb.

There's no denying that his muscular stewardship transformed the crumbling, near-bankrupt Chelsea he bought for £1 in 1982 into a sufficiently swanky concern to attract Roman Abramovich and the modest nest egg he'd chiselled from the oil and mineral reserves of the former Soviet Union. Nor could anyone deny that Ken's ungodly gift for picking fights provided plenty of amusement in the course of that journey.

It was a rare sign of Kenneth's commitment to democracy that no individual or group was spared his belligerence. For years his programme notes, in which I occasionally had the honour to feature, were a fortnightly delight for fans of petty score-settling. He also had the courage to ban Peter Osgood and Ron Harris – heroes of the 1970 FA Cup final win over Leeds United on which Chelsea fans have been so admirably loath to dwell at mawkish length – after taking umbrage at imagined criticism. Who knew that it was a classic trait of the archetypal bully to have the thinnest of skins himself?

Most memorable of all the Batesian eccentricities was the foray into social experimentation that saw him propose the electrification of a fence to shock fans minded to invade the pitch into thinking again. It offers a useful insight into the workings of his humanitarian world view that the idea suggested itself to Ken while visiting his cattle farm.

It would be foolish, having said that, to affect grave concern for the sensibilities of the *animali* of that era, when the Stamford Bridge faithful's expression of anti-racist sentiment was the chant 'We all agree/Our coons are better than your coons.'

As for the followers of Leeds, who used to mark visits to White Hart Lane with hissing noises intended to echo the sound of Zyklon B escaping into Nazi death chambers, and chanted a ditty about Tottenham's Jewish fans returning to Auschwitz for another dose, perhaps they too have been civilised by Papa Bates' tough love. For all that, much as with Tony and Cherie, it's hard to avoid the conclusion that they and Ken deserve a marriage made in hell.

22

Alan Shearer

The irony about Shearer's three distinct careers is that it is the only one in which he was competent (though as a striker he was rather more than that) which continues to invoke the rage.

As a pundit, he is of course abysmal. No one outside the Sleepeasy Care Home for Retired Sporting Dimwits more formally known as BBC Sport, and his loyal army of professional self-pitiers on Tyneside, could dispute that. In four years of perching on the *Match of the Day* sofa, never once has he trawled his mind and dredged up a thought of the vaguest insightfulness or originality.

If he stays welded to that sofa for another fifty years, until the effects of old age oblige the studio manager to cut out the seating bit from underneath and replace it with a commode, he will never say anything about football that hasn't been apparent to the sighted for several minutes. You might as well ask Pam Ayres to write a sonnet to shame the ghost of Shakespeare. Try as he might, and for all we know he might be trying his little heart out, the grey matter simply isn't there. The blessing, for the generous-hearted among us, is that the very last person to be aware of his luminescent inadequacy in this field is Mr Shearer himself.

The same appears to go, miraculously, for his brief and catastrophic dipping of his toes into the frothing waters of football management. Already assumed by 97 per cent of the viewing audience to know nothing about the tactical and psychological issues on which he is lavishly paid to lecture others, he swiftly removed any residual doubt by becoming a manager.

This Mr Shearer did achieve with inarguable success. It's hard to cite alternative names who, having yielded to the cries of 'Send for the Messiah' in April 2009, when Newcastle had eight games in which to save themselves from relegation, could have failed in the modest task that was his charge. Almost invariably a new coach elicits sharp improvement from even the most dismal and depressed of squads, and Newcastle's fixture list was hardly daunting. They needed only to win a few home games in front of the self-proclaimed 'most passionate fans in the world'. The late Barbara Cartland would have kept them up. So would Lamb Chop, Shari Lewis's ovine glove-puppet sidekick. Even David Pleat might have done it. Abundantly clueless, Shearer could rouse his team to no more than five points from that octet of fixtures.

His return to the *Match of the Day* studio brought to mind the pipe dream of *Seinfeld*'s George Costanza on walking into his office one Monday morning having resigned the previous Friday with a savage tirade at his boss. It was George's hope that, startled by his brazenness, no one would mention that he had disqualified himself from the right to draw his paycheque.

It didn't work for Costanza, but Shearer had better luck. After spending a couple of months establishing beyond dispute that he was better qualified to lecture Titian on brush technique, and Gerald Ratner on how to destroy a thriving business with one four-letter word, than football coaches on how to coach football, he resumed his seat as if he'd never been away. No one said a word, and enveloped in this *omerta* he simply continued as if it had never happened.

Fatiguing as the resumption of his opinion-forming career has proved for those already wearied by the winsomeness of Gary Lineker and by Mark Lawrenson's deranged faith in his own wit, it is, as I said, for his playing days that Shearer lives in infamy, despite the natural talent for scoring goals.

Passing over that irksome goal celebration – head down, one arm aloft, charging towards the faithful in the stands – two incidents within a couple of months demand attention. The first, in April 1998, involved Neil Lennon, then of Leicester City, whom a sequence of camera shots appeared to suggest that Shearer had kicked viciously in the face while he lay prostrate.

Had Shearer not been the England captain at the time, the Football Association disciplinary committee might have agreed with this received wisdom. As it was, it accepted Shearer's explanation that he was trying to free his leg from Lennon's grasp when the unfortunate contact between boot and face was made.

So it was that Mr Shearer retained the armband for France '98, where he committed the most heinous act of World Cup treason since Alf Ramsey threw away a quarter-final victory over West Germany by taking off Bobby Charlton in 1970.

In the last-sixteen match, England memorably met Argentina. Each side converted a penalty in the first ten minutes (England's by Shearer, as nervelessly reliable as ever from twelve yards), before Michael Owen sensationally scythed through the Argie defence with the fearlessness of infancy to put England 2–1 ahead. When Paul Scholes slid a sitter the wrong side of the post after about half an hour, my cousin Nick and I turned dismally to one another and simultaneously acknowledged that that was it with a reciprocal 'It's over, old boy, we're out.' If the gods of football see a gift like that rejected, they don't forgive. They wait for the appropriate moment, and kick the miscreant team hard in the cobblers.

So it proved. Zanetti equalised in the final moments of a peerlessly melodramatic first half, laconically finishing a cunningly worked free-kick move; and early in the second David Beckham's petulant leg-swipe at Diego Simeone was rewarded with that infamous red card.

Yet England, typically roused by misfortune, contained Argentina with relative ease, even threatening to steal the game. They should have done so when, with a few minutes to go they won a corner on their left. Taking a rare break from the physio's room, Darren 'Sicknote' Anderton swung over a high, in-swinging cross which Sol Campbell rose to nod into the Argentine net. As the England players enveloped him, those of us who had embarked on a delirious lap of honour were startled, on returning to the telly, to find Argentina breaking against a five-man team, and more astonished that the scoreline in the top left of the screen still read 'England 2 Argentina 2'.

The reason soon became apparent. While the ball was in flight, Shearer had risen in unison with the Argentine keeper and elbowed him in the face. Had he not done so, Carlos Roa couldn't possibly have reached the ball, and the goal would have stood. Whether England would have held on we cannot know, but the way those ten men were playing suggested that they might. In the event, it went to extra time and penalties, and I wouldn't dream of insulting your intelligence by stating how that panned out.

In melding idiocy to the malevolence that always underscored his game, Shearer prevented England – more impressive that night under Glenn Hoddle than young readers might perhaps believe – from reaching a tough but perfectly winnable quarter-final against Dennis Bergkamp's Dutch.

Somewhere in all this we may sense a portion of rough divine justice on familiar Greek tragic lines. The payback had been delayed, but the FA's droll acquittal over the assault on Neil Lennon's face hadn't wiped the slate clean. It had merely sent an embossed, gilt-edged invitation to Nemesis, who waited patiently until Shearer used another limb to confirm his inherent nastiness to punish him, and more pertinently us, for the original crime.

Shearer himself has never shown an iota of penitence for either offence. But if he thinks the rest of us have forgotten or forgiven, he shows a more impressive gift for self-delusion than for punditry or football management.

21
Billy Bowden

The New Zealander may or may not be the least competent of the current Test umpires, as Australian and West Indian squads have voted him in the past. We could argue his claims against those of Rudy Koertzen, Daryl Harper, Darrell Hair and others until stumps are drawn. What brooks no argument is that Billy Bowden is the creepiest official in cricket, or any sport, in this age or any thus far.

Primarily, of course, it's his finger. The other gestures – the crumb-sweeper arm wave to denote a four; the six-phase hop with both arms aloft for a six; the rubbing of the crotch until his white coat tents out at the front to inform the scorer of a leg bye (I may have made one of those up) – are irksome enough. Here, they inform us, is a man desperate to prance in the spotlight denied him during an ineffably mediocre playing career.

Often he seems to exhibit the only child's craving for attention, which perhaps explains his habit of travelling the planet with both parents in tow – a mild eccentricity in a middle-aged man, yet an endearing one. Filial piety is such a noble thing that his religiosity can be excused. He has described Jesus Christ as 'always my third umpire … He's there behind me, beside me, in front of me.' What with propelling Jonathan Edwards (see no. 60) to a triple jump Olympic gold, guiding Kaka to Champions League glory and so on, the Son of Man has always taken a close interest in sport. Being obliged to examine ultra-slo-mo pictures of a tight run-out would hardly bother Him.

All in all, then, this angular self-dramatist would barely make the cut as a minor panel in the Bayeux Tapestry of sporting peculiarity were it not for the index finger of his right hand.

When someone shouts 'Howzat?' and Bowden concludes that the batsman is out, up it comes, with the upper half bent over the lower to make the shape of a crook.

Bowden claims that arthritis compels him to make it that shape, and perhaps this is true. More likely, what with the Lord being his shepherd, the crook is a private sign between him and his Saviour – the umpiring equivalent of the Jesus fish on the back of the car.

Whatever its genesis, purpose and meaning, let no one deny this: the very last place on earth you would wish to see that crooked finger is outside your child's school gates at 3.30 p.m.

20
Derek Thompson

Of all the television entities cited as Primary Inspiration for Alan Partridge, the Channel 4 racing presenter and on-course commentator would stake the mightiest claim were it not for two things. Firstly, the title clearly belongs to Fred Dinenage, as anyone who saw his Sky TV documentary on the Kray twins – a riot of unintended hilarity the like of which you would scarcely believe – must agree. Incidentally, you can earn a decent living betting suckers on the spelling of Fred's surname. No one believed that either, pre-Googling. And secondly, returning to TV's Tommo, he doesn't have the intellect. If Partridge had an elder brother known to the family as Durhh even before suffering severe neurological damage in a point-to-point fall, for that role Mr Thompson would be cast to type. But he doesn't.

What Tommo does have is an unyieldingly smug and patronising grin that seldom vacates his features, and an eerie knack for speaking fluently on the telly. That what he says is almost invariably cobblers is not, at least for his employers, the point. The ability to talk to time without stumbling is a glib yet precious one in live broadcasting, and in twenty-five years I can't recall him drying on air. He is the oilman's wet dream. He never stops gushing

Off air, things have sometimes gone less smoothly. His obituary will doubtless centre on his role in the 1997 libel trial brought against the *Sporting Life* by Kieren Fallon and the trainers Jack and Linda Ramsden, the trio taking umbrage at that extinct newspaper's suggestion that they had fixed their horse in a handicap. Tommo was subpoenaed to repeat his claim that Mr Fallon, in the gents of a Newmarket pub, had told him that he 'pulled' the horse (deliberately prevented it from running its race). Possibly identifying Tommo as the last man on earth in whom anyone wearing a jacket that does up at the front would confide a criminal conspiracy while targeting the Armitage Shanks, the jury found for the plaintiffs.

This may have suggested an alternative revenue stream for one whose appetite for money, as we shall see, is unquenchable. Tommo could market himself as a courtroom double agent, ostensibly appearing as star witness for the prosecution in the covert quest for unlikely acquittals. So credible a witness to anything is he that, were he to testify to having been present at a murder recorded in minute detail on CCTV cameras, with the defendant holding his passport up to the lens while yelling, 'And now, members of the jury, behold my Kalashnikov!' there would be enough reasonable doubt for a verdict of not guilty.

Perhaps the more satirically minded of obits will also touch on his role in the Great Tipster Stakes, a competition I oversaw while writing the diary column for the *Guardian*. Here an interest must be declared. My late father-in-law John Tyrrel also broadcast on Channel 4 racing, to whose viewers he was known as JT, long before John Terry usurped the initials. When he died in Newmarket in 1995, Tommo raced to the house to offer condolences, and to beg JT's widow to delay the funeral for more than a week, until the first day on which he could be certain to attend. This, at some inconvenience, she duly did.

The mystery of Tommo's non-appearance at the church was not resolved until hours after the service, when my brother-in-law and I chose to pay our most private respects by spending an hour in a bookmaker in Newmarket High Street. Any plans to make a missing person's report and ask the police to put out an All Points Bulletin for a Caucasian male, about forty-five years old, with an infuriating smirk were happily forestalled when a familiar voice drifted out of the speakers. Tommo, having demanded the postponement of the funeral to a time convenient to himself, had waged a fierce internal battle and then decided to earn a few bob from commentating on behalf of the bookies' satellite service SIS at an exceedingly minor meeting at Uttoxeter.

When, a week later, a newspaper reported that the watchdog for premium-rate telephone lines had criticised Tommo's 0898 tipping service, I naturally felt obliged to do what Tommo himself would inadvertently do for Mr Fallon two years later, and clear his name. The rules for the Great Tipster Stakes were simple enough. Each morning I would ring Tommo's line and get his tips for the day – tips generally introduced with a long and waffly profit-maximising reflection on how he'd met 'my great mate Willy Ryan' (a jockey) in a pub, or on the gallops, and been put onto a 'steering job' (such a dead cert that the jockey need only point it towards the winning post).

I would then ring my wife at work to relay the races concerned. She would blow up the relevant race cards on the photocopier, buy a quarter of a roasted chicken from the canteen and cut it into pieces, placing one beside each horse's name on the card. Our then ten-month-old West Highland white terrier Steptoe, whom she took to work, would then be unleashed, and whichever piece of chicken he ate first would be his selection.

After a month the Westie led Tommo by about £100. By the end of Royal Ascot, the puppy was almost £400 clear (a lead he comfortably nursed to the winning post) thanks to winners in large handicaps at 12–1 and 16–1, and an each-way touch on a 66–1 shot. Tommo, meanwhile, was out of luck, as a bewildering sequence of odds-on chances proved themselves fit for steering only to the nearest Uhu factory.

While Steptoe was gracing the front page of the *Racing Post* and appearing on an ITV weekend magazine show to pick National Lottery numbers, Tommo was being greeted at race tracks with cries of 'Woof, woof!', one of which led to a minor skirmish in a bar.

His resilience was no more in doubt, however, than his Olympian *chutzpah*. One afternoon we both appeared on a Radio 5 Live show, and a five-minute debate about the cosmic uselessness of Tommo's premium-rate phone line concluded with him giving out the number over the air.

For all that, it would be not only needlessly cruel but inexcusably misleading to portray Tommo as purely a mercenary. He has his altruistic side too, as this reply to an enquiry about his work regime in a recent *Times* questionnaire makes plain: 'In the mornings … I update various telephone tipping lines,' confided Tommo. 'I'm frequently asked to open new betting shops, and it's a job I absolutely love because it allows me to put something back into a world that has given me so much.' Purest Partridge. On reflection, perhaps Fred Dinenage has cause for concern after all.

19
Michael Schumacher

Whether or not this pastiche of German cockiness is the greatest driver in the modern history of Formula One (and most would opt for Ayrton Senna there), he is indubitably its most viscerally repugnant. Given the abundant roll-call of horrors that sport has produced, this – and not the seven world titles and ninety-one race wins – is the achievement for which he deserves to be remembered.

One cannot be exposed for a millisecond to that prissy, smug little face without the hydrochloric acid rising to assail the oesophagus in disgust. Partly it's the chin – modelled directly on the Wicked Witch of the West's – to have a threatened Jimmy Hill freezing the TV picture while he scurries off for his ruler. More than that, it is the various incidents that pose the question provoked by his namesake compatriot Harald 'Toni' Schumacher (see no. 16) as to where the line between ruthless gamesmanship and attempted murder should be drawn.

The most infamous of these came in 1994 when, deeply affected by Senna's fatal crash a few months earlier, he collided with Damon Hill, his one remaining challenger for the world championship, to take them both out of the final race of the season in Australia. Any lingering doubt as to whether this was a deliberate act of cheating was squashed when Murray Walker declared it, bless him, an accident.

There have been enough subsequent 'accidents' to suggest that Schumacher's control of his steering wheel is on a par with that of a ninety-two-year-old whose short-sightedness has caused him to mistake a quart of Scotch for his Parkinson's medication. Three years after the Hill abomination, Schumacher again found himself leading the son of a former world champion, in Jacques Villeneuve, by a single point when the closing race began in Spain. Would you believe it, he steered his Ferrari into Villeneuve's Williams, although this time he himself was the only one obliged to retire, and Villeneuve finished third to win the title.

If that outcome seemed a rare nod towards the existence of a benign deity, his return to F1 in 2009, three years after retiring, hinted blessedly at more brutal and ancient gods. His hubris has been punished in the traditional matter, Nemesis working her magic by disabusing the world, if not yet Schumacher himself, of the notion that at forty he can defy the effects of middle age on his reflexes. It isn't his failure to make a single podium that has humiliated him. It's being outraced time after time by teammate Nico Rosberg – yet another world champion's son; the rejection of nepotism is one of so many enchantments in F1 – that firmly establishes his abundant failure to turn back the clock.

His response to this late acquaintanceship with inadequacy was endearingly predictable, and suggests that, to borrow Harold Wilson's putdown of Tony Benn, he immatures with age. Where the two potentially fatal 'accidents' detailed above were marginally mitigated by having some purpose, his driving Rubens Barichello off the road at the 2010 Hungarian GP, leaving the Brazilian a few inches from colliding with a concrete wall at 180 mph, was motivated purely by petulant spite. Such is his reputation for self-righteousness that his confession to having made 'a mistake' was celebrated throughout this apology for a sport as an act of wondrous graciousness.

Whether Schumacher will extend this new humility to accepting that he is too old and too slow to drive anything but the hearse into which he has so narrowly avoided placing various rivals, it remains too early to know. If so, he will at least have a driving-related diversion to occupy him in retirement. In one of those exquisitely subtle ironies you require the German sense of humour to appreciate fully, Michael Schumacher is an ambassador for an FIA-supported campaign aimed at reducing reckless driving around the globe. Its name, drolly enough, is 'Make Roads Safe'.

18
John Terry

Where in the name of all the saints do you begin with the erstwhile Churchillian bulldog captain of England? Perhaps by gratefully observing, on behalf of a troubled industry, that without him (and his engagingly *Minder*ish family; the dad charged with dealing cocaine, the mum done for shoplifting; can't wait for his twins to grow up) our noble tabloids would have been in even graver strife in recent years. This is the Jordan of association football.

Purely as a central defender in the yeoman mould, he remains an enigma. Where he has so often looked masterly leading the Chelsea back line these past dozen years, twice voted best defender (2005 and 2008) in a Champions League laden with world-class players, in two consecutive World Cups he has turned in performances worthy of pre-half-time substitution in the Hackney Marshes League Division 73, as played on swampland pitches requiring flippers rather than boots, without lines, match officials or nets.

Clearly there is a psychological kink. After the 2006 World Cup, when he presaged the disaster against Germany in 2010 by allowing a harmless ball down the middle to bounce over his head and gift Sweden a goal, an acquaintance in a Turkish baths offered some insight. This man, claiming to know a close friend of his, reported that on his return from the 2006 tournament Terry told him that he never felt comfortable in the competition. He just felt he didn't belong on the grandest stage.

No surprise there, you may think. For decades, men who play consistently well in their club strips have been transformed into Conference footballers by the simple expedient of pulling on an

England shirt. Yet with Terry, this contra-intuitive nervous nelliedom presents at club level too. Since no one else slipped while taking a penalty during the 2008 Champions League final shootout between Chelsea and Manchester United, as Terry did before missing the kick to win a trophy they went on to lose, we may assume that the problem lay not with the turf but in his head. The man – and as a loud and proud Englishman, the adherence to tradition does him credit – is a choker.

Of the above-mentioned 2010 performance that deserved to be rewarded with a 9–2 German victory, rather the 4–1 that richly flattered England, I feel unqualified to write. But then, I'm not sure who is, other perhaps than Agatha Christie. Certainly The Mysterious Disappearance of John Terry mirrored no public event in British history so eerily as that author's eleven-day vanishing act in 1926 before turning up, without explanation, at a Harrogate hotel.

Yet perhaps this is unfair. More likely, Terry had been told shortly before kick-off that NATO had slapped an exclusion zone banning him and Matthew Upson from the centre of England's defence, and quite possibly the entire England half. At times, especially in the second half, he appeared to have left the pitch entirely, taking to a touchline lounger for a Solero ice lolly, perhaps, and a flick through the *Racing Post*. It is a small exaggeration to say that it would have made no difference to the outcome, and might even have improved things, had Fabio Capello replaced him at half time with Wee Jimmy Krankie. On its own merits, let alone weighing competence against reputation, this may have been the most abysmal individual performance in World Cup history.

Yet, unforgettable as this was, Terry will be remembered more for his off-pitch offences. The instant collapse of his one-man mutiny against Fabio Capello nicely illustrated the complementary character traits of aggressive egomania and rampant cowardice. The attempt to disguise the seething resentment about losing the captaincy in the rags of altruistic patriotic concerns fooled nobody.

How he came to hold the captaincy – a position rightly regarded as a great office of state, since it precisely replicates the duties and responsibilities of the regimental goat – would be a three-pipe mystery had the appointer concerned not been Steve McClaren. Anyone else might have recoiled from giving the job to a man who marked his arrival as a Premier League star by joining equally drunken team-mates in crudely taunting American tourists in a London hotel a few days after 9/11.

To that boorishness he was swift to add the sexual generosity (inviting a groupie into the back of his Bentley, allegedly to extend his largesse far beyond the signing of a match programme) that would eventually, via those twice-weekly trysts with former teammate Wayne Bridge's girlfriend, cost him the captaincy.

His other tabloid triumphs include the ostentatious blowing of £13,000 in a few hours in a Surrey Coral's in the company of that same Mr Bridge, and an acquittal over charges resulting from injuries sustained by a nightclub bouncer. When, knowing all this, Mr McClaren announced his captaincy pick by proclaiming: 'I'm certain I've got the right man in John Terry,' he was in a narrow sense correct. If there is an unwritten expectation placed on anyone appointed as a national leader, that must be to represent and reflect those being led. Who better, you will ask, to do so on behalf of the English professional footballer than a man well known as a boozer, gambler, brawler and cuckolder? To this extent, he was to the England footballer what Churchill's defiance was to the East Ender standing outside the smoking husk that had been her home, smiling bravely for the cameras of Pathé News. He personified as well as anyone ever has the sovereign belief that to be young, obscenely rich and worshipped for playing football is to receive an access-all-areas pass to instant gratification.

John Terry, roaring lion of Stamford Bridge and toothless tiger of England, was for a decade the leading paradigm of all that was most repellent in the Premier League as it hurried its descent into the Eurotrash can of sporting life. The sadness – for us, you suspect, rather more than for him – is that when given the chance to justify the bizarre national fascination with his private endeavours with a public display of central defending, he excused himself from the fray and allowed the Germans to invade English territory unchallenged. Some Churchill.

17

Pete Sampras

Give a monkey a typewriter and infinite time, the old saw posits, and eventually he will type the complete works of Shakespeare. Give a baboon a tennis racket and a mere dozen years, the modern fact relates, and he will become the most successful player in tennis history.

If Pete Sampras was never as 'myriad-minded as Shakespeare' (see Simon Barnes, no. 98), he was, until Roger Federer emerged to displace him, the holder of the all-time record for major titles with fourteen. The oddity is that, despite so immense an achievement, you can't shrug off the feeling that Sampras missed his true vocation. Had he joined the CIA at nineteen, rather than becoming the youngest US Open champion, the outsourcing of interrogation to electrode-wielding Syrians would never have been required. Half an hour in his company, recoiling as that tongue flopped down in the familiar great ape manner, and the operative known to his al-Qaeda chums as Hassan the Unbreakable would have begged for a copy of *The Bin Laden Rough Guide to Hindu Kush Hideaways* and a marker pen.

Seldom has sport known such a chasm between stellar success and the pleasure it provided. The two were in such dramatically inverse proportion to one another that the Sampras age felt like tennis's answer to O'Brien's vision of the future ('imagine a boot stamping on a human face – forever') in Orwell's *Nineteen Eighty-Four*.

Watching this genetic throwback crush opponents with mechanical joylessness raised the mental image of a bunch of Tokyo's leading artificial-life scientists wondering how he could have snuck through quality control with the emotions microchip unactivated. If the same might have been said of Bjorn Borg, in fact the Swede was always Vulcan in *Star Trek* terms, using the glacial persona to subjugate the violent feelings bubbling beneath. Sampras took the part of the android Lieutenant Commander Data.

His fans might argue that huge servers are invariably a shade boring to behold, and they'd have a point. Watching Roscoe Tanner or Goran Ivanisevic was never entrancing. Even so, Tanner had the good grace to forge a second career as a crook, doing a bit of bird for passing dud cheques, while Ivanisevic was never less than engagingly loopy on court and, rather more, off it.

Sampras, on the other hand, was constructed on the Steve Davis blueprint, but without the self-parodic charm the Nugget came to develop. From that ruthlessly reliable serve-and-volley game to the taking of the Colgate-TV-commercial wife, here was a man who cleaved to rigid predictability like a toddler to a comfort blanket.

His claims to have pre-empted Federer to the title of tennis's GOAT (greatest of all time) were always less persuasive than they seemed. For one thing, Sampras was blessed by the timing of his birth. Had he been born a decade earlier, the competition would have included Borg, Jimmy Connors, John McEnroe and Ivan Lendl. A decade later, and he'd have run into Federer himself, as well as Rafael Nadal. His one genuine long-term rival, Andre Agassi, was never a threat on Wimbledon courts so fast and low-bouncing back then that they rendered grass-court tennis a form of hypnosis. Meanwhile, his efforts on clay were, as one sage put it, 'like sumo wrestling on ice'. His failure to reach a single French Open final highlights the versatility of all the above-mentioned, who reached Grand Slam finals on all surfaces.

It is due only to the shameful laxity of tennis's regulations that he ever won anything at all. Were the sport properly regulated, the opening point of each match would have obliged the umpire to announce: 'Code violation, tongue hanging down, warning Mr Sampras.' A penalty point, a penalty game and disqualification would have ensued before the first changeover.

Sampras cannot be held accountable for the ATP's refusal to police the game adequately, but he can and must be blamed for keeping to himself every iota of the joy he claims to have felt on winning major titles, and for imbuing a decade of men's tennis with the visceral excitement of a call centre on the outskirts of Arbroath dedicated to handling complaints about malfunctioning colostomy bags.

What little we know of the private Sampras was only recently revealed by the man he beats in this book's rankings as he did for so long in tennis. In his lively autobiography, Agassi reminisces about Sampras tipping a Los Angeles car valet to the tune of one dollar. 'I envy Pete's dullness,' he went on, dipping a delicate toe into the pond of irony. 'I wish I could emulate his spectacular lack of inspiration.' No one, not even Ivan Lendl, ever has, and God willing no one will.

16

Harald 'Toni' Schumacher

Anyone shocked to the verge of an ague by Nigel de Jong's kung-fu kick on Xavi Alonso's chest in the World Cup final of 2010, and mystified by referee Howard Webb's leniency in showing only a yellow card, cannot have seen or must have forgotten the source of this German goalkeeper's infamy. On reflection, it has to be the former. No one who witnessed Schumacher's attack on France's Patrick Battiston in the 1982 World Cup semi-final could forget it without a helpful nudge from Alzheimer's. To this day, it remains hard to identify precisely in terms of the English criminal law: a sweet-natured prosecutor might have gone for GBH, a flintier one for attempted murder.

With the match tied at 1–1 when Battiston was put through on goal by a typically exquisite Michel Platini pass, Schumacher charged out of his area to intercept him. This, to his credit, he did. Less to his credit, Battiston had already sent the ball the wrong side of the post by the time Schumacher launched a curiously hybrid challenge melding elements of cage-fighting with an *outré* manoeuvre from surrealist modern ballet. The goalkeeper raised both arms, propelled himself into the air like a longjumper leaving the board, twisted his body sideways in flight and slammed into Battiston's windpipe with his hip.

Mr Webb may take comfort for his indulgent handling of de Jong from the memory that the referee in the 1982 match, the Dutchman Charles Corver, showed Schumacher no card at all. Bizarrely, he couldn't even rouse himself to give France the minuscule consolation of a free kick, awarding West Germany a goal kick. Most observers felt that this fell tantalisingly short of what strict justice required: a call to Interpol and the removal of Schumacher, long before extra time and the subsequent penalty shootout, to a cell in The Hague.

What elevated Schumacher's efforts to a crime against humanity was his response. While Battiston lay chillingly still on the turf, with his French colleagues taking him for dead on the admittedly fanciful grounds that, as Platini later put it, 'he had no pulse', the German stood by his goalpost waiting to take the goal kick as if congratulating himself on his heroic patience. As the paramedics gave Battiston oxygen, he affected not the vaguest concern. Had somebody closed Battiston's eyes, lifted a blanket over his head and intoned, 'Time of death, 4.32 p.m.' into a tape recorder, Schumacher would have shrugged and muttered something about typical French malingering. And possibly lit a cigar.

All that said, it would be wrong to suggest that he sustained this indifference to the near-fatality his spite had provoked. When told later that Battiston had not only suffered severe damage to his vertebrae (he did not play again for more than a year), but also lost two front teeth in the assault, he did, to his eternal credit, dredge up the contrition lacking on the pitch. 'If that's all that's wrong with him,' said Schumacher, 'I'll pay for the crowns.' All heart.

Although he insists to this day that the challenge was fair and that he was attempting to get the ball, Schumacher later ground out an apology through the most heavily gritted of teeth, and this Battiston graciously accepted. Four years later the countries met again in another World Cup semi-final, and while the Frenchman nobly claimed that the incident was 'forgiven and forgotten', he faintly undermined the latter half of that Jesusy sentiment by adding that he intended to keep a minimum distance of forty metres between himself and Schumacher at all times. In fact he didn't. With the Germans leading 1–0 late in the game, he had a chance to equalise from close range. This moment of cathartic retribution at hand, inevitably the ball struck Schumacher's legs and bounced to safety, allowing West Germany to break and score again.

The one tiny shard of justice to emerge from this amorality tale is this: the only thing for which Schumacher is remembered, and ever will be, is miraculously coming closer to committing homicide with his hip than his namesake (see Michael Schumacher, no. 19) has yet managed with a Formula One car. Whether that disturbs him, who but he can say? All one can do is recall the sight of the mustachioed poster boy for deranged German arrogance lolling about near his post while Battiston seemed to be dead, and make a wild guess.

15

Kevin Pietersen

The irony about Pietersen's claims to Britishness, about which he seems as sceptical as anyone else, is this: for all the suspicion about the speedy Zola Budd-esque switch, he has proved his commitment to his adoptive country beyond all doubt. There is a grand tradition whereby young British men emerge into the international sporting arena as the finished, world-class article, even as Athena sprung fully formed from the head of Zeus, and then fizzle out. Michael Owen is one leading example, while Wayne Rooney's international career seems to be taking the same trajectory of the vertical lift-off swiftly followed by the corkscrew spin down to earth. Andy Murray, it breaks the heart to observe, may be on a similar if less dramatic flightpath.

Pietersen, unlike the above, was no teenager when he announced himself as a generational talent in the Ashes series of 2005, though at twenty-five he was still a toddler in Test cricket terms. Whatever the reason for the nationality swap from South African, his debut series was magnificent primarily, though not solely, for his Ashes-winning 158 in the final Test at The Oval. Made under pressure as intense as any cricketer can ever have experienced, it may stand as the greatest maiden century in Test history. England had chanced upon the most naturally gifted attacking batsman in a decade, and his subsequent achievements in becoming the fastest man ever to reach 1,000 and 2,000 one-day runs and to amass 5,000 in Test matches seemed little more than the *amuse-bouches* for a glorious banquet to follow. And then the fizzling began.

Half a decade later, he appears to have sacrificed his potential to challenge for a place in the All Time Test XI, or at least the squad of twenty-two, on the altar of his egomania. Signs of the narcissistic profligacy that has at times made him a Test match irrelevance, and even cost him his Twenty20 berth, come and go. Every now and again, he reminds us of his greatness, as with a quite majestic double hundred against India in the summer of 2011. But the cockiness, the brusqueness, the self-adoration and the thoughtless shot selection (he might have been out seven times en route to that Oval 158) have not vanished, nor have the doubts over the true motivation for his switch from one country to another. He claimed it was in principled protest at the black and coloured quota system that was keeping him out of the South African team. Those who suspected more mercenary grounds have seen nothing to disabuse them since.

Of Pietersen's short stint as England Test captain, little need be said. If those who appointed him had forgotten the precedent of Ian Botham (see no. 42), and failed to understand that the self-obsessive qualities essential for individual brilliance do not lend themselves to the thoughtfulness required to lead others, that was not Pietersen's fault. To you and me, it may seem obvious that making your star performer captain is a reliable recipe for a bad captain and an ex-star player desperately out of form. However, you and I tend not to be England selectors or chairmen of the England and Wales Cricket Board.

Anyway, just as with Steve McClaren and his England job, you cannot blame a man for failing to know his own limitations. Pietersen's conceit inevitably led to a personality clash with a coach, Peter Moores, for whom he couldn't find the strength to disguise his contempt. The two were simultaneously sacked, and that was that. The surprise, to Pietersen's credit, is that he didn't walk away from the side in dudgeon, although with hindsight it might have been better for all concerned had he done a Kevin Keegan queeny flounce.

What he did instead was throw away the potential to become one of Test cricket's all-time greats. Watching a man of such preposterous natural talent devote himself to Twenty20 self-enrichment has brought to mind the notion of Van Gogh, at the height of his powers, anachronistically electing to model his work on that of Jack Vettriano.

That Pietersen's first foray into the Indian Premier League led to the injury that ruled him out of almost the entire Ashes series of 2009 seemed an indecently cute potted commentary on the warped priorities of both him and of cricket itself. He has become a disappointment like few in memory, and an embarrassment to the country he loves so deeply that he left South Africa for its glorification.

That, at least, is what he would have us believe. Those who doubt that he'd be on the first plane to Harare with a passport application in his pocket if Robert Mugabe offered him £1 million to become Zimbabwean are directed to an interview he gave *GQ* magazine not so long ago.

'Do you get weird fan mail?' asked the interviewer.

'Yeah, pictures of girls with their tits out.'

'That's outrageous.'

'I know,' agreed Pietersen with a snigger. 'But look, it's your nation, not mine.'

Precisely.

Whether Pietersen would have shown more application and commitment had he stayed in South Africa and defied that quota to become a fixture in its Test side we will never know. Perhaps the lure of easy money would have been resistible had he played for a country to which he felt emotionally bonded. More likely, perhaps, contemplating the Olympian self-regard (his interview persona reminds me of Hollywood stars with contractual clauses dictating that no crew member may look them in the eye), he would have succumbed to the temptation of the Indian Premier League all the same.

The solitary benefit to emerge from Pietersen's involvement in that cattle auction has been the most exquisitely perfect nickname in sport. One Indian headline-writer, tiring of him relentlessly throwing away his wicket with insanely stupid strokes in the cause of personal wealth, called him 'Dumb Slog Millionaire'. He will need quite a few more double centuries in Test cricket to avoid warranting that as the inscription on his gravestone.

14

Mark Lawrenson

For all but the most determinedly overgrown of schoolboys, the jettisoning of adolescent ambition is an unavoidable stage in male development. Reluctantly, at forty-six, and despite still enjoying the odd fantasy, I have come to accept that I will never win the Premier League for Spurs with a forty-five-yard Roberto Carlos-style free kick, take the unified world middleweight title with a controversial split decision over Marvelous Marvin Hagler in the car park of the MGM Grand, or conclude a maiden Test appearance by taking 9 for 27 (with a mixture of pace, swing, off breaks and leg spin) against the Australians in Melbourne.

So by what preternatural act of will does Mark Lawrenson sustain the conviction that if he just ploughs on long enough, a grateful nation will acclaim him football punditry's answer to Mark Twain? Even at the Algonquin Round Table *de nos jours* that is the *Match of the Day* studio, ranged against the comedic might of Gary Lineker and Alan Hansen, he comes a distant third. If Supersonic Sid Little joined the panel, Lawrenson would be fourth. Stick Margaret Beckett on the sofa and he'd limp in fifth. Indeed, it's hard to imagine the *MOTD* pundit capable of lifting him off the bottom spot. An aggressive pancreatic tumour in a Perspex box might do it. You could argue that one both ways.

Yet the man whose one and only comedic success story ended the day he shaved off the disco queen moustache still labours under the belief that he is football's Dorothy Parker. In fact, he is and will always remain its David Brent.

As with his Wernham Hogg role model, it is often hard to discern whether Lawrenson's misfiring attempts are rooted in nastiness or foolishness. A recent comment on *Football Focus*, when he suggested to Garth Crooks that he would struggle to gain entry to South Africa for the World Cup, hints darkly at both, though there is a less unkind explanation. Typically, comedians remain trapped in the era when they broke through. In the 1990s I saw Ken Dodd on stage, leaving some two hours later when, almost a third of the way through his set, Doddy unleashed a zinger about Harold Wilson's Lavender List. Until his death a few years ago, Bernard Manning was still cracking gags about Sid Vicious and the Cresta bear. Perhaps, then, it's understandable if Lawro finds himself stuck in the late 1970s, when apartheid was all the rage and he was doubtless delighting the Liverpool dressing room with a waggery that seems a touch out of its place and time today.

There is an admirable side to Lawro. In recent years his work as a match summariser has seen him handle the role of John Motson's carer, subtly correcting his more egregious errors and gently steering him away from the more obvious commentary cul-de-sacs, with surprising sensitivity.

Yet elsewhere an underlying edge of casual cruelty is often as palpable as the inverse proportion between the effort invested in a gag and the mirth it induces. 'He was more "Take aim" than Ben Haim' sticks in the memory, if only because it's touch and go whether it even technically qualifies as a pun. Conversely, at least for graduates of Colemanballs Studies, his spontaneous efforts can be unintentionally droll. 'Ireland will give 99 per cent … everything they've got,' seemed refreshingly understated in an era when 110 per cent has become an emblem of dilettantism. 'You need at least eight or nine men in a ten-man wall' confirmed why he never applied for the vacancy when Carol Vorderman left *Countdown*.

What the Eeyore of football punditry would be like were he not sufficiently aware of his gamma-male status to be subdued in the presence of Alan Hansen doesn't bear contemplating. For all that, was David Brent ever quite so nauseating as when dancing in the shadow of Chris Finch?

13

Audley Harrison

If few heavyweights since Muhammad Ali have talked a better fight than Audley, fewer still have fought a sequence of worse ones. Next to the chasm in class between this leisure management graduate's mouth and his fists, the Grand Canyon is a crack in a paving stone.

Audley's courage in defying the endless ridicule that has attended his professional career festoons him with credit. Had he shown the same resilience and willingness to endure pain in the ring, he might have challenged Rocky Marciano's unbeaten record.

I was in the Sydney boxing arena the night he won his Olympic superheavyweight gold, and the consensus among the hacks present was that he had the talent to succeed in a laughably weak weight division. What no one could have predicted was that losing the amateur's protective headguard would affect him much as the removal of stabilisers affects the four-year-old yet to master cycling. Down he went again and again, in the estimation of the public if not always to the canvas.

After turning pro, his gift for self-promotion earned a £1 million ten-fight deal with the BBC, but long before it expired his reputation was lying on the pavement, knees bleeding, crying for its mummy.

The tantalising thing is that he appears to have just the two minor failings: an aversion to being hit, and a disinclination to hit others. Although the combination hints at a commendable grasp of Christ's injunction not to do unto others what you'd rather they didn't unto you, one can't help feeling that moral objections to a sport predicated on the infliction of brain damage are better expressed by opponents of boxing than by those taking money to box.

This pacifism, though splendid in other contexts, has played its part in earning him the three nicknames that must suffice as his reward in the absence of a title belt. Between them, the trinity of 'A-Farce', 'Fraudley' and 'Audrey' capture the mixture of con-man, big girl's blouse and shambolic underachiever.

Picking the precise moment at which the towel should have been thrown in on his career isn't easy in so fearsomely crowded a field. But perhaps pride of place goes to the February night in 2007 on which he contrived to walk into a sucker punch thrown by the statuesque Michael Sprott, a delightful chap from Reading flattered by the term 'journeyman', and with the mobility of a geriatric ox with rheumatoid arthritis.

Heroically impervious to the jeers that night, Audley soldiered on, his tenacity finally rewarded with a world championship bout with David Haye. Keen to avoid either of the Klitschko brothers for as long as possible, Haye prefers to enrich himself in the meantime at zero risk to his physical and financial health. The best of British luck to Audley with that fight. Should he somehow win it (as he very well might, so long as he has the foresight to hire a sniper), or indeed survive beyond round five, my humblest apologies for doubting him.

Until that biblical miracle unfolds, the fact remains that not since Noah glanced up at the skies on day twenty-four of the flood and told his missus, 'It's clearing up, girl, I'm sure of it. Now, where did you put the Ambre Solaire?' have human affairs known a more dazzling triumph of hope over experience than Audley Harrison's insistence on battling on in search of a world title. That quest – much like the heavyweight division itself, only more so – is a joke that had long ago delighted us enough.

12
Tim Henman

Curiously enough, it is not primarily for being Tim Henman that Tim Henman edges into the top dozen. Were he no more than a mildly irritating, faintly conceited, blithe, complacent and studiedly anodyne eternal prep-school boy from Oxfordshire, he would be lucky to rise above the mid-thirties.

What promotes him to a berth among the elite is his status as the leading emblem of Englishness in modern sporting history, and his uncanny gift for inducing self-loathing in those, like me, who cannot resist the lure of cheap patriotism when it comes to the playing of games.

Nothing crystallised this like the afternoon of 8 July 2001, the third of three consecutive days on which he and Goran Ivanisevic played their rain-delayed Wimbledon semi-final. On the Friday, Henman had come back from a set down to lead the adorably eccentric Croat two sets to one, taking the third 6–0 in a quarter of an hour, and standing a few minutes from reaching the final in the fourth when the rain drove them off court. On the Saturday, Ivanisevic took that fourth set, and when they resumed the next day, such was the tension that I took to the bath, leaving the door to the bedroom ajar so as to follow events solely by gauging the flow of points from the crowd reaction.

Such was my desperation to see a British player in a Grand Slam final that I was physically incapable of watching, lest someone I couldn't stand lost to someone I admired. As of course he did. For no sounder reason than holding the same passport, I and millions of others like me were shamed by tribal loyalty.

It wasn't Henman's fault that he provoked this avalanche of self-disgust. Of course it wasn't. Yet it's impossible not to resent him for his role of catalyst, unchanged one iota himself as he effected a gruesome psychochemical reaction in the rest of us – the Centre Court dummies who continued yelling 'Come on Tim!' long after he retired; the congregants on Henman Hill playing out the annual mystery play of disappointment; the hacks and broadcasters pitiably asking McEnroe and Becker and Cash year after year if this might be Henman's year, and gratefully taking them for serious rather than polite when they answered that it might; the wretches at home in their armchairs and baths making deals with gods in whom they didn't believe on behalf of a man on whom, were he aflame, they wouldn't have wasted a drop of urine.

Technically, it's hard to doubt that he had the sort of talent and all-court game which, had he been born in Australia, France or Spain (anywhere, really, but here), would have propelled him to a couple of Grand Slam titles. The one he unquestionably should have taken came late in his career, oddly on the red clay of Paris, much his least favourite surface. How he failed to do so pinpointed classical English frailty to perfection.

In the French Open of 2004 he had shown unwonted resilience by twice coming from two sets behind to reach the semifinal. There he faced the world's leading clay-courter of the moment, and hot ante-post tournament favourite, the Argentine Guillermo Coria.

As he would prove in the final, where he miraculously contrived to lose from a winning position to his obscure compatriot Gaston Gaudio, Coria was no paragon of mental strength himself. He buckled beneath the pressure at the start, and Henman's flawless serve-volley game saw him a set up and leading 3–1 with a break in the second. And then, needless to add, he collapsed and lost eleven games in a row. Had he jacked it in then, and dropped the fourth set, like the third, 0–6, it would have been less inexcusable. But no. In pursuit of maximising the torment, he revived himself, with help from the fawn-like Coria, and served for that fourth set at 5–4.

There are nine-year-old girls with serious muscular disorders who would, halfway through their second lesson with the club pro, have served with more pace and accuracy than a man more than once ranked number four in the world did then. He might as well have gone underarm. He was broken with ease, and there would, mercifully, be no more flattering to deceive. Echoing Stuart Pearce and Chris Waddle taking penalties to put England into a World Cup final they could hardly have lost, Henman cemented his reputation as the choker's choker. He looked at victory, and recoiled in abject terror. He was the Aristotelian ideal of English sport.

Since retirement he has become a central part of the BBC's Wimbledon coverage, where his adenoidal, faintly Estuarine twang picks up from where he left off on Centre Court by lending an additional layer of irksome blandness to a warehouse already overstocked with that commodity as it is. In punditry as on court, he lacks the sharpness and commitment of Greg Rusedski, who with a fraction of Henman's natural gifts reached a Grand Slam final (the US Open in 1997, where he lost to the enchanting Pat Rafter the day after Diana's funeral). Still, at least with Henman's opinionising, which shies away from trenchancy as if it were enriched uranium, there's none of that dismal sense of talent betrayed by character. He may safely be acquitted of the charge of not speaking his mind, after all, on the defence known to the criminal law as 'the doctrine of impossible intent'.

11
José Mourinho

On his first day at the psychiatric hospital, the new consultant walks into a ward and finds this fella sat up in bed with one arm tucked beneath his nightgown. 'Right then,' says the doctor, 'who are you supposed to be?' '*Supposed* to be, you fool?' says the patient. 'I'm Napoleon.' 'I see. And who told you that?' 'Jesus!' he says. And the fella in the next bed says: 'I never told you no such fucking thing.'

The compendium of stale northern club-comic gags is replete with references to those who confuse themselves with Christ, but until recently one thought this mental-illness stereotype to be as outmoded as those about the obese missus and the battle-axe mother-in-law. And then, on arriving in Milan as the new manager of Internazionale, José Mourinho told an interviewer: 'Even Jesus isn't loved by everybody.' In fairness, he was responding to the interviewer's observation that the difference between God and Mourinho is that God doesn't think He's Mourinho. But in every good joke lies a kernel of truth, and encapsulated in this vaudevillian exchange are the two qualities that make the Portuguese pretty boy as hard on the ear as he is easy on the eye.

Whether the delusional paranoia is more or less irksome than the rampant narcissism is a tough call, and probably an unnecessary one, since the two have a cosily symbiotic relationship. It is Mourinho's mystification at the failure of others to share his self-estimation, you suspect, that persuades him that any criticism can be motivated only by envy or malice.

Undoubtedly there is method in his madness. Creating a heightened sense of they're-all-out-to-get-us hysteria is a team-building tactic as old and hackneyed as the gag about the man who thinks he's Christ. The bunker mentality doesn't always pay off (I believe that ultimately Herr Hitler, for instance, found it a disappointment), but countless football coaches have successfully used the trick. With Mourinho, you suspect that this is one of those happy unions between business and pleasure – or if not pleasure, compulsion. This man genuinely believes that there is a global conspiracy against him, and no one would scream for the smelling salts were he to include among his enemies the Mossad, JFK's putative second assassin, the NASA mob who mocked up the moon landing in a TV studio and the Bilderberg Group, that sinister collation of plutocrats and their political hand puppets who meet each year in some forest to bond with communal peeing and primal screaming.

It goes without saying that Mourinho's ability as a coach, although primarily defensive, borders on genius. His record in three countries, in both domestic football and more remarkably in the Uefa Champions League, beggars belief. Thus far his efforts in a fourth, Spain, as manager of Real Madrid, where he has somehow scaled a new apex of deranged nastiness, have been dwarfed by the peerless achievements of Barcelona. Although there is no shame in this (the 1950s Hungarians and 1970 Brazilians could not have lived with Barca's brilliance), and for all the sporadic flashes of charm and wit, this eternal adolescent is a cholera on football. As graceless in victory as he's petulant in defeat, he has shamed himself time and again with the viciousness of his ravings, and the lack of even affected contrition when they have their desired effect.

Some of his paranoia-induced naughtiness has been comically trivial. A while ago, after Mourinho used a handcuffs gesture to hint with characteristic subtlety that the referee was shackled by bonds of loyalty to Inter's opposition of the day, the Italian authorities asked themselves the Dionne Warwick question. They concluded that they did indeed know the way to ban José, and excluded him from the touchline for three games.

Other offences have been less banal. Memorably odious was his taunting of Arsène Wenger as 'a voyeur'. Mourinho cannot have been unaware of the disgusting false rumours to which Wenger is still subjected by the *chanteurs* of opposing teams, or of the word's sexual connotations. However preposterous Wenger's overreaction to a taunt that anyone vaguely normal would imperiously have ignored, the Portuguese's subsequent wide-eyed profession of ignorance fooled nobody, his little boy's pants-on-fire winsomeness having lost whatever appeal it had long before.

Yet nothing has exposed the scale of his derangement like the case of Anders Frisk, the Swedish referee Mourinho suggested spoke, in some nebulously dodgy manner, with Barcelona coach Frank Rijkard during half time of the first leg of Chelsea's 2005 Champions League tie. The Chelsea fan base is not the most genteel, and the neo-Nazi death threats against Mr Frisk were predictable, if not inevitable, from the moment he was accused of corruption. Mourinho demonstrated his repentance for this poisonous accusation when Uefa banned him from subsequent games by sneaking into the dressing room hidden in a laundry basket. Even when Mr Frisk galloped into retirement at twice the speed of his Grand National-winning namesake, Mourinho offered no hint of regret.

Paranoia, egomania and a gift for management are hardly unfamiliar footballing bedfellows. Brian Clough, to whom Mourinho has routinely been compared, was another product of that *ménage à trois*. Among the distinctions between them, however, isn't merely that Cloughie had the vodka bottle for an excuse for the lunacies that marked his latter years, but that he was always fiercely intolerant of the petulance and histrionics Mourinho did nothing to discourage. Cloughie, who would have thrown Didier Drogba and Arjen Robben out of Nottingham Forest by the earlobes for their diving, was never less than a purist. Mourinho, for all his undeniable brilliance, will never be more than a cynic, and the 'enemy of football' of Uefa's description.

10

The Henman Parents

Long before Botox came the Henman Parents. By the force of their personality alone (and I find that it helps to think of them as a single entity), and with no need for botulinum-based serum injections, their faces were immovably frozen for a decade and more as they gazed down upon their lad on Wimbledon's Centre Court.

No one has ever won a sponsorship deal for watching sport, so far as I know, and no one now ever may. If it didn't happen when Jane and Tony Henman's Players' Box presence was as fixed a feature of the Season as Royal Ascot and Henley, with a purveyor of choicest embalming fluid paying them to have the company slogan 'You'd Die To Look Like This!' tattooed on their foreheads, the odds must be that it never will.

If Tim hit a screeching forehand cross-court winner on match point, they stared impassively down. If he lost a crucial tie-break by netting a backhand volley the late Margaret Rutherford would have instinctively punched away, down they impassively stared. Had Tim called over a ball boy during the changeover and instructed him to replace the Robinson's barley water with a crack pipe and a couple of crystals, impassively and down is how they would have stared.

In all the years they sat there watching their issue torture this country with his rich talent betrayed by mental infirmity, nothing penetrated their icy detachment. Had the tournament referee walked out, ashen and solemn, to announce that a nuclear warhead hijacked by terrorists had left its silo in Turkmenistan and was due on Centre Court in twenty-three minutes, Tony might have glanced impatiently at his watch and muttered something Blimpish about the folly of trusting the punctuality of anything from the former Soviet Union, while Jane rang the vicar's wife to excuse herself from flower-arranging duty on Saturday evening. But I doubt it. More likely, they'd have sat there, silently, staring impassively down.

The only recorded evidence I can locate of any form of emotional engagement from the Henman Parents came a few years ago when their picturesque Oxfordshire village was threatened with a development of eco-friendly homes nearby, and they led the protests themselves, with Tim chipping in for good measure. And there lies a hint of their Nimbyish horror. Somewhere in those frozen faces – his the length of Nicolas Anelka's viewed through a fairground mirror; hers bringing to mind one of those glacial P.G. Wodehouse aunts who could open an oyster shell at a dozen paces with a single glance – lay contempt for all but those to whom I imagine them referring, in the dialect known as Sloanear B, as PLU (People Like Us). It wasn't merely on their boy whom they were looking impassively down, you felt, but on all of humanity. It was as if any show of feeling was the sort of indulgence not to be expected from provincial solicitors and their wives, and unforgivably common.

Somewhere in all this studied aloofness lay an echo of the historic problem with British, or rather English, tennis: the rigid determination of the professional middle classes who run the sport and control the clubs to keep it to themselves. Had the Williams sisters been born to farm labourers in rural Oxfordshire, the only things they'd have stood any chance of ever serving would have been accompanied by the question, 'Fries with that?'

Stiff-upper-lippery is fine in its place, of course, and can even be heroic. When Tim lost his best chance to reach a Wimbledon final in 2001, after rain prevented him finishing off Goran Ivanisevic in their semi, the Parents' stoicism did them credit. Had weather intervened when my son stood ten minutes from reaching a final against Patrick Rafter he'd have started favourite to win when the weather intervened, I'd have rent my garments like a Trojan widow and screamed, 'Why, why? Oh God, why?' at the heavens. Jane and Tony stared impassively down as the match was suspended, and again when it resumed with the inevitable outcome.

What was so offensive about this sporty pair – she a former junior tennis champ, he a keen hockey player reputed to tend towards the careless when other people's ankles come within range of his stick – is that they could no more celebrate the good times than mourn the bad. What possible point can there be to having children if you can't go crazy when they do something wonderful?

Six times their Tim reached a Grand Slam semi, and their mouths didn't rise by more than an aggregated 1/24th of an inch. Queen Victoria looked happier on the first anniversary of Albert's death than these ice monsters managed in almost fifteen years, and then with what was, even by her unfortunate menstrual standards, a peculiarly excruciating cycle.

And so, to those who snottily moan about Judy Murray going bananas when watching Andy, and allowing her shows of maternal emotion to leaven the sombreness of that *Prisoner: Cell Block H* warder's haircut, I offer these three words of rebuke: The Henman Parents.

9

Geoffrey Boycott

At a private-dining-club dinner in London about a decade ago, Geoffrey Boycott took to the stage for one of those chats with a broadcaster which buffers paying a couple of hundred quid a head expect with the brandies and, back then, Cuban cigars. Once Boycs had treated us to a typically self-effacing appraisal of his works, we in the audience were invited to put questions.

I'd had a few, and raised a hand. 'Do you think you might have made something of your cricketing career,' I asked him, a shade wearied by the boastfulness, 'if only you hadn't been so riven by self-doubt?' He looked a little stunned, but the ironic penny dropped and he quickly recovered to deliver a cogent and persuasive mini-lecture on the paramount importance of self-confidence for the sportsman.

Looking back, I wonder whether this facetiousness was as misguided as it was childish. Could the rampant egomania that defined Boycott's batting, and later his media work, actually be the mechanism of a genuinely self-doubting man to disguise his insecurities? With Boycott, unlike such other top-ranked narcissists as Didier Drogba and Kevin Pietersen (see no. 15), there's a sub-tone of desperation beneath the bombast and conceit, and a barely containable rage bubbling away under the surface, that hint at uncertainty.

Perhaps failing the 11-Plus explains it. Being almost arbitrarily written off as second rate so young does wicked things to a developing child, which is primarily why some of us on the woolly-minded, bleeding-heart liberal left regard the idea of adding more grammar schools to the few survivors as a retrograde anathema. Six decades after he failed the exam, it torments John Prescott to this day, and his filthy temper palpably stems from the intellectual insecurities, however misplaced, of a man with the words 'Don't you dare call me thick or I'll slap you in the chops' forever visible in the imaginary speech bubble above his head.

With Boycott, it's harder to be sure. Perhaps he failed the 11-Plus because he spent his every waking moment practising the forward defensive with his Yorkshire village mates, and didn't gave a damn which school he attended so long as it came with a cricket pitch attached. Or it could be that he was born a wildly conceited arse. If and when Professor Steve Jones gets round to answering the question I've been posing for fifteen years (if it really is all about genetics, how did we get from Sigmund Freud to Clement in two generations?), maybe he'd care to share his thoughts on Boycott.

The temper is every bit as filthy as Prescott's. There are times when he is summarising a cricket match (at which he is superb) or commentating on it (at which he is not) when some perceived idiocy pushes him close to apoplexy, and he sounds tempted to rip off the microphone and charge to the crease to give an errant batsman a slap.

Whether or not he did that, repeatedly, to his lover Margaret Moore in their bedroom at the £1,000-per-night Hôtel du Cap in Antibes (she was paying) one evening in 1996, we cannot be sure. Mrs Moore claimed that, enraged by her repeated demands for marriage, he held her to the floor and punched her some twenty times in the face. Boycott has always denied it, insisting that though he was infuriated by the nagging, he stormed out of the room, and that she did the damage to herself by falling to the floor.

The justice system of France twice sided with Mrs Moore, first in a trial which Boycott grandly declined to attend, and then, despite his appearance, on appeal. All you can say with any confidence is that if a man can become ferociously cross about an overly defensive declaration, it isn't beyond imagining that he might lose his rag with an insistent would-be spouse, as those Gallic courts concluded.

Boycott by and large survived that episode, thanks partly to the ensuing throat cancer he appears to have licked. He coped with illness with unwonted dignity, in public at least, and the resultant sympathy persuaded broadcasters and newspapers which had initially dropped him like a stone to refer the dismissal to the third umpire of public opinion. It proved a more malleable appellate court than the one in France.

Those who work with him report that he has mellowed, and by more than his brush with mortality. Eventually, after many years of openly maintaining relationships with two women – 'They are both too important in my life. I am different from other men,' as he put it (and who would argue with that self-analysis?) – he married the one by whom he had been blessed with a daughter. He wasn't perhaps quite as ostentatiously thrilled as most of us would be on hearing he was about to become a father for the first time. 'Nobody made me as angry as Rachel,' he later recalled, 'when she told me she was going to have a baby. I just didn't want it, but rather than argue,' he went on, usefully underlining the innate restraint he insists precluded him from striking Mrs Moore, 'I walked away.' Once the child had put the nasteries of babyhood behind her, he selflessly deigned to enter her life, and the two are now believed to be close.

If he is indeed a less peevish, truculent and intolerable colleague than once he was, this may come as Pyrrhic consolation to those who remember him as a player, both in the dressing room and at the crease. His Olympian self-centredness saw him reinterpret cricket not as a team sport but as an individual game devoted solely to his own glory. One of the all-time great opening batsmen, he would have been greater still had he now and then deployed his stroke-making talent (and he had plenty, as a couple of savage one-day knocks revealed) in the cause of the group rather than obsessing about his batting average.

Where he might be remembered today for his unrivalled work ethic and powers of concentration, and a batting record of genuine magnificence over several decades, the memories for middle-aged buffers like myself revolve around entire summers spent in a semi-coma watching him take five hours over a chanceless 24; his refusal to play for England in the mid-1970s in umbrage at being passed over for the captaincy, a job in which he had been a monumental failure with Yorkshire; and a penchant for running out teammates at pivotal moments.

If he regards himself as a tremendous servant to club and country, the truth is that he made club and country a servant to him. He was the perfect representation of what is really going on in a football striker's head when he blethers about not caring about scoring so long as the team wins.

For all the above, it's hard not to hold a certain fondness for him. Any pundit who speaks his mind, let alone with the disdain for self-editing associated with the professional Yorkshireman, is a thing of beauty in a world where punches are remorselessly pulled in the boys' club of the commentary box. More than this, though, the bewilderment of the lonely child clings poignantly to him even now, at seventy, as it always did.

Few if any sportsmen in my lifetime have made as many enemies as Geoffrey Boycott. What he would be the last person to acknowledge, and perhaps to comprehend, is that the very worst of them was himself.

8

Sir Alex Ferguson

Glasgow's estimable gangland lost something special, you can't help suspecting even now in his dotage, the day the Govan shipyard worker plumped for a very mediocre career as a professional footballer. What a magnificent enforcer he would have made, this parfit gentil knight with the twin talents for demented raging for no apparent reason and the nursing of grudges. Swap the hairdryer for a knuckleduster or flick knife, and there isn't a goon on the Clyde – not even Mad Malchy 'Maddest of the Mad' McMadman, winner of the Joe Pesci Clockwork Clown for Murderous Overreaction at this year's McPsycho Awards bash at the Glasgow Hilton – who wouldn't hide under the table as the silhouette of that claret-reddened proto-W.C. Fields hooter imbued the drawn blinds with a roseate hue.

Perhaps I exaggerate a little. Ferguson, it must be admitted, has mellowed a little over recent years. His muted reaction to Manchester United's annihilation in the 2009 Champions League at Barcelona's hands hinted at a man who, pushing seventy, has almost learned how to be gracious in defeat. Such, perhaps, is the transformative power of gentrification on even the most deranged of souls.

And gentrified, to a degree that must startle his old shipyard workmates, Sir Alex has certainly become. Not since Brian Clough rode around Derby in the early seventies preaching Old Testament socialism from behind the wheel of a gold Rolls-Royce has football known a political paradox merchant in Ferguson's league. Sir Alex enjoyed the cosiest of relationships with New Labour, as the entries accorded to Mr Tony Blair (see no. 48) and Alastair Campbell (see no. 80) confirm. The claims of both – Blair that he picked Ferguson's brains about sacking Gordon Brown as Chancellor; Campbell that Ferguson regularly rang his Man-United-supporting teenage son to discuss team selection – come, as must any pronouncement from either, stamped with the traditional 'HazFib' warning. Even so, what with Sir Alex being a self-proclaimed lifelong leftie, there may be a shred of truth in the existence of these friendships, if not the finer detail. 'I am almost as passionate about politics as I am about football,' he wrote in the *Daily Mirror* shortly before the general election of 2005. 'I have never forgotten where I come from, or how fortunate I have been to get where I have …'

Well, that's how he sees it. Sir Alex's journey from the tenements of Glasgow to the royal enclosure at Ascot is a warming tale of meritocracy that would be warmer still but for the incident that perhaps captures him – the greed, the nastiness, the conceit and the demented arrogance – as well as any.

In 2003, Sir Alex hired lawyers over Rock of Gibraltar, one of history's greatest racehorses, in which he had been given a stake by the Irish racing plutocrat John Magnier and his business partner J.P. McManus, one of history's finest and most afeared punters.

At this point, it should be stated that the gift came with no strings attached. The fact that the Irishmen appeared to be sniffing around Manchester United at the time, possibly contemplating a hostile takeover bid, and that if this was so the adored manager's support would have been essential to its success, was the purest coincidence. Had it been anything else, searching questions might have been asked – by Manchester United, the Stock Exchange, and even maybe by a generally sycophantic football press – as to what an employee of a public company could be thinking in accepting such largesse from men possibly contemplating buying a controlling interest in that company against the wishes of the board.

Anyway, they allowed the horse to run in Ferguson's racing colours, and very sweetly gave him a half share in its winnings (some £600,000, all tax free) – quite an act of friendship from these splendid altruists, yet nothing like enough to sate the odious old bruiser. When in 2002 the horse was retired, having won a record seven consecutive Group One races, Sir Alex decided that his share in the Rock extended beyond the prize money. He was entitled, he felt, to half the income it generated at stud, a sum estimated at anything up to £40 million.

For once in his life, Ferguson found himself outgunned. Gigantic fish in his own pond though he is, he was a minnow up against a pair of blue whales in the ocean of contention that ensued, and all his bluster was pointless. The Irishmen seemed more saddened than enraged by his avarice, and after they had peppered Fergie's lawyers with intriguing technical questions about many transfers in which he had been involved – all entirely above board beyond doubt – the case was settled. They never did buy the club.

Perhaps a touch chastened by that humiliation, Sir Alex has never scaled such heights of rapacious monomania again. Although he continues his babyish boycott of the BBC, in retaliation for impertinent enquiries into the dealings of his football agent son Jason in a 2004 documentary, the toddler-tantrum rants at referees are more scarce. He hasn't repeated the shaving of David Beckham's eyebrows with a flying boot, and has even marginally downscaled his mission to castrate every England coach by denying him players for friendlies on such compelling injury grounds as a broken fingernail, a grazed Bentley wing-mirror or the faintest stirrings of pre-menstrual tension.

For all that, regardless of the cuddly old gramps figure he occasionally now plays, and despite very sporadic shows of affected humility, Alex Ferguson remains monumentally charmless living proof of the ancient axiom, which I've just this minute invented, that a man's success as a football manager will always lie in direct inverse proportion to that manager's success as a man.

7

Bernie Ecclestone

Even after decades of exposure to the Great Dictator of Formula One, it's hard to make sense of his existence as an organic life-form. The unlikely combination of that insane acrylic wig, the improbably wizened frame and the startling sprightliness for a man newly turned eighty suggest a Pixar trainee's first crack at an alarming yet oddly endearing human–bird hybrid with access to an elixir for the forthcoming blockbuster *Dorian Gray's Ugly Great-Uncle Goes to Jurassic Park*. Precisely how one such tiny man came to own one huge global sport remains a source of rich bemusement. Somewhere online, no doubt, is a cogent account of how he came by Formula One and the billions it has given him; but frankly, who has the strength to care when there is so much cheap merriment to be had at Little Bern's expense?

Of his annual efforts to make Grand Prix racing less tedious by tinkering with its arcane rules, scoring systems and technical specifications, all that need be said is that they invariably produce the reverse result. Every plan to produce more overtaking, for instance, produces less. If he'd had his way, and the title was awarded not on points at all but on the number of race wins, it would be over with eight races left in any season dominated in the manner stomach-churningly pioneered by the younger Michael Schumacher (see no. 19).

The most recent meisterplan to improve the sport was perhaps the best yet. Shortly before the start of the 2011 F1 season, Little Bern floated the idea of spraying 'artificial rain' – or, in English, 'water' – onto the track for ten laps in the middle or at the end of each race. Clearly he had a point. F1 only comes alive these days when drivers are aquaplaning through the air and at grave risk of death. Yet it was a point so riven with lunacy that it inspired one facetious dunce (me) to anticipate his proposal of, among others, the following innovations as well:

Sunday Drivers

Every twentieth lap, a fleet of twenty-four Morris Minor 1000s, each driven at no more than 13mph by pipe-smoking nonagenarians of the sort who make the outskirts of Bath such a weekend motoring joy, will join the race in a figure-of-eight formation. Any driver who attempts to overtake this formation will suffer a time penalty of twenty minutes behind the Safety Caravan, as occupied by Margaret Beckett and her husband Leo.

Potholes

Whenever a Toro Rosso or McLaren is leading, a circular gap in the tarmac, with a radius of no less than 4.5 metres, will be created on the blind side of the next chicane by a controlled detonation.

Penalty Notices

If any pit stop for new tyres and/or refuelling extends beyond 6.2 seconds, the team traffic warden will affix a parking ticket to the windscreen. The driver may not leave the pit lane until he has rung a call centre and paid the fine by credit or debit card. Diners' Club will not be acceptable.

The Libyan Grand Prix

Mr Ecclestone will strike a deal with Colonel Gaddafi for this exciting addition to the calendar. Held on the streets of central Tripoli, this will conclude after seventy-five laps or when eighteen drivers have been wounded by rebel gunfire. In accordance with Mr Ecclestone's stated preference for dictatorship over democracy, drivers tear-gassed by troops loyal to Colonel Gaddafi will be deducted 50 per cent of any championship points previously won.

Professor Pat Pending

The mad scientist from *Wacky Races* will join each race on lap twenty-two, with his Convert-A-Car 3 transformed at two-lap intervals into the following: a bouncy castle, a scimitar the height of Nelson's column, Mount Rushmore, and a giant, glowing ball of weapons-grade plutonium. Penelope Pitstop may also race, although only the wrong way round the track and in a Sauber. She may not use her Compact Pussycat 5, the retractable lipstick device failing to conform to current specifications.

Temporary Blindness

Between laps twenty-five and thirty-three, drivers who started from an odd position on the grid (pole, third, etc.) will be rendered sightless by a film of treacle caused to dribble down their helmets by remote control, and solidified by a blast of liquid nitrogen from a canister sited within the steering wheel. Unsighted drivers may take team guidance over their radios, but any instructions as to steering must be given in ancient Etruscan.

In Bernie's defence, albeit that he is responsible, Formula One's primary function is medicinal. In an episode of *House MD*, Hugh Laurie's Vicodin-addicted diagnostician treats a woman driven to death's door by ten sleepless days and nights. The entire premise of the series, that House is a rampant genius, falls apart when he fails to treat her on admission with a tape of the first Grand Prix of 2010 from China.

If the dullness of the racing places pressure on Little Bern to compensate by providing off-track entertainment – and not merely with the annual ritual of the insane publicity-seeking innovation that comes to nothing – to this challenge he rises majestically. In 1997, his £1 million bribe to New Labour to reverse its policy to ban cigarette advertising came close to destroying Mr Blair's premiership in its earliest infancy – a heroic near-miss, many might think, though hardly Little B's intention at the time.

His next important foray into the geopolitical arena came when defending his friend Max Mosley, then the president of F1's governing body the FIA (and excluded from this book through sympathy for a start in life in which both his parents were interned within his first month). Mr Mosley would make 'a super Prime Minister', declared Bernie soon after those false Nazi fetish allegations were first aired, before adding a refreshingly original insight into the man his chum's parents so richly admired. 'Apart from the fact that Hitler got taken away and persuaded to do things that I have no idea whether he wanted to do or not,' declared this underrated modern historian, 'he was able to get things done.' On this intriguingly novel portrayal of the Führer as a weak-willed dupe so far as the Holocaust was concerned, if otherwise a paradigm of strong leadership, Little Bern was pleased to expand. 'If you have a look at democracy,' he added, 'it hasn't done a lot of good for many countries, including this one.'

Boldly eschewing Denis Healey's advice about holes and the time to cease digging, he then responded to the World Jewish Congress's demand that he resign from his position as F1 global overlord with startling versatility. First he apologised, with all the crushing sincerity of Hughie Greene praising a palsied spoons-player on *Opportunity Knocks*, for having been 'an idiot'. He then underlined his freshly minted pro-Semitic credentials by observing, of the Jewish people and the 2008 global financial meltdown, 'It's a pity they didn't sort the banks out. They have

253

a lot of influence everywhere.' So much for the Tel Aviv Grand Prix. Farewell the aborted embryo of Gefilte Racing.

On the other side of the PC-gone-mad balance sheet, having said all that, Bernie has long been in the vanguard of neo-feminist thinking. 'You know, I've got one of those wonderful ideas,' replied the Andrea Dworkin *manqué* when asked about female motor-racing drivers. 'Women should be dressed in white like all the other domestic appliances.' Why he was divorced by Slavica, a foot taller than him at six feet two inches, and in the Mrs Merton 'What first attracted you …?' sense quite the Debbie McGee to his Paul Daniels, we will never know.

That must have come as a grievous blow to Little Bern, but rather than retire to his bunker with the revolver, he chose to follow the teachings of the distastefully democratic Winston Churchill and kept buggering on. He will do so, one suspects, until the elixir runs dry. God willing, that day won't dawn for many years. Without its Great Dictator and the endless mirth he generates, what possible point to Formula One could there be?

6

The Offside Rules of Rugby Union

The consolation for those of you who have spent decades in the futile quest to comprehend when and why an egg-chaser is or is not offside is that you are in excellent company. There are international referees of twenty years' standing who are precisely as baffled as the rest of us, and award penalties on an entirely arbitrary basis.

For here is sport's closest answer to Mornington Crescent, the game played on Radio 4's *I'm Sorry I Haven't a Clue* in which Barry Cryer, Graeme Garden and the others spout gibberish about the consummately arcane rules concerning fictitious journeys on the London Underground. New listeners to the show tend to be mystified by the panelists' and audience's appreciation of the infinitely complex nuances, until finally the penny drops. The joke, in its entirety, is that there are no rules at all. Everything is made up on the spot, for no more compelling reason than to confuse the outsider.

So it is in rugby, with one minor difference: the rules of offside do appear to exist, if their Wikipedia entry is any guide. Even so, they make half as much sense as Mornington Crescent.

Insofar as my researches have produced any dividends, I am pleased to offer this helpful guide in easy-to-follow bullet-point form.

- When a side is in possession, a player is offside if a) he is in front of the ball carrier; b) he receives a pass or collects a kick from a teammate with a birthday in October, January or May; and c) he regards *The Big Lebowski* as the Coen brothers' finest movie.

- That player shall be deemed onside, however, regardless of the above, if he is obstructed by an opponent who has been on holiday to Thailand or Laos within the last five years. The referee will ask to check said player's passport for immigration stamps. Failure to provide the passport will, for the purposes of offside, constitute an admission that he has not.
- In open play, a player can become onside, so long as he is retreating when receiving a kicked ball, if he is passed by the original kicker or another player on his side who was behind the ball at the time of the kick, and if a Boeing 777 has been sighted overhead within the previous twelve minutes.
- However, if an Airbus 380 has also been sighted during that period, the player will be deemed offside unless his zodiac sign features a living creature other than a bull.
- In any other part of play (scrums, rucks or mauls), players are offside if they are in front of the offside line. This is an imaginary line parallel to the Equator which runs through the hindmost foot of the hindmost player in the scrum/maul/ruck. However, if a player who would otherwise be offside performs a triple salchow after the fashion of Robin Cousins, and yells 'Archimedes!' at the point of landing, he shall be deemed onside.
- At a line-out, only players in the line, a receiver and a thrower from each team are permitted within five metres of the line, and will be deemed offside if they encroach unless they are wearing a prime number on their shirt and had a chicken bhuna with pilau rice and a brinjal bhajji within the previous week. A keema nan, although strongly advised by the RFU (Rugby Football Union), is for the purposes of this rule regarded as an optional extra. Mango chutney, on the

other hand, will cause the player to be deemed offside regardless.

- If a player kicks the ball out of hand from the dead ball area, players can be in front of the kicker and remain onside as long as they do not leave the dead ball area before the ball has been kicked, can recite the first chorus of Bonny Tyler's 'Total Eclipse of the Heart' verbatim, and have a phobia of Hazel Blears, as certified by two independent psychiatrists.

That, by and large, is that, and I hope it helps. There is something called the 'Experimental law variations', which you can read up on yourselves if the fancy takes you. According to a spokesman for the Lucasian Professor of Mathematics, Stephen Hawking was planning to devote his next magnum opus to deconstructing these particularly enigmatic variations, but has reluctantly concluded that building a time machine would be less demanding.

5

Arsène Wenger

Never in the field of British public life have so many taken so long to rumble one distempered Alsatian. For almost a decade after Arsène Wenger became the manager of Arsenal, he was almost universally celebrated for what the media chose to see in him rather than for what he was. Bamboozled by the haughty, beaky-nosed aspect of an Oxford don, the press portrayed the lunatic as the Premier League professor, an aloof yet good-natured philosopher-king.

The truth was always otherwise. If the early glories he brought to Arsenal smoothed the more abrasive edges, he would eventually be revealed to all as every bit as unhinged as Alex Ferguson. In fact, Wenger's ego may be the larger and more uncontrollable of the two. Where Ferguson is an arch pragmatist, ever ready to change personnel and stratagems when circumstances demand, Wenger's obstinacy has visited years of comparative failure on his club and its fans. He will change nothing, ostensibly from an overwhelming purist commitment; but really, as we have come to see, from an unshakable faith in his own flawlessness.

That the man is a coach of genius few would deny. His teams produce exquisite football, and his eye for affordable young foreign talent is unmatched. Aesthetics alone win nothing but admiration, however, and even that has faded as his refusal to balance the flair of his babes in arms with grizzled experience has become less a point of principle than a form of self-harm on nose-cutting, face-spiting lines.

The difference between Arsenal's perennial near-misses and tangibly metallic success has been the couple of experienced, stress-hardened twenty-eight-year-olds he has adamantly refused to bring in. His approach to football management appears to have been modelled directly on the Charge of the Light Brigade, which drew from Marshal Bosquet the judgement: '*C'est magnifique, mais ce n'est pas la guerre.*'

Noxiously bubbling away beneath the professorial façade, meanwhile, and too often bubbling over, is the three-year-old throwing a tantrum in the confectionery aisle of Tesco. There is no more graceless and infantile loser in English football, which is saying something, and the charge sheet of touchline outbursts at rivals is long and humiliating. The self-pitying post-match whining is more so, that fabled ocular deficiency more so still, and the staggering dearth of self-awareness perhaps most of all.

If one incident captures all of the above, it came in April 2006 during a north London derby at White Hart Lane, with Arsenal and Spurs locked in combat for the fourth and final Champions League spot. When Spurs took the lead with two Arsenal players prostrate in their own half, Wenger was sent berserk, by the belief that not only should Spurs have put the ball out of play, but that their manager Martin Jol had been honour-bound to compel them to do so, presumably by telepathic communication, from his dugout.

Having squared up to the droll Dutchman, necessitating the involvement of peacekeeping stewards, he refused to shake hands at the end of the match, and then accused Jol of lying about not having seen the injured players. This, needless to spell out, from the man whose failure to see any misdemeanour committed by an Arsenal player had long since seen Arsène Wenger Disease listed in the *Dictionary of Ophthalmic Disorders* as 'An expedient form of temporary, selective blindness from which the sufferer will recover the moment it becomes convenient to do so.'

Myself, I blame this internal personality conflict – one minute the pure soul floating above the fray, the next a superannuated

259

version of the nineteen-year-old John McEnroe – on his birth-place. Growing up in the historically disputed province of Alsace-Lorraine, unsure from one week to the next whether he was French as his passport insisted, or German as his surname suggests – cannot have been easy for so fragile a psyche. If his way of resolving the conflict was a conscious decision to meld Teutonic arrogance and aggression with Gallic *froideur* and imperiousness, the combination is not a pretty one.

Chuck a portion of paranoia into this unlovely mix (his hysterical overreaction to José Mourinho's admittedly mischie-vous claim that Chelsea had compiled a dossier on him; see no. 11) and the question of beside which of him and Ferguson you'd prefer to be trapped on a flight fom London to Sydney becomes tricky.

On balance, I'd go for Fergie, who hints at the capacity to enjoy a joke, however crude and malevolent. Wenger, on the other hand, is humourless even beyond what might be expected from a Franco-German hybrid who in his sixties still spends every leisure moment studying tapes of football matches played elsewhere.

His level of obsessiveness is not unique among coaches, but other OCD sufferers can at least appreciate the absurdity of a grown man who can think of nothing but a game. Interviewed before the 1990 World Cup, for example, Argentina coach Carlos Bilardo spoke of a recent wedding he had attended. Milling about outside the church while the bride and groom and their families lined up for the photos, he grinningly recalled, he became increasingly anxious, until he could take it no longer. 'No, no, that's all wrong!' he heard himself shrieking at the photographer. 'For God's sake, put an extra man at the end of that wall!'

There's something endearing about the anecdote and the droll self-knowledge its telling suggest. Had Wenger been among the guests in Buenos Aires that day, far from being tickled by his own lunacy, he'd have harangued the best man, made the brides-maids cry and picked a fight with the photographer for not putting the priest on the end of the wall in the first place.

4

Alan Green

At school, a classics teacher told a story from his wartime days with the Indian Army to illustrate the central importance of what he knew as 'the words of command' (see John Inverdale. no 24).

During a lecture about Marconi radio technology, a Colonel Carruthers points his baton at the blackboard and declares: 'Now, gentlemen, as you can see, the first connection must be made between this point, A, and this one, B. After this … er, yes, Major Chatterji?'

'Excuse me, sir, but surely you mean between A and C?'

'Precisely, the initial link is between A, here, and C, there. Major Vindakji, you have something to add?'

'Forgive me, Colonel, I mean no offence, but I think the first connection is surely between C and D.'

'Quite right, Major Vindakji. C is connected with D. Now then … what is it, Lieutenant Patel?'

'Apologies, Colonel, but surely the first connection can only be B with D.'

'Indeed, Lieutenant, I'm delighted you took the point. So, as I was saying …'

A few more interruptions ensue, the lecture ends, and as the students are filing away one turns to another and says, 'I tell you what though, Pandit, that Carruthers doesn't half know his stuff.'

'The words of command', in other words, is an ineffably British principle whereby it matters not one iota if you speak incessant cobblers, so long as you speak it with absolute confidence in your own omniscience. Pull off this trick, and you will invariably be taken at your own estimation.

And so to Alan Green, the Colonel Carruthers of football commentary and also, alas, opinionation on Radio 5 Live. Greeny, as he prefers to be known, may uncannily resemble fellow Ulsterman Eamonn Holmes's cockier. more corpulent elder brother, but he lacks a shred of the self-deprecating charm and Wildean wit that make Eamonn so unending a joy.

What he does have, in industrial quantities seldom seen outside a large Chinese city during Let's-put-up-a-127-storey-shopping-mall-by-Sunday-lunch week, is impregnable self-belief. That this lies in inverse proportion to his talent is itself the diametric reverse of the point. A large segment of any British audience will always be suckers for the words of command. The curious thing is that this seems to include his bosses at the BBC.

As a commentator, it must be admitted, Greeny often strays into the gentle meadows of adequacy. Technically, he is fine, and can be relied upon to identify a player from the name on the back of his shirt. At his best, in fact, he's pretty good, though not a patch on the late Bryon Butler or the later Peter Jones; or the extant Geordie John Murray, by light years the outstanding commentator of his generation.

Greeny's best is a captive beast very seldom allowed its freedom, however, because very seldom is a match sufficiently captivating to disabuse him of the belief that the players, coaches and officials have conspired to ruin his afternoon or evening.

Questions of mental health are often raised in this book, psychosis and sporting success being such lascivious bedfellows. With Greeny, the regret is that journalism lured me away from a career in psychiatry, and that I am therefore in no position to diagnose Narcissistic Personality Disorder, the condition of which some suspect Mr Tony Blair (see no. 48) of being a victim. It is defined by *The Diagnostic and Statistical Manual of Mental Disorders* in the US as 'a pervasive pattern of grandiosity, need for admiration, and a lack of empathy … The narcissist is described as being excessively preoccupied with issues of personal adequacy, power, and prestige. Narcissistic Personality Disorder is closely linked to self-centredness.'

Greeny self-centred? Pah! Yet barely a game goes by without weary expressions of rage that he, Alan Green, should be forced to endure the incompetence arrayed before him by players and the referee for no other reason than to cause him psychic pain.

Instructive here is an aural vignette from the 2010 World Cup, when a colleague asked him why, with England playing like the Executive Committee of the Council for Partially Sighted Dyspraxics, Joe Cole had not been used in the first game against the USA. 'I know, I know,' harrumphed Greeny, the cocktail of two parts disbelief to one part disdain topped off with the olive of wounded outrage. 'Joe Cole was on my team sheet for the USA game. I had him on my team sheet.'

On reflection, he had a point. While Greeny had spent the previous twenty years sat in a little box with a microphone pressed to that capacious gob, Fabio Capello was fiddling about managing teams to league titles in Italy and Spain and winning European Cups. Who was this know-nothing Italian dilettante to defy the will of Greeny? Had Greeny not made himself abundantly plain on the matter? Joe. Cole. Was. On. HIS. Team. Sheet. How much clearer could this have been? It reminded me of Mr Blair's livid puzzlement when finally realising, after a meeting with Jacques Chirac, that France would never join him in Messrs Bush, Cheney & Rumsfeld's delectable mission in Baghdad. 'He just doesn't get it, does he?' thundered Mr T, and how history has vindicated him there.

Over Greeny's hosting of post-match phone-ins, I must necessarily lightly brush. If your pain threshold is higher than mine, I salute you. Without powerful sedatives of the sort more commonly given to those undergoing colonoscopy, three minutes is my strict maximum. That these are invariably three minutes in which Greeny patronises callers blessed with the sense denied Don Fabio to echo his opinion in every respect, while brusquely dismissing any Capelloid imbeciles who do not, should need no spelling out. The hectoring tone, betraying the conviction that his every insight is so unquestionably correct that disputing it must be evidence of obtuseness or malice or both (do any of you read the *Daily Mail* columnist Melanie Phillips?), is adequately familiar from his commentaries.

The self-aggrandisement rivals the arrogance and mono-mania, and barely a broadcast goes by without Greeny remind-ing the audience of what he calls his 'feud' with Alex Ferguson, in the belief that his half-share in this minor spat elevates him to the status of the Manchester United manager. Whether this is a genuine feud, or Greeny being outraged at finding himself on the wrong end of the lofty contempt he more commonly doles out, is anyone's guess.

The stories of his nastiness towards colleagues are many and predictable. Not long ago he fell out with Graham Taylor, not the sharpest stud on the boot but a good and gentle man, for lightly teasing him on air. More infamously, his maltreatment of Mark Saggers, with whom he once refused to share a plane, drove one of 5 Live's better broadcasters into the arms of its rival TalkSport.

And then there is the low-level racism that has at times drawn a gasp of amazement – not so much because it is particularly vile, or particularly surprising that Greeny finds himself trapped, like so many bombastic dullards in late middle age, in an era before political correctness entered its straitjacket; more because blithely mouthing such outmoded thoughts on air seems an astounding show of cocky self-unwareness even for him.

The broadcasting regulator Ofcom censured him in 2004 for suggesting that the Cameroonian midfielder Eric Djemba-Djemba was talking comic pidgin English during a Socratic dialogue with a referee. Another time, he referred to the number on the shirt of Man City's Chinese defender, splitting few sides with 'Number 17 – that'll be the chicken chow mein, then.'

However many thousands of annual hours the BBC has to fill with live sport, one Peter Alliss must surely suffice.

The question of how and why Alan Green's bosses are willing to put up with the queeny tantrums, imperious behaviour towards colleagues and occasional forays into the arena of seventies stand-up intrigues many, as it has for perhaps too long. The answer is depressingly simple. The words of command hold sway today in BBC high command as much as they did in Colonel Carruthers' lecture room in Calcutta in 1942.

3

Sebastian Coe

Perhaps it's the striking resemblance to the young Dustin Hoffman – short, wiry, swarthy, huge schnozz, arrogant, chippy, aloof and desperately driven – but I could never watch Coe run without drifting into a *Marathon Man* fantasy involving a root canal, Laurence Olivier's drill and a dearth of any dental anaesthesia. Anything, you felt, anything at all, to wipe the born-to-succeed smugness off that blandly handsome face.

In the glittering life story of Lord Coe, it fell to Steve Ovett to take the part, perhaps against type, of *der Weisse Engel*. In the days when the two bestrode middle-distance running like chalk-and-cheese colossi, there was a touch of the Lennon–McCartneys about the choice you had to make between the posher, more superficially appealing pretty boy and the even chippier, more abrasive yet somehow more intriguing perpetual outsider.

So when Ovett drilled deep into the roots of Coe's cavernous self-esteem by bucking the odds to defeat him in the 1980 Olympics 800-metre final in Moscow, Coe's agony was as pleasing, to the sweeter-natured among us, as Ovett's typically muted joy.

Coe's response a few days later showcased both the best and the worst of him. Recovering from so brutal a challenge to his sense of supremacy to best Ovett – regarded then as unbeatable over 1500 metres – was truly magnificent, and even heroic.

Celebrating that victory by staring murderously up at the Moscow stadium press box, holding up a lone index finger to indicate that despite the doubting Thomases he remained number one, stormed over the borderline between stout defiance and rampant megalomania. If ever a watching child needed a cautionary tale about the incestuous relationship between individual sporting greatness and undiagnosed psychosis, here it was.

With the brace of Olympic golds, a clutch of world records, a clean record on drugs (some hacks tried to get him for blood doping, but never succeeded), and a large slice of athletics immortality, the decent thing for Coe to do on retiring was to vanish and devote himself to making a fortune from endorsements, motivational speaking and health clubs. All the above he has done, with the sole exception of the vanishing. But then, obscurity was hardly a serious option for such a monster ego as his.

Neither was a brief stint as a Conservative MP (there's something enduringly repellent about the Tory sportsman: see Colin Montgomerie, no. 46), nor a briefer one as William Hague's supposedly cool mate (technically 'chief of staff') during Hague's unhappy leadership of the party. Who can forget the time Coe appeared with his arm in a sling after suffering severe damage to the limb at Mr Hague's hands, or possibly feet, on the judo mat – at the very time Mr Hague was flailing around for a way to rebrand himself as a man of steel and energy?

The good voters of Torbay tired of Coe in the Labour landslide of 1997, yet the advent of Mr Tony Blair would lay the ground for his *coup de grace*. Insofar as Coe's saddling of an innocent city with the 2012 Olympics goes, here I underestimated him. The only thing his little lordship's masterminding would win him, I once wrote (as he was insolent enough to remind an audience in a victory speech), was the *Légion d'Honneur* from chief bid rival France.

If only. Instead, in 2006 he was rewarded for winning that bid with a KBE to add to the MBE, OBE and peerage already trousered. London, meanwhile, was rewarded with the misery of incessant roadworks, and the country with a bill likely to nudge £25 billion, if not more, for an event 99.99 per cent of the population will watch only on telly. To all but a minuscule minority, in other words, it will be impossible to differentiate the London Games from Olympics held in Athens, Atlanta, Beijing, Montreal, Ulan Bator or Chad. If any of you can identify the faintest flavour of Londonness, Englishness or Britishness during the seventeen days the 2012 Games are televised, I am pleased to offer you an all-expenses-paid trip to Lord Coe's childhood home in Sheffield, with tea with David Blunkett thrown in. Unfortunately all the expenses will have to be paid by you, just as with the Games themselves, but it's still a prize worth winning.

The new stadia will be a herd of white elephants, the 'regeneration' of east London will prove the usual mythology, obese schoolkids will not be motivated to take up the 10,000 metres by watching a bunch of Kenyans, and we will all be obliged to endure months of jingoistic drivel while the Exchequer is further impoverished in the cause of international willy-waving of the sort which fading post-imperial powers such as ours like to confuse with genuine global relevance.

For all this, the credit goes to Sebastian Coe, that insanely driven marathon man of self-regard. Does anyone have the number of a decent, God-fearing Nazi dentist?

2

The England
Football Team

For their various crimes, individuals involved in the cataclysmic World Cup campaign of 2010 will of course be held responsible. It is a misnomer, after all, that football is England's national sport. The national sport of England is a nameless amalgam of self-pity, moral outrage and scapegoating, and this book would betray itself if it failed to reflect this by recognising the contributions of John Terry (see no. 18) and others.

However, both individually and collectively this entry trumps those, and on this basis. The identity of the personnel involved in any given World Cup disaster is irrelevant. It is such an immutable fact of life, if not a cosmic law, that England will underperform in major tournaments that the specific details of any one failure are incidental. If you lose a loved one in a motorway crash, do you really care if the coroner establishes the cause as tyre blowout, engine failure or driver error? A little, perhaps, but the inquest and its findings must take a distant second place to the stark fact that the loved one is dead.

England have been the World Cup living dead since losing to the part-timers of America in their first crack at the competition in 1950, and have franked that form at all eleven of their subsequent appearances on foreign soil. Even in 1966, they needed colossal luck by way of a linesman's indulgence. Looking back from the vantage point of stout middle age, I cannot help wondering whether that goal from 1966 is better analysed in terms of Greek tragedy than football. When Oedipus murdered his father Laius at the crossroads, and later usurped him in his mother Jocasta's bed and upon the throne of Thebes, his appropriation of what was not rightly his brought a curse upon his house. So it was with the Geoff Hurst shot that bounced down from the crossbar and onto the line. England were gifted something golden and lustrous that was not justly theirs, and have been punished for the ensuing hubris ever since.

So much for the pretentious theorising. The plain fact is that England had been relentlessly mediocre in all World Cups before '66, never beating a global giant in a knockout match or reaching the semi-finals, and after it settled snugly into the pattern of mishap and failure that peaked in Bloemfontein in the summer of 2010. To spare the torment, we'll hurry through the catalogue of disaster as swiftly as possible.

On the night of 14 June 1970, my six-year-old self sat on his parents' bed watching the rematch between England and West Germany from León, Mexico, on the old black-and-white telly. It was the first match I ever saw. It was also, with hindsight and humiliating to admit, the most central formative experience of my life. It wasn't just the wonderment of the grainy pictures or the intoxicating buzz and fractional delay on the satellite feed, much though these added to the evening's epic quality. It wasn't even that England's two first-half goals led to permanent emotional enslavement to Spurs, both being scored by Tottenham players (Alan Mullery and Martin Peters). It wasn't purely that this was when I fell in love with the game that would come alarmingly to dominate my life. It was how the course of the match and its outcome entrenched in even so young a subconscious the understanding that Englishness and sporting excruciation must forever travel hand in hand.

With England leading 2–0 in the second half, Alf Ramsey tempted fate by taking off Bobby Charlton to rest him for the semi-final. Fate, needless to say, found itself unable to resist, and responded with a fearsome smack in the chops. After Peter Bonetti's goalkeeping howler and Uwe Seeler's looping backward-header had brought Germany level, my parents had the common decency to send me to bed to cocoon me from the horrors inevitably to ensue in extra time. But the walls were thin. I could make out Gerd Müller's injury-time winner, and sobbed myself to sleep, as I did three years later when Jan Tomaszewski, the Polish 'clown' of Brian Clough's estimation, produced perhaps the finest goalkeeping display Wembley ever knew to prevent England qualifying for the 1974 World Cup in Germany.

Four years later, we failed to qualify again. We did make it to Spain in 1982, going out in the second group stage after sterile goalless draws against Spain and West Germany, and in Mexico four years later lost to Maradona's brace (Hand of God followed by Feet of Genius).

And so to Italia '90, the one from which many of us haven't the remotest hope of ever beginning to recover. Dismal in all three group games, undeserving last-minute victors in the last sixteen over Belgium, for whom Enzo Scifo hit the inside of the England post with the regularity of a hyperactive woodpecker, and dismantled by Cameroon, Roger Milla and all, in the quarters, somehow we limped into the semi-final against newly reunited Germany. The peculiar poignancy of that penalty shootout defeat is that having played so well against the eventual champions, awaiting us in the final was an Argentine side so toothless, with winger Claudio Caniggia suspended, that even accursed England might have found it beyond them to locate a path to defeat.

The most thunderous England traumas seem to come at twenty-year intervals. So it was that (after unlucky last-sixteen defeat on penalties to Argentina in 1998; feckless capitulation to ten-man Brazil in the 2002 quarters; and dismal last-sixteen shootout defeat to Portugal in 2006), 1970 and 1990 duly gave way to 2010 and that horrendous 1–4 dismantling at the brutal hands of the Hun. Admittedly that last-sixteen defeat saw

England shrug off the bonds of sullen mediocrity to scale a Himalayan zenith of defensive incompetence. But as I said, the details of the team's individual failures are barely relevant. At heart, with the odd unique flourish, it was the identical old story: England, as always, had progressed as far as it took to meet one of the global giants, and no further.

The debate that followed the Germany game, on the phone-ins and newspaper message forums, was one we've had so often that it qualifies more as an elongated haiku. 'What's wrong with England,' to borrow from Victoria Derbyshire on Radio 5 Live the morning after, 'and how can we fix it?' The replies were wearyingly familiar. 'Bunch of money-fixated prima donnas … only care about their clubs, not their country … too many foreigners in the Premier League … foreign managers can't invoke Dunkirk spirit … should have played a different system … robbed by the officials …' Every four years, if not every two, we have this ritualistic debate, and two or four years later it's *déjà vu* all over again. And always, always, always, we end up returning to 1966.

So did I at half time against Germany. If the Russian linesman caused a curse to be placed on the House of England by awarding them a goal that wasn't, I insanely concluded, now being denied a goal that clearly was had to be the equivalent of Oedipus putting out his own eyes (the blindness here belonging to the Uruguayan referee and linesman). Here was the blood price for robbing Germany forty-four years ago paid at last. Liberated from the curse we would come out for the second half and beat the Germans for the first time in a knockout game since – when else? – 1966. The symmetry was indecently perfect. The trouble was, I was looking at the wrong curse.

The reason England always underperform in World Cups (and European Championships) has nothing to do with a Sophoclean curse, or the players being jaded due to the rigours of domestic and European club competition and lack of a winter break, or being callous mercenaries, or badly coached, or perpetual victims of dreadful decisions. All the above have played some part down the decades, but always a peripheral one. Nor is it that they are poor players. They're not. Generally, they range from the good to the outstanding, impressing year after year in the Champions League, a more technically demanding competition than any World Cup. No one disputes that Wayne Rooney, in his Man United shirt, is among the planet's best five players, or claims that Capello won loads of Scudettos and La Liga titles, and a European Cup, without having a clue how to organise a defence.

The underlying problem with England footballers, then, can only be that they are English. And the reason England can never match expectations is that the fans, being English, cannot comprehend that those expectations are unrealistic – not because the players can't play well enough, but because when playing for England, being English, they cannot play at all.

No country that loses a great empire forgets its imperial glory in a hurry, or recovers from the loss of self-esteem in centuries, if at all. And no country in history has fallen in status so quickly and so devastatingly as this one. In 1939, Britain's empire remained, geographically at least, the largest in human history. Nine years later, during the arctic winter of 1948, Britain was literally on the verge of famine. Unable to feed its own people, the government was reduced to importing from the former colony of South Africa a canned fish, the snoek, so disgusting that even a starving populace not known in times of plenty for its culinary fussiness could not eat it.

Where being born an Englishman had so recently been regarded as hitting the jackpot in the lottery of life, it was now a losing ticket. England learned her place in the new world order in many ways during those drab and dismal austerity years, one being the 3–6 defeat at Wembley to Puskas's legendary Hungarians in 1953, when bread was still being rationed.

That would end a year later. The rationing of success in international football would continue, with that one oasis in '66, without end.

Since the war, Britain has known a single brief period of genuine vibrancy and self-confidence, and that was in the swinging mid-sixties. The 1970s, which saw the defeat in León yield to successive World Cup finals absenteeism, also saw national self-belief at its lowest ebb, with the country riven by industrial and social unease. When Mrs Thatcher's monetarist tough love produced an economic revival of sorts, England's World Cup form revived with it, peaking in 1990 a few months before the whisky-sodden old haddock was ousted. Then came the Major recession, mirrored by the sweet but preternaturally clueless Graham Taylor's failure to take us to the 1994 World Cup. In 1998, with the false flower of Blairite optimism still in bloom, came the false dawn under Glenn Hoddle in France, when much like New Labour the team flattered to deceive. In 2002, the government's glow was fading, and so was the team under Sven in Japan. Four years later, the boom times were ending, and so was the iron pyrites generation we fools misidentified as golden. In 2010, the worst economic slump since the 1930s was perfectly mirrored by the slump in form in South Africa.

Every World Cup performance has echoed the national mood, perhaps because nowhere in sport is national mood and character so clearly unveiled as at a World Cup. Brazil, now poised to become a major economic power, have become tedious and sombre grown-ups. The French are as arrogant and quixotic as ever, preferring to be atrocious rather than mediocre if they know they cannot be excellent. The Germans ... but enough of them already.

If English defeatism were only evident in football, it might be dismissed as an anomaly. But it covers the sporting spectrum, as other entries in this book confirm. Tim Henman losing eleven straight games and the match from a set and a break up on Guillermo Coria in a French Open semi-final, Paula Radcliffe failing to finish at all when odds-on to win the Beijing marathon, Colin Montgomerie taking five shots from the middle of the final fairway when four would have won him the US Open … our sports stars aren't afraid of losing. It's the prospect of winning that terrifies them.

To those raised in this defeatist culture, it's what we know and what, collectively, we do: failing to build sports stadia on time, if at all, or plug oil leaks off the coast of Louisiana, or install multi-billion-pound NHS computer systems that work, or educate our children to read and write, or care for our elderly so that they have dignity in decline, or electrify lines decades after the Japanese had bullet trains. The beauty of it is this: losing gives way to the enveloping warmth not only of self-pity and moral outrage, but also the unspoken resentment that foreigners who failed to fight Hitler, or allied themselves with him, came out of the war so much better than we did. Our reward for winning was gloom, grime and grinding poverty. While we were rationing bread, the French were feasting and Japan was thriving. As for the Germans …

These things are seldom said these days, and perhaps seldom consciously thought. But somewhere in the national psyche they bubble away and shape the twin tracks on which the English soul trundles: the misplaced sense of superiority born of the muscle-memory of Empire, and the more powerful sense of inferiority that has trickled into the national DNA since 1945. We were wartime winners, and our reward was post-war defeat. Can our sportsmen and women be held any more responsible than the rest of us for confusing the two?

So, if England qualify for Brazil 2014 (and on the World Cup/economic model outlined above, don't bank on it), and crash out of it to the first major football nation they meet, try not to blame the players, the coach, the match officials, the ball, Fifa, the tactics or any of the other magnets for displacement by which we are always attracted. Blame fate. Blame the sweep of history for an era in which we still can't begin to make sense of our post-imperial place in the world. Blame England and Englishness. Blame the shirt.

1
Peter Alliss

Astride the highest plinth in the pantheon of sporting horror sits the girthular sage of golf. One syllable from Mr Alliss – more often than not the 'Oooooh' that prefaces his sub-sub-sub-Terry Wogan flights of fancy – and it becomes impossible to resist the lure of a fantasy involving a pitching wedge, a pat of butter, a pair of latex gloves and a pioneering method of attaching a permanent shooting stick to the human form.

A chronic sufferer of the disorder known throughout Harley Street as APS (Audible Pipe Syndrome), the Socrates of snug-bar philosophy is technically the BBC's chief golf commentator. In effect he is less a commentator, however, than an archetype of misplaced English arrogance of a rankness that would – were what he must know as 'the PC Brigade' a more effective military outfit than he might have us believe – have been wiped out long ago.

Admittedly, Mr Alliss does now and then deign to refer to events taking place on the course, though without the will or the capacity to vary the tone he once lavished on the fairway adventures of Brucie, Tarbie and Little Ron in that unlamented era when Pro-Celebrity Golf was such a fixture on BBC2. Moments of the highest drama, and even of what equates in sport to personal tragedy, are handled with the same chucklesome winsomeness he once deployed to mock Mr Corbett for slicing a fairway wood into the Wentworth trees. When Jean van der Velde did his Devon Loch act at the 1999 Open at Carnoustie, for example, taking a triple-bogey seven at the last when needing six for the title, Mr Alliss might have been describing some hilarious 1976 bunker byplay involving Kenny Lynch, a tea towel and an impression of Lawrence of Arabia. The tone, at once both enraging and stultifying, never varies. He has the emotional range of the resting actor who lost out on the 'Mind the gap' gig for St James's Park tube station due to lack of emotional range.

It was on the first day of that same 1999 Open that Mr Alliss had the grace to offer me the most surreal moment of my life so far. Picking up on an interview he'd given a golfing magazine, I had written my annual piece about how he was less a describer of golf than a bouncer stationed outside its holiest portals, deploying the air of twittish condescension designed to repel anyone under fifty years of age and not suitably middle-class who might otherwise be tempted to go in, and so preserving it for his own demographic group in the manner of the snottier golf clubs keeping out the local riff-raff.

He couldn't understand the modern lack of respect for the police, he had confided to the magazine: he himself always addressed officers as 'sir' regardless of even a half-century age gap. Nor could he comprehend the BBC's obsession with sex. Who, he asked, wants to know what lesbians get up to? To this attemptedly rhetorical question, it seemed to me, there was a perfectly literal answer: every straight man in Britain other, apparently, than himself.

The article appeared on the Thursday of the first round, and I was dozing after lunch in front of the telly that day when the familiar droning began. 'Ooooh, oooooh, now I'd like to say hello to an old friend …' it began, and the subconscious help-fully filled in the rest before he had time to do so himself: '… an old friend, Sandy McTavish, ninety-seven years young. You've not been so chipper lately, Sandy old horse, but we hope the hip replacement goes well, and that we'll see you for a beaker of the warm south at the nineteenth very soon.' These personal messages to obscure ancients were so frequent, as they remain to this day, that it could be nothing else.

Yet it was. 'Ooooh, oooooh, now I'd like to say hello to an old friend,' went this particular shout-out, 'Matthew Norman of the *Evening Standard* in London. Spicy writer, spicy writer. Saucy young fella. He's had a few words for me in the paper today,' he went on, and I was by now fully awake. Recalling the classic *Candid Camera* sketch in which a snooker ball flew out of the TV set and landed in the lap of a man sitting in his armchair watching *Pot Black*, I peered behind the telly to inspect it for a recording device, or possibly a pygmy Rory Bremner. Neither was visible.

I can't say how long he rambled on about me, or what precisely he had to say, other than that he concluded this oration with what was presumably meant as a menacing reference to hearing from him again before handing over to Alex Hay following Bernhard Langer down the ninth.

It said something instructive that he saw nothing peculiar in treating millions of viewers to his thoughts about a journalist of whom almost none of them had heard, and of no conceivable interest to the few who had. What it said, of course, is that he treats the BBC commentary box, in which he surrounds himself with pinheaded sycophants of the style of 'Esther's Nancies' on *That's Life* – Mr Hay, now departed, being the leading sycophant back then, and a man to whom the only question worth asking as he emerged from a commentary stint at Mr Alliss's side was, 'Hey, Hay, find any polyps up there?' – as his personal fiefdom.

Palpably, a large chunk of his audience admires and even worships this most reliably divisive of national figures, finding the folksy homilies as endearing as his reduction of major tournament golf to a trifling amusement. It is no such thing. At its best, golf is as vicious and brutal a trial of nerve as there is in sport, and a uniquely rigorous test of psychological strength. I've never seen any sportsman, even in a World Cup penalty shootout, crushed by stress as absolutely as Bernhard Langer was when he stood over, and inevitably missed, his five-footer to retain the Ryder Cup for Europe in 1991. In the US Masters of 1996, Greg Norman suffered the closest thing to a self-contained nervous breakdown you will ever see on live television outside the *Big Brother* house as he converted a six-stroke lead over Nick Faldo after fifty-four holes into a five-stroke defeat after the full seventy-two. Van der Velde's self-destruction, for all the farcical gloss as he removed his shoes and socks to play a shot from a creek, was a moment of epic catastrophe that deserved sympathy, rather than the 'stupid boy' dismissiveness of Captain Mainwaring, or a throwaway 'More Jacques Tati than Jack Nicklaus.' Alliss destroyed the moment, as he does almost every moment, with the default tone of irritation of the suburban golf-club bore blethering on about the difficulty of getting a replacement air filter for the Lexus.

The extent of Mr Alliss's casual racism is hard to gauge, but one can hardly expect the patron saint of the string-backed driving glove to comprehend why routinely referring to Oriental golfers as 'inscrutable', or euphemising to insist that a clearly swearing Tiger Woods is 'talking Swahili', might be irksome to that brave band of PC Brigadiers who slipped past him at the door. This hardly makes him a Pringle-sweater-clad Bernard Manning, and it behooves us to make allowances for a man pushing eighty (he enters his ninth decade in February 2011) who lacks the imagination to understand why words spoken with no active intention to offend might do so nonetheless. We are all of us prisoners of our age and upbringing, and a lifetime in the cocoon of professional golf is no ideal training to adapt to refinements in mores and sensibilities.

Even so, it remains impossible to hear Peter Alliss sermonising about life's little foibles from his commentary-box-bully pulpit without picturing him sat on his bar stool at the nineteenth holding forth to a gaggle of admirers about that halcyon era, between the abandonment of National Service and the arrival of mass immigration, when rock and roll and the contraceptive pill had yet to be introduced, children still routinely developed rickets, homosexual sex was a crime and lesbianism unheard of, and the Kray twins made the streets of the East End safe for little old ladies to walk; about how, while he has many dear friends of a dusky hue, dear old Enoch was talking perfect sense.

Mr Alliss is and will to his dying breath remain the paradigm of self-indulgent nostalgia for the falsely recalled paradisial era that was the 1950s. He is the editorial column of the *Daily Mail* given legs and voice, and of a less appealing entity than that I cannot conceive.